CHILDREN IN THE DIGITAL AGE

CHILDREN IN THE DIGITAL AGE

Influences of Electronic Media on Development

Edited by
Sandra L. Calvert, Amy B. Jordan,
and Rodney R. Cocking

PRAEGER

Westport, Connecticut
London

Library of Congress Cataloging-in-Publication Data

Children in the digital age : influences of electronic media on development / edited by
Sandra L. Calvert, Amy B. Jordan, and Rodney R. Cocking.
   p. cm.
   Includes bibliographical references and index.
   ISBN 0–275–97652–1 (alk. paper)
   1. Mass media and children. 2. Computers and children. 3. Internet and children.
  4. Video games and children. 5. Child development. I. Calvert, Sandra L. II. Jordan,
Amy B. (Amy Beth) III. Cocking, Rodney R.
   HQ784.M3C455 2002
   303.48'34'083—dc21   2002019509

British Library Cataloguing in Publication Data is available.

Library of Congress Catalog Card Number: 2002019509
ISBN: 0–275–97652–1

First published in 2002

Praeger Publishers, 88 Post Road West, Westport, CT 06881
An imprint of Greenwood Publishing Group, Inc.
www.praeger.com

Printed in the United States of America

∞™

The paper used in this book complies with the
Permanent Paper Standard issued by the National
Information Standards Organization (Z39.48–1984).

10 9 8 7 6 5 4 3 2

In memory of John C. Wright, our friend and esteemed colleague. His love of children and his dedication to our field made us all so much richer.

Contents

Figures and Tables   ix

Acknowledgments   xi

Introduction   xiii
    Ellen A. Wartella

I. Media Usage Patterns   **1**

1. The Impact of Computer Use on Children's and
   Adolescents' Development   3
   *Kaveri Subrahmanyam, Patricia M. Greenfield, Robert
   Kraut, and Elisheva Gross*

2. American Children's Use of Electronic Media in 1997: A
   National Survey   35
   *John C. Wright, Aletha C. Huston, Elizabeth A.
   Vandewater, David S. Bickham, Ronda M. Scantlin,
   Jennifer A. Kotler, Allison Gilman Caplovitz, June H. Lee,
   Sandra Hofferth, and Jonathan Finkelstein*

II. Behavioral Effects of Media   **55**

3. Identity Construction on the Internet   57
   Sandra L. Calvert

4. Adolescents, the Internet, and Health: Issues of Access and
   Content   71
   Dina L. G. Borzekowski and Vaughn I. Rickert

5. Political Socialization in the Digital Age: The "Student Voices" Program   83
   Emory H. Woodard IV and Kelly L. Schmitt

6. Violent Video Games and Aggressive Thoughts, Feelings, and Behaviors   101
   Craig A. Anderson

III. Cognitive Effects of Media   **121**

7. "We Have These Rules Inside": The Effects of Exercising Voice in a Children's Online Forum   123
   Justine Cassell

8. Developmental Implications of Commercial Broadcasters' Educational Offerings   145
   Amy B. Jordan, Kelly L. Schmitt, and Emory H. Woodard IV

9. Children's Online Reports about Educational and Informational Television Programs   165
   Sandra L. Calvert, Jennifer A. Kotler, William F. Murray, Edward Gonzales, Kristin Savoye, Phillip Hammack, Susan Weigert, Erin Shockey, Christine Paces, Melissa Friedman, and Matthew Hammar

10. The AnimalWatch Project: Creating an Intelligent Computer Mathematics Tutor   183
    Carole R. Beal and Ivon Arroyo

IV. Family and Consumer Media Models   **199**

11. The Development of a Child into a Consumer   201
    Patti M. Valkenburg and Joanne Cantor

12. Family Boundaries, Commercialism, and the Internet: A Framework for Research   215
    Joseph Turow

13. A Family Systems Approach to Examining the Role of the Internet in the Home   231
    Amy B. Jordan

Index   249

About the Editors and Contributors   255

Figures and Tables

FIGURE

1.1 Teens' and Adults' Self-Reported Purposes for Using the Internet between 1995 and 1998   6

2.1 Minutes per Week of Educational Program and Noneducational Cartoon Viewing by Age and Gender   46

2.2 Minutes of Video Game Play of Each Type by Age and Gender   48

6.1 Single-Episode General Aggression Model   105

6.2 Multiple-Episode General Aggression Model: Long-Term Effects of Video Game Violence   106

6.3 Average Effects of Violent Video Games, Adults and Children Combined   110

6.4 Average Effects of Violent Video Games, Children Only   111

6.5 Relation between the Violent Content Difference between the Violent and Nonviolent Video Game Conditions and the Effect on Aggressive Behavior, Experimental Studies   113

7.1 Excerpt from Junior Summit Entry Form   128

7.2 Technologies of the Online Forum   133

11.1 Percentage of Parents Experiencing a Purchase-Related Conflict with Their Child in a Store   206

TABLE

1.1 Metrics of Internet Use by Generation and Gender   8

2.1 Number of Minutes Viewed per Week in Each Program Type by Age and Gender 44

5.1 Adjusted Posttest Means Comparing Outcomes for Treatment versus Control Groups 94

8.1 Objective Items in the Educational Strength Scale 151

8.2 Commercial Broadcasters' 1998–1999 E/I Programming in the Philadelphia Broadcast Area 154

9.1 Frequencies of Programs Viewed and Favorites by Age and Sex 174

9.2 Means and Standard Deviations for Lessons Learned and Educational Strength of Report 176

Acknowledgments

This collection of essays would not have been possible without the support of a wide variety of individuals and organizations. We would especially like to thank Cheryl, John, David, Adam, and Julia for their support during the preparation of this book. We also gratefully acknowledge the financial support of the following private foundations and government agencies who were instrumental in making the studies in this book possible.

The National Institute of Child Health and Human Development provided support to the University of Michigan's Institute for Social Research, the Hogg Foundation for Mental Health provided support for John Wright, and the William T. Grant Foundation provided support for John Wright, Aletha Huston, and Elizabeth Vandewater. The Entertainment Software Ratings Board also supplied game descriptions and game ratings.

The Smith Richardson Foundation and Georgetown University provided support for Sandra Calvert.

The Pew Charitable Trusts and the Annenberg Public Policy Center provided support for Emory Woodard and Kelly Schmitt.

Merrill Lynch and other sponsors of the MIT Media Lab provided support for Justine Cassell.

The National Science Foundation Program in Gender Equity provided support for Carole Beal.

Chapters 1, 2, 4, 8, 9, 11, and 12 are reprinted with the permission of Elsevier Science for articles printed in the *Journal of Applied Developmental Psychology*, 2001, Vol. 22, No. 1.

Introduction

Ellen A. Wartella

The new media are here. This collection of essays presents some of the latest research on children and interactive media, and collectively are an acknowledgment of the vast changes children's media environments have undergone in the past decade. While television may yet be the medium children spend the most time with, it is clear that video games, the Internet, computer interactive products, and interactive toys have made considerable inroads on children's out-of-school leisure time. This collection brings together a range of studies and reviews that address contemporary public policy concerns about children's use of interactive media and the ways in which the new media have become the established media in children's lives.

As with earlier periods of research on film, radio, and television, these studies of the newer interactive media reflect the shifting public concerns about children's use of technologies and exposure to potentially harmful content. They examine implications of which demographic groups of children are gaining access to interactive media most quickly, how much time youth are spending with these media, what other activities are being displaced, and what specific content preferences are evidenced by children of different ages and genders. Further, this collection addresses recent public concerns about the impact of networked environments on both cognitive and social development. For instance, children's learning from specially produced video games and computer programs are examined as are studies of adolescent identity formation and adolescents' development of a sense of community across distances and cultures.

Public discussions are of both promises and perils: interactive technologies may improve children's learning and speed cognitive development but these same technologies may expose children to content that is violent or unsafe or that may infringe on their privacy. Questions about the role of interactive media in shaping healthy social relationships are addressed in these essays through examinations of how children's use of networked environments may shape their sense of identity and their development of peer and family relationships. The longstanding public concern about the role of violent media content, and in particular violent interactive video games, is addressed by one set of authors.

Two hallmarks of this collection stand out. First is the extent to which the authors are interested in locating children's use of interactive media in the context of children's maturation in terms of cognitive, social, and emotional growth. This is indeed a developmentally oriented collection of studies. Particularly gratifying is that these studies of interactive media and children incorporate this developmental perspective in order to understand the role of media within the entire context of children's growth. While a developmental perspective has been popular in studies of children and television since the early 1970s, it is important that this tradition continues and grows with the study of new media. Furthermore, it is increasingly significant that our understanding of the role of media in children's growth be integrated into the larger literature and history of child development. This will only happen when media research on children adopts a developmental perspective.

Second, it is increasingly clear that how children use and interact with technologies will be the focus of future research, surpassing concerns regarding actual amount of time spent with these technologies. Children easily adopt interactive technologies into their lives quite often earlier than their parents. They also engage in a variety of kinds of activities including entertainment, education, and communication. This suggests that how children engage with different kinds of content with new interactive media as early adopters will become an increasingly important topic of study.

These essays demonstrate that we are quickly reaching the time when research on children and "media" will not be categorized by medium. The promise of convergence—that the same appliance can bring us broadcast television, cable television, the Internet, and other interactive content—will only make more manifest what is already obvious—that we should be studying children's exposure to different content in the media rather than media use per se. Children are using a wide variety of appliances and interactive platforms that provide them with educational content, gaming, dramatic fare and other genres of entertainment content, and the opportunity to communicate about what they are using in the media while being engaged. Children's content use and not media use is what is most important.

As an example of these hallmarks, consider the extent to which these essays relate children's media use to developmental trends and basic developmental processes. For instance, some of the research presented here examined whether and how interactive media use affects children's cognitive development and how to create the most effective computer programs to aid children's learning of mathematics. Furthermore, other research questioned what is the developmental trajectory that describes children's understanding of various marketing strategies used in television and other advertising directed at children. These are fundamental questions regarding the role of media content in influencing children's learning about the world and media in the context of cognitive processing and cognitive development with an emphasis on content rather than time spent with a medium.

These essays point to many directions for future research and they enlighten our current understanding of the powerful role interactive media play in children's lives. It is my hope that scholars from all disciplines will be inspired by this collection to address the questions raised by these authors and continue the tradition of the developmental approach to the study of children and interactive media.

Part I

Media Usage Patterns

Chapter 1

The Impact of Computer Use on Children's and Adolescents' Development

Kaveri Subrahmanyam, Patricia M. Greenfield,
Robert Kraut, and Elisheva Gross

I really want to move to Antarctica—I'd want my cat and Internet access and I'd be happy.
—16-year-old HomeNet participant, 1995

The time is ripe to assess the impact of home computer use on child and adolescent development. Over the past few years, a growing number of U.S. households have added electronic games, home computers, and the Internet to other technologies—the telephone, radio, TV, and stereo system—that consume children's time. Furthermore, the Annenberg Public Policy Center has reported that among U.S. households with children aged 8 to 17, 60% had home computers, and children in 61% of households with computers had access to Internet services; in other words, 36.6% of all households with children had Internet services, more than twice the percentage of that in 1996 (Turow, 1999). When a national sample of children and teenagers was asked to choose which medium to bring with them to a desert isle, more children from 8 to 18 chose a computer with Internet access than any other medium (Rideout, Foehr, Roberts, & Brodie, 1999).

Surveys of parents suggest that they buy home computers and subscribe to Internet access to provide educational opportunities for their children, and to prepare them for the "information-age" (Turow, 1999). Although they are increasingly concerned about the influence of the Web on their children and express disappointment over their children using the computer for activities such as playing games and browsing the Internet to download lyrics of popular songs and pictures of rock stars, they generally consider time wasted on the computer preferable to time wasted on TV, and even consider children without computers to be at a disadvantage (Kraut, Scherlis, Mukhopadhyay, Manning, & Kiesler, 1996).

While the research on whether computers are a positive influence in children's lives is mostly sketchy and ambiguous, some initial findings are beginning to emerge. This chapter begins with a discussion of the time spent by children on computers and the impact of such computer use on other activities such as television viewing. Then we review the available research on the effects of computer use on children's cognitive and academic skill development, social development and relationships, as well as perceptions of reality and violent behavior.

We present data from the HomeNet project, which was a field trial by researchers at Carnegie-Mellon University, who studied household use of the Internet between 1995 and 1998 (Kraut et al., 1996; Kraut, Patterson, Lundmark, & Kiesler, 1998). By reducing economic and technological barriers to the use of computers and the Internet from home, this study examined how a diverse sample of families would use the technology when provided the opportunity for the first time. Starting in 1995, the study provided 93 families in the Pittsburgh area with home computers and connections to the Internet, then collected data about them for two years through in-home interviews, periodic questionnaires, and automatically whenever members of these families went online. The goal was to provide a rich picture of the factors encouraging or discouraging use of the Internet, the manner the Internet was used, and the impact of such use over time. The sample included 208 adults and 110 children and teenagers (ranging in age from 10 to 19 years), hereafter referred to inclusively as teenagers. Here we present data on teenagers' use of the Internet.

In examining the impact of computer use, we have primarily looked at two popular applications of the computer, including games and the Internet. Because games played on a computer are similar to games played on other platforms (e.g., stand-alone game sets such as Nintendo and Sega or hand-held games, such as Gameboy), we use the term "computer games" inclusively to refer to all kinds of interactive games regardless of platform. Even the distinction between games and the Internet is getting blurry as interactive games can be played on the Internet. With the expected convergence of different media in the near future, assessing the impact of computer technology on children will only get more complex and challenging.

TIME SPENT ON COMPUTERS

Understanding the impact of computer use requires good estimates of both the time children spend on computers, and the time taken away from other activities. Time-use data on children's use of computers has been gathered mostly through self-reports and reports by parents. Despite their overall usefulness, particularly for sampling a large number of people, self-report data are beset by problems of accuracy and reliability stemming from memory limitations and inaccurate estimations on the part of respondents; these problems are further accentuated when studying children. In contrast to the self-report methods, more reliable methods include the Experience Sampling Method, in which participants were paged and asked to record their activity when paged (Kubey & Larson, 1990), and computer-based means of tracking computer use, where the software records the person using the computer, the applications used, and web sites visited. However, these methods are also more expensive and time-consuming to carry out, and raise concerns regarding privacy.

Parents in the Annenberg survey report that children (between 2 and 17 years) in homes with computers spend approximately 1 hour and 37 minutes a day on computers, including video games (Stanger & Gridina, 1999). In the HomeNet study, machine records of weekly usage averaged across approximately two years of data between 1995 and 1998, show that among the teens who had access to the Internet at home, usage averaged about three hours a week during weeks when they used it, and over 10% used it more than 16 hours a week. Teens in the study were much heavier users of the Internet and all its services than were their parents.

The teens used the Internet for school work, for communication with both local and distant friends, and to have fun, especially by finding information related to their interests and hobbies. As seen in Figure 1.1 teenagers were more likely than adults to report using the Internet for social purposes. For example, teens were more likely to report using the Internet to communicate with friends, meet new people, get personal help, and join groups.[1] They were also more likely to use the Internet to listen to music, play games, and download software. In contrast, adults were more likely to use the Internet for instrumental purposes such as getting product information, purchasing products, or supporting their employment. Teens also used the Internet for instrumental purposes, such as doing school work and finding educational material.

Variation in Use by Age, Gender, Ethnicity, and Social Class

The time that a particular child spends on a computer and their activities on the computer may depend on age, gender, ethnicity, and social class. In a national survey of children and teenagers from 2 to 18, the percentage of children who reported (or were reported by their parents) to have used a computer out of school the day before rose with age: from 26% in the 2 to 7 age range to 44% among the 14- to 18-year-olds (Roberts, Foehr, Rideout, & Brodie, 1999). Interestingly, while more boys than girls reported using (or were reported to use) computers *in school* the day before, there were no gender differences in percentages using a computer *out of*

Figure 1.1
Teens' and Adults' Self-Reported Purposes for Using the Internet between 1995 and 1998

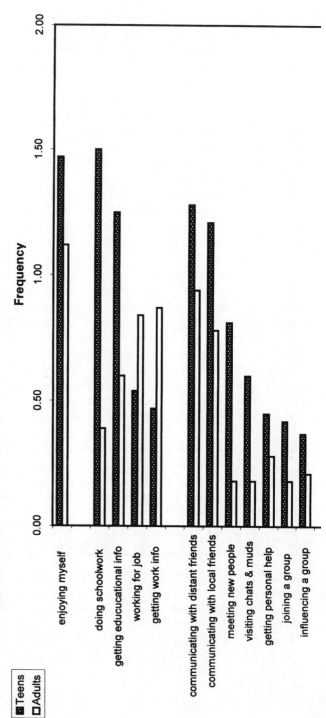

getting hobby info
learning about local events
reading the news
downloading
playing games
listening to music
viewing sex-oriented materials

getting product info
buying something
making money
advertising
selling something

Table 1.1
Metrics of Internet Use by Generation and Gender

Weekly Usage Measure	Teenage Boys	Teenage Girls	Adult Men	Adult Women
Percent active per week	58%	44%	37%	35%
Number of Internet sessions	5.30	2.93	1.41	1.45
Hours online	4.00	1.51	0.82	0.57
Session length in minutes	37.98	30.83	33.54	28.13
Hours on e-mail	1.70	0.84	0.25	0.22
Percent online time using e-mail	43%	56%		
Unique web sites visited	11.17	3.89	4.34	1.93
Mail messages sent	3.79	2.51	0.32	0.49
Mail messages received	3.40	1.95	0.22	0.28
Newsgroup messages sent	0.36	0.14	0.01	0.00
Newsgroup messages read	4.55	2.59	0.39	0.17
Listserv subscribed to	0.20	0.28	0.08	0.06
Listserv messages sent	0.03	0.01	0.00	0.00
Percent using a MUD or IRC	38%	25%	0%	0%
N (windsorized)	31	44	67	88
N (All)	43	67	92	116

school. However, the percentages of children using a computer the day before were significantly higher for White than for Black or Hispanic children. The percentages of children with reported computer use the day before also rose significantly as neighborhood income and parental education increased. Living in a single-family or two-parent household was not a significant factor.

The core audience for computer game systems, such as Nintendo or Sega, has always been boys between the ages of 8 and 14. Boys are five times more likely than girls to own a Genesis or Super Nintendo computer game system (Elmer-Dewitt, 1993). Boys have always and continue to spend more time playing computer games (Funk, 1993; Harrell, Gansky, Bradley, & McMurray, 1997; Roberts et al., 1999). The gender disparity in the amount of time spent playing computer games is greater for 14- to 18-year-olds than for 8- to 13-year-olds.

With regard to the Internet, boys in the HomeNet study were substantially heavier users than girls even though girls had equal access to the technology (see Table 1.1). For example, across the two-year period, on average, the teen boys were active on the Internet for 58% of the weeks, compared to 44% for the teen girls. Boys outstripped girls in nearly every type of usage, from hours on electronic mail, to web sites visited, to newsgroup messages sent and received. Only in subscriptions to listservs did girls slightly edge out the boys.

Other evidence suggests a more even gender distribution in non-game uses of the computer. For instance, a recent national survey of teenagers between 13 and 17 years, conducted by the Gallup Organization in conjunction with CNN/USA Today and the National Science Foundation, found that although boys were more likely to report playing video games on a daily basis, the same number of boys and girls reported using a computer on a daily basis (U.S. Teens and Technology, 1997). Furthermore, both boys and girls reported equal levels of computer usage and expressed equal levels of confidence in their computer skills.[2] Similarly, Roberts et al. (1999) found parity between the two genders for reported use of the computer for school work; indeed, there is a consistent (albeit statistically nonsignificant) trend for older and younger girls to use the computer a bit more for school work than boys.

Indeed, the Internet provides certain activities that strongly contribute to a more equal gender balance in computer use. Again, Roberts et al.'s (1999) data suggest that younger girls and boys (between 8 and 13) use computers similarly *except* in levels of gaming. When in-school and out-of-school use data are aggregated, there are no gender differences in this age group in the use of the computer for chatting, visiting web sites, using e-mail, doing school work, or using the computer to do a job. The picture is similar for the 14- to 18-year-olds, except that older boys visit significantly more web sites than do older girls.

Significance of the Gender Gap in Computer Game Playing

Despite the trends in other aspects of computer use, computer games continue to be more popular among boys. It is hard to know the extent to which this is cause or effect of game design and marketing. For example, in an address at CILT99, the CEO of Lucas Learning admitted that their products are designed exclusively for boys (Frank Evers, personal communication, 1999). Because computer game playing might be a precursor to computer literacy, and the belief that computer literacy will be increasingly important for success in society, the "gender imbalance" in computer game playing has been a topic of much recent discussion.

Efforts of the software industry to create girl games with nonviolent themes and female protagonists have largely been unsuccessful with the exception of Barbie Fashion Designer. Based on an examination of research on games that girls and boys design and on research on their play styles, and television and reading preferences, Subrahmanyam and Greenfield (1998) proposed that the Fashion Designer was successful because it contained features that fit in with girls' play and their tastes in reading and literature. In contrast to boys' pretend play, which tends to be based on fantasy, girls' pretend play tends to be based more on reality, involving themes with realistic-familiar characters (Tizard, Philips, & Plewis, 1976). Thus, by helping girls create outfits for Barbie, the computer became a creative tool that fits well with girls' preferences for more reality-based pretend play. The success of the Fashion Designer along with the growing popularity of the Internet among girls suggests that they are not turned off by computer technology. Instead, they just need applications that appeal to their interests.

Displacement of Other Activities

The little research on whether time on computers displaces other activities such as television viewing, sports, and social activities, has mainly focused on the relation between computer use and television viewing. According to the 1999 Annenberg survey of parents regarding Media in the Home (Stanger & Gridina, 1999), children still watch more television (2.46 hours/day) than use computers (0.97 hours/day) and video games (0.65 hours/day). Although comparisons of media use in homes with and without computers were not made, data suggested that the majority of the homes (68.3%) had both a television and a computer. The survey by Roberts et al. (1999), based on aggregating in-school and out-of-school media uses, confirms the pattern of greater time spent watching television than using computers. The preference for the computer mentioned earlier may therefore be more a portent of things to come, rather than a reflection of current usage.

Nonetheless, when children in homes with and without computers have been compared, it is reported that children who use computers may watch less television than nonusers (Stanger, 1998; Suzuki, Hashimoto, & Ishii, 1997). For instance, the 1998 National Survey of Parents and Children on "Television in the Home" by the Annenberg Public Policy Center (Stanger, 1998) found that children in households with computers watched television an average of 2.3 hours per day compared to the children in homes without computers, who watched an average of 2.9 hours per day.[3] Other studies suggest that computer use does not reduce much television viewing. For example, a study by Nielsen Media Research (1998) found little change in household television viewing after the household gained Internet access. Instead, many Americans report a preference for simultaneous television and computer use. For example, Media Metrix (1999) found that among households with a home computer, 49% used their computer and watched television simultaneously. Because of the growing trend to link the content of various media, computer use may even lead to an increase in television viewing (Coffey & Stipp, 1997). We need more research on the impact of computer use on television viewing as well as on other activities.

COMPUTER GAMES AND THE DEVELOPMENT OF COGNITIVE SKILLS

Many computer applications, especially computer games, have design features that shift the balance of required information-processing from verbal to visual. The very popular action games, which are spatial, iconic, and dynamic, have things going on at different locations. The suite of skills children develop by playing such games can provide them with the training wheels for computer literacy, and can help prepare them for science and technology, where more and more activity depends on manipulating images on a screen. We now summarize the experimental evidence for the role of computer games in developing cognitive skills. Although the term "cognitive skills" encompasses a broad array of skills, most of the research has focused on components of visual intelligence, such as spatial skills and iconic representation. These skills are crucial to most video and computer games as well as many computer applications.

Computer hardware and software evolve so quickly that most of the published research on the cognitive impact of game playing has been done with the older generation of arcade games and game systems. Despite advances in interactive technology and the capabilities of current computer games, the fundamental nature of computer games has remained unchanged. The current generation of games continue to include features that emphasize spatial and dynamic imagery, iconic representation, and the need for dividing attention across different locations on the screen. Therefore, the nature of the effects of computer game playing that stem from structural features of the medium would likely remain the same—although the strength of the effects on visual intelligence could change with increasing sophistication of the graphics.

Spatial Representation

Spatial representation is best thought of as a domain of skills rather than a single ability (Pellegrino & Kail, 1982) and include skills such as mental rotation, spatial visualization, and the ability to deal with two-dimensional images of a hypothetical two- or three-dimensional space. Skills in utilizing two-dimensional representations of hypothetical space are central to a variety of computer applications, including programming and computer and video games. As these skills may be important to being able to "read" and utilize the information on computer screens, repeated practice on these applications (particularly computer and video games) may enhance selected spatial skills.

Overall, the research suggests that spatial skills are related to video game playing (Greenfield, 1994; Okagaki & Frensch, 1994; Subrahmanyam & Greenfield, 1994).[4] Not every video or computer game will help develop any or all spatial skills. Computer game playing will only enhance a particular spatial skill if the game utilizes that skill. In principle, skills can only be enhanced by game playing if these skills have reached a certain level of maturation. However, to our knowledge, only one study comparing the cognitive impact of games on children of different ages has been carried out and they found no changes in effects between fifth-, seventh-, and ninth-grade students (McClurg & Chaille, 1987). All three age groups showed improved mental rotation, a spatial skill, as a result of playing two computer games.

In a study of 10½- to 11½-year-olds, Subrahmanyam and Greenfield (1994) found that practice on a computer game (Marble Madness) reliably improved spatial performance (e.g., anticipating targets, extrapolating spatial paths) compared to practice on a computerized word game called Conjecture. Marble Madness involved guiding a marble along a three-dimensional grid using a joystick, skills that are key components of visual spatial tasks.

Iconic Skills

Another skill embodied in computer games is iconic or analog representation—or the ability to read images, such as pictures and diagrams. Indeed, images are frequently more important than words in many computer games. In a cross-cultural study carried out in Rome and Los Angeles, Greenfield, Camaioni et al. (1994) found that playing a computer game shifted representational styles from verbal to iconic. In the study, undergraduate students played the game Concentration either on a computer or on a board. Those who had played the game on the computer used more diagrams in their descriptions of an animated computer simulation, whereas those who played the game on a board offered more verbal descriptions. Both iconic and spatial representation are crucial to scientific and technical thinking; these modes of representation enter into the utilization of all kinds of computer applications.

Visual Attention

Another skill incorporated in playing computer and video games is divided visual attention, the skill of keeping track of a lot of different things at the same time. Greenfield, deWinstanley et al. (1994) explored the effect of video game expertise on strategies for divided visual attention among college students. Divided attention was measured by measuring participants' response time to two events of varying probabilities at two locations on a computer screen. Participants who were expert computer game players had faster response times than novices. Playing an action game also improved strategies for keeping track of events at multiple locations. Overall, the study showed that more skilled video game players had better developed attentional skills than less skilled players.

Although this research focused on college students, computer and video game playing could have similar effects on children and help develop the skills for occupations that require expertise in divided visual attention (e.g., instrument flying, military activities, and air traffic control). However, there is no research that actually documents a link between video game playing, attentional skills, and success in academic performance or specific occupations. Furthermore, much of the research on the impact of computer games on cognitive skills has only measured the effects of game playing immediately after practice, and does not address questions about the cumulative impact of interactive games on cognition.

Nonetheless, selective increases in nonverbal or performance IQ (Flynn, 1994) scores during the last century seem to relate, in part, to the proliferation of imagery and electronic technologies in the environment that has occurred in this period of time (Greenfeld, 1998). Many computer games develop the same skills that are tested in nonverbal IQ tests such as the Wechsler and the Stanford-Binet. Okagaki and Frensch (1994) found improvements in the skill of spatial visualization among males as a result of playing the video game Tetris. The skill of spatial visualization developed by the video game Tetris and the Object Assembly subtests of the Wechsler intelligence tests for children and adults are similar. Future experimental research should be designed to test whether there is a direct, causal connection between repeated computer game playing and rise in nonverbal IQ performance.

HOME COMPUTER USE AND ACADEMIC PERFORMANCE

In this section we examine the impact of computer use on children's performance in academic areas such as math, science, language arts, and writing. Teenagers in the HomeNet sample reported that the most common educational use of computers was simple word processing for school assignments. In addition, students used links to the Web to find information for various class reports. For example, one student found information on Pittsburgh's role in the underground railroad for a Black History Month assignment. While students in clubs (e.g., the school newspaper) sometimes used Internet communication to coordinate meetings or to distribute shared materials (e.g., assignments or stories), this was far less common than using the computer for writing, printing, and research. Stand-alone educational software programs aimed at fostering children's creative expression, memory, and spatial awareness were used even less frequently.

Surveys indicate that parents generally believe computers to be an educational resource. According to Turow (1999), 70% of the parents in households with computers said that children can discover fascinating and useful things on the Internet and 60% said that children without access to the Internet were at a disadvantage compared to their peers who had Internet access. Parents in the HomeNet study said they appreciated the new educational resources that the Internet provided their children, but at the same time worried about erosion of standards (e.g., reading short articles online rather than books) and about the credibility of online information. One mother marveled at the wealth of information that her middle school–aged son was able to discover, but also worried that the sheer abundance of the information was devaluing research and critical thought. Others worried that the information was biased and unbalanced.

Several studies provide preliminary evidence that computer use is positively correlated with academic achievement, but fails to clarify this relationship. Sparks (1986) reported significant differences between the computer literacy test scores of high school students who had educational software at home and those who did not. She further determined that presence of video games and word processing software on a student's home computer were not significant factors in computer literacy scores. Computer use by a male adult in the home was positively correlated with male and female students' computer literacy scores.

Rocheleau (1995) analyzed survey responses from seventh to twelfth graders. Students with home computers reported higher overall grades and better grades in math and English than did students without home computers. Given that a home computer is correlated with parent education and socioeconomic status levels, it is noteworthy that when only children with home computers were examined, heavier users reported better overall grades, better grades in math and English, and did better on a test of scientific knowledge. Another study that compared the out-of-school activities of 5- to 12-year-old students deemed generally academically "successful" and "unsuccessful" found that unsuccessful boys spent more time watching television and playing video games than their academically high-achieving peers (Madden, Bruekman, & Littlejohn, 1997).

One program of note is that of Cole (1996) who has been experimenting with the use of electronic communication and games with children in both classroom and after-school settings for nearly 15 years. The after-school programs are called "The Fifth Dimension," and include the typical uses of home computers, such as educational software, computer games, searching the Internet, and Multi-User Domain (MUD) activities. Subject matter includes social development, geography, communications, reading, writing, math, social studies, health, technology, language, and problem solving (Blanton, Moorman, Hayes, & Warner, n.d.). The electronic games and Internet activities are based in a total social and cognitive environment that includes a ladder of challenges. Program effects include advances in reading and mathematics, computer knowledge, following directions, grammar, and school achievement tests (Summary of cognitive evaluation studies, n.d.). Although Cole's programs are set in after-school settings, his results indicate that well-designed games and Internet activities for home use can have a lasting impact on children's academic performance.

The emergence of the Internet and resulting educational innovations has spawned research focused on the educational impact of projects that integrated home and school computer use through school-driven, technology-enriched curricula (McGarvey, 1986; McMahon & Duffy, 1993). Initially, qualitative studies praised programs like the Classroom of Tomorrow and the Buddy System Project, citing descriptive evidence that home-school computer curricula increased parent-teacher interaction, bolstered students' self-esteem and motivation for learning, and greatly facilitated learning for students with ADHD and other learning disabilities. However, later follow-ups, attempting to quantify these findings, have found no significant relationship between academic achievement and participation in such projects (Miller & McInerney, 1995). Given that the evidence shows mild positive effects of home computer use on academic performance, we need research to understand fully these effects.

EFFECTS ON SOCIAL DEVELOPMENT AND RELATIONSHIPS

In the following sections, we examine the various ways in which computer use impacts social development, from the impact of game playing on the development of friendships and family relationships to the impact of the Internet on relationships and psychological well-being.

Impact on Friendships and Family Relationships

Interaction with peers has an impact on children's interpersonal skills, their poise, and social competence (Dworetzky, 1996). By age 7, children tend to spend as much time with peers as they do with adults (Griffiths, 1997). Because of the solitary nature of most computer activities, concerns have been raised that children might form "electronic friendships" with the machine, instead of friendships with their peers, hindering the development of interpersonal skills. The fact that more than one-fifth of all children between 8 and 18 report having a computer in their bedroom (Roberts et al., 1999) indicates that the computer may often be used in solitude. Indeed, Roberts et al. found that, among junior high and high school students, over 60% of all computer time is spent alone; however, much of this time is spent in online social interaction (e.g., Pew Internet and American Life Project, 2001).

Few studies have examined the effect of children's time on computers on their social skills and friendships. The extant research suggests that frequent game players actually meet friends outside school more often than less frequent players (Colwell, Grady, & Rhaiti, 1995). In addition, no differences have been found in the social interactions (Phillips, Rolls, Rouse, & Griffiths, 1995) of computer game players versus nonplayers. In other words, game playing did not impact the social networks and characteristics of interactions among children. Less is known, however, about the long-term effects of excessive computer use among the 7% to 9% of children who play computer games for 30 hours a week or more (Griffiths & Hunt, 1995).

The impact of computer use on family dynamics is also of interest. In an early study conducted during the 1980s, 20 families with new home computer game sets were interviewed for their opinions about the benefits and dangers of playing games (Mitchell, 1985). The results suggested that computer games did have an impact on family interaction—they brought the members together for shared play and interaction. An important question is whether this is still true now that computers and game sets have multiplied in numbers, have become more routinized in the home, and are usually located in personal spaces, such as bedrooms. Current research on this topic is needed.

Children and teens are often more sophisticated than their parents in their knowledge of and ability to navigate on computers. For instance, 62% of teenagers between ages 13 and 17 said that they could operate electronic equipment or computer software without any help, and 54% reported that they or a sibling were responsible for programming the VCR in their family (U.S. Teens and Technology, 1997). In the HomeNet study, teenagers were more likely to help their parents with computers than parents were to help their children, with boys disproportionately helping their fathers and girls disproportionately helping their mothers (Kiesler, Lundmark, Zdaniuk, Kraut, Scherlis, & Mukhopadhyay, 1998). Further research is needed to assess the impact that such role reversals may have on family dynamics and interactions.

Use of Computers for Communication

Research indicates that in households with access to the Internet, use of the computer to communicate with others (via e-mail, chat rooms, etc.) is an increasingly popular activity, especially among teens. A 2001 report of teen Internet use reported that 92% of online American teens use e-mail, and 74% use instant messaging (Pew Internet and American Life Project, 2001). Indeed, for one-fifth of respondents to the Pew survey, instant messaging replaced the telephone as the principal means of communication with friends.

Similarly, teenagers in the HomeNet sample reported that keeping up with both local and distant friends was a very important use of the Internet for them (see Figure 1.1). Interpersonal communications via e-mail were more important to them than information acquisition via the Web. Many of the keep-in-touch communications described by teens involved small talk—gossip and news of the day, with a here-and-now flavor. These communications exist for the pleasure they bring, rather than for their instrumental benefits. A teenage girl who was keeping up with a pen pal she met online, described the small-talk nature of her conversations with him as "stupid stuff—what's happening in his life; what's happening in my life."

Use of the Internet for interpersonal communication also sustained interest longer than other types of activities—that is, use of e-mail dropped less over the first two years online than did other uses of the Internet, such as visiting web sites. Teens and adults who used e-mail more heavily than they used the Web were more likely to still be using the Internet after their first year. These observations suggest that e-mail is the primary Internet application that keeps both teens and adults coming back to the computer.

Although it is clear that the Internet is frequently used for social purposes by teens, it is not immediately obvious whether these social uses add to or diminish teenagers' stock of social resources. The influence depends in part on whether the social uses of the Internet supplement or substitute for other sources of social contact that teens have. Early research focusing on the Internet suggested that use of the computer was associated with declines in social involvement and psychological well-being. For example, analyses of longitudinal data from the HomeNet study (Kraut et al., 1998) found that as participants spent more time online, they experienced greater declines in social and psychological well-being. In particular, greater use of the Internet was associated with small, but statistically significant, declines in social involvement as measured by communication within the family and the size of people's social networks, and with increases in loneliness, the psychological state associated with social isolation. Greater use of the Internet was also associated with increases in depression.[5] Among teenagers, greater use of the Internet was also associated with declines in social support.

There are at least two plausible and theoretically interesting mechanisms for the initial effects of declining social involvement and increasing loneliness, but additional empirical evidence is needed to establish which, if either, is correct. The first is that the time that people devote to using the Internet substitutes for time that they had previously spent engaged in social activities. This interpretation is consistent with the finding that people who use the Internet more spend less time talking to other household members, but is ambiguous to the extent that time on the Internet is spent communicating with others. This leads to a second explanation, which is that by using the Internet, people are substituting poorer quality social relationships for better ones, that is, substituting weak ties for strong ones (Krack-hardt, 1994).

"Strong Tie" versus "Weak Tie" Relationships

Among the HomeNet participants, all of whom were Internet neophytes, the majority of online social relationships had their roots outside of the Internet and predated their access to the Internet. Thus, online communications were used primarily to keep up with close friends and close family members, what sociologists term "strong ties" (Granovetter, 1973). In addition, use of the computer for e-mail in these online relationships supplemented the telephone and face-to-face visits, but rarely replaced these older communication modes. For example, teens in the study told researchers they would hurry home from school to have e-mail conversations with the friends they had just left. After going off to college, students frequently used e-mail to correspond with their parents and high school friends.

While most communications involved "strong tie" relationships, new online relationships in the HomeNet sample were also created, representing relatively weak ties with strangers, acquaintances, or nonintimate kin. Research shows that these types of social contacts typically provide less consequential social support than more intimate ties (Wellman, Salaff, Dimitrova, Garton, Gulia, & Haythornthwaite, 1996). The creation of such "weak tie" relationships reflect the fact that, in contrast to earlier telecommunications technologies for interpersonal communication, the Internet contains several popular communications applications that encourage strangers to communicate with each other, including Usenet newsgroups, listservs, MUDs, and chat rooms. The important similarity among these services is that they provide public spaces on the Internet where people gather, meet each other, communicate, or observe others communicating, and occasionally form new relationships.

In the HomeNet study, those who participated more in Usenet newsgroups, MUDs, and chat rooms were more likely to report using the Internet for meeting new people. Adults made more of their new online relationships through Usenet newsgroups and listservs, meeting people as a side-benefit of more nonsocial motivations to get information about hobbies or work. In contrast, teens made more of their new online relationships through MUDs and chat rooms, which they said they frequented for the express purpose of interacting with strangers.

Compared with adults, teenagers were found to be heavier users of MUDs and chat rooms, even after accounting for teens' greater use of the Internet overall, and were more likely to report using the Internet to meet new people. Because adolescence in the United States is typically characterized by experimentation with social relationships and an expansion of peer groups (Brown, Mounts, Lamborn, & Steinberg, 1993), teens' use of the Internet for this social experimentation appears consistent with their developmental needs.

Research on the relative strength of online relationships is unclear. The HomeNet study suggested that when online relationships exist, they are typically "weaker" than comparable relationships people report having offline. For example, participants in the HomeNet study reported feeling less close to the person with whom they had the most frequent electronic communication than to the person which whom they had the most frequent face-to-face communication. Similarly, participants in a study by Parks and Roberts reported that they spend less time "together," either in person or by computer, with someone they meet online, than they did in their "real world" relationships, and they described their online relationships as existing for a shorter time (Parks & Roberts, 1997). Moreover, compared with their real world relationships, participants reported that the online relationships had less breadth and predicted that they would be less likely to endure. In the HomeNet study, the online relationships created by the participants typically remained in the electronic domain. Less frequently did relationships that started online result in face-to-face meetings, but there were some exceptions. One teenage boy in the sample dated one of the girls he met in an America Online (AOL) chat room and took her to his senior prom, although he did not keep up contact with her afterwards.

Data from other studies reveal different trends. For example, McKenna and Bargh (1998) report that socially anxious and lonely people find more honest and intimate human relationships with others on the Internet than in the real world, and they tend to successfully integrate these online relationships into their offline lives. Rather than examine newcomers to the Internet as in the HomeNet study, McKenna and Bargh surveyed experienced Internet users who had chosen to engage in online communications. Furthermore, people who locate their "real selves" online versus offline, that is, those who "share aspects of themselves with Internet friends that they cannot, or do not, express with people in their daily non–'Net lives' are more likely to form strong attachments with online acquaintances, and to integrate these people into their offline lives" (McKenna, 1999, p. 1).

Changes in Effects Over Time

The original HomeNet study was conducted from 1995 to 1997. Follow-up research with the participants showed that use of the Internet did not have the same effects later on as it had initially. That is, during respondents' first year or two, the more hours they were using the Internet per week, the more their psychological and social well-being declined. During the next 12 months, further use of the Internet was associated with smaller declines in psychological and social well-being or even improvements. For example, during the initial period, a greater amount of time spent online was associated with increases in loneliness, but subsequently was associated with declines in loneliness (Kraut, Kiesler, Boneva, Cummings, Helgeson, & Crawford, 2002).

A subsequent longitudinal study conduced in 1998–1999, which replicated the design of the original HomeNet research with a larger sample, found that the effects of Internet use were generally positive over a range of dependent variables measuring social involvement and psychological well-being—size of local and distant social circles, amount of face-to-face communication, community involvement, trust in people, positive affect, and unsurprisingly, computer skill (Kraut et al., 2002). On the other hand, heavier Internet use also was associated with greater stress, less local knowledge, and lower desire to live in the local area. In general, having more social resources amplified the benefits that people got from using the Internet. For example, the effects were more positive for extraverts as compared with introverts; extraverts had larger increases in community involvement and self-esteem, and larger declines in loneliness, negative affect, and feelings of time pressure. Although the Internet did not have better or worse effects with age, the outcomes that improved most differed for teens and adults. While adults increased their face-to-face communication with others and their emotional closeness to distant friends as they used the Internet more, teens gained more social support and increased their family communication.

There are two competing explanations for these reversals. First, as with many dynamic processes, people individually and collectively may have learned to use the Internet more wisely later in their experience than they did early on, in ways that are better aligned to their true interests. Second, the technology and social provisions of the Internet have also changed. For example, during 1995 and 1996, when respondents were using the Internet for the first time, MUDs and chat rooms were the two most popular real-time communication services. Because these services connected anyone who logged into a common site, they increased the likelihood that users would communicate with strangers. Later, two new AOL real-time communication services gained in popularity: Instant Messenger and ICQ. Both of these services increase the likelihood that people will communicate with others they already know. In addition, the growth in the online population meant that the close friends and relatives of study participants were more likely to have an Internet account in 1998 and 1999 than in 1995. This explanation is supported by recent studies of school-based (Gross, Juvonen, & Gable, 2002) and national probability samples (Pew Internet and American Life Project, 2001) of adolescents, which report that teens largely use the Internet to exchange instant messages and e-mail with known friends. Gross and colleagues, who used a daily report methodology to examine use in an Internet-saturated community (where over 90% of participants had home Internet access) found that Internet usage was unrelated to well-being. Distinguishing between these alternative explanations and understanding the vast spectrum of people's experiences with the Internet, as reflected in different studies, will require additional research.

EFFECTS ON PERCEPTIONS OF REALITY

Simulated worlds created by electronic games, computers, and, more recently, the Internet are broadening the breadth of children's experiences from real to virtual. Through electronic games, children interact with simulated characters and creatures; through the Internet, teens assume multiple identities to interact with strangers—and even robots—in the simulated worlds of MUDs and chat rooms. At an extreme, real life is now reduced to two letters, "rl," and real-world experiences are merely a window on the computer screen. Next, we discuss how this shift affects children's development, and especially, their perceptions of reality and violence.

Shift from Real Life to Simulation

Computerized games and the Internet are moving children into a world where the distinction between real life and simulation is not always clear. One impact of this blurring of reality and virtual reality may be that children will have more difficulty in distinguishing between what is real and what is simulated. In addition, they may become desensitized to behaviors perpetrated in artificial and simulated worlds, such as aggression, violence, and killing.

One of the first computer games to thrust children into the realm of simulation was SimCity, soon followed by SimAnt (1991), and SimLife (1992). The game of SimLife is a simulation of evolutionary processes. As one 13-year-old put it, "You get to mutate plants and animals into different species. You get to balance an ecosystem. You are part of something important" (Turkle, 1995, p. 169). On the other hand, Turkle found that some children, and even adolescents, may have difficulty understanding the boundaries between real and artificial life (p. 169). For example, one 10-year-old thought that the creatures in SimLife were "a little alive in the game," and that if you turned off the modem, they would go away, but if the modem stayed on, the creatures could "get out of your computer and go to America Online." Such confusion concerning the definition of life was not limited to young children. A 15-year-old said that the point of the game was to show that you could "get things that are alive in the computer," and that just as "we get energy from the sun, the organisms in the computer get energy from the plug in the wall."

The rise in popularity of small interactive game-toys, such as virtual pets, represent a new level in the integration of computers into the social world of children through simulation (Richard, 1998; Turkle, 1995). A virtual pet is a hand-held, gender-neutral interactive electronic game that requires the owner to take care of it to prevent it from "dying." The game is somewhat more popular among girls, most likely due to its theme of nurturance. It beeps to attract attention and displays various icons to indicate its immediate needs for food, sleep, play, or medicine.

Like other computer games and software, virtual pets have specific cognitive requirements: the screen presents an iconic code whose meanings and functions must be mastered by the child, contributing to cognitive socialization to the world of computers. The beeps socialize the child to respond to the same signal that they will respond to as "wired" adults with beepers, cell phones, and voice-mail (Richard, 1998). To a much greater extent than other computer games, children are stimulated to think of the virtual pets as "real." This is because the virtual pets require constant attention to stay alive, so children must take the game with them wherever they go. Indeed, some parents use virtual pets as training to take care of a real animal.

The actual psychological effects of virtual pets have not been studied systematically. Nonetheless, the popularity of simulation, or "virtual life," has continued with the advent of the "Furby," which is an electronic toy with fur, eyes, and ears, a 200-word vocabulary, and the ability to interact in its environment to a limited extent.[6] Systematic research is needed to assess the impact of such simulations and virtual pets on children.

The phenomenon of integrating simulated life into real life in the domain of electronic games is being reinforced on the Internet. There, robot-like programs "run around" MUDs interacting with "real" characters operated by real people, but sometimes indistinguishable from them (Turkle, 1995). Based on an extensive set of interviews, Turkle (1995) discusses the identity issues created by role-playing in MUDs. People create multiple characters as they participate in different or even the same MUD. For example, one Midwestern college junior interviewed by Turkle played four different characters across three different MUDs: a seductive woman, a "macho cowboy" type, a rabbit of unspecified gender, and a furry animal. He described how the various computer screens, or windows, make it possible to turn pieces of his mind on and off: "I just turn on one part of my mind and then another when I go from window to window . . . 'rl' [real life] is just one more window, and it's not usually my best one" (Turkle, 1995, p. 13).

This effect is a continuation of a phenomenon that was begun by television. In the 1970s, *Newsweek* reported interviews with children who thought the real world was boring compared with the televised world (Waters, 1977). At about the same time, Joshua Meyrowitz (1985) pointed out that televised characters, especially on recurring series, were becoming a part of our social world and influencing human relations and politics in the real world. In relation to children and families, Meyrowitz thought that television's behind-the-scenes look at adults in general and parents in particular would break down children's respect for adult authority. Similarly, he saw other hierarchical authority structures being broken down in the same way: male-female, White-Black are two examples he develops. Perhaps the equality between people of all ages and statuses in the screen world of computers further breaks down authority structures and promotes even more equality than television did. Such equality could cause problems in socializing the next generation: children might be less willing to accept their parents' ability and right to guide and direct their actions. This is an important issue for future research.

There is some suggestion that the Internet is reaching an increasingly young audience and socializing them to form multiple identities in a simulated social world. Although most MUD players are in their teens or twenties, it is no longer unusual to find MUDs where 8- and 9-year-olds "play" such grade-school icons as Barbie or the Mighty Morphin Power Rangers (Turkle, 1995).

There are others who suggest, however, that most MUDs are not used for experimenting with identities. For example, Schiano and White (1998) conducted observations, interviews, and a survey of users in LambdaMOO, one of the largest and oldest role-playing systems. Respondents estimated that they spent approximately 60% of their time online in social interaction, a percentage that was reliably higher for females than for males and that increased with the length of time participants had been frequenting LambdaMOO. Even though LambdaMOO allows participants to log in under multiple identities, approximately 50% of participants reported having only a single identity under which they communicated. For most people this identity was a slightly idealized, fanciful, or distorted view of themselves. Of the 50% of participants who communicated under multiple identities, most had only a single additional character. In observations made of over 4,000 different individuals over a two-week period, over 75% used only a single character during that period, and of the minority who assumed multiple characters, over 80% of their participation occurred while they logged in under their main character. Thus, one can calculate that during this two-week period, less than 5% of the online behavior in LambdaMOO represented people acting out multiple alternative identities. The strong majority of respondents reported that most of the time they communicated by "being yourself" rather by "role playing." Such a role-playing system might seem a developmental outgrowth of children's fantasy play, which eventuates in adult drama and film. However, what appears different is, first, that people have an opportunity to play an improved or otherwise modified version of themselves, something that theatrical roles rarely if ever afford. Second, a role-playing system such as LambdaMOO presents a unique social situation in another way: One never knows whether one is interacting with a character that is a real self or with a character that is someone's alternative identity. In such a MUD, the distinction between fantasy and reality, so hard-won in childhood, may be blurred.

A related concern is the prevalence of sexually explicit dialogue, and even simulated activity by children and teens on the Internet. Numerous public listservs, message boards, and web sites, including sites geared toward more mature populations, offer teens the opportunity to share questions, concerns, and experiences regarding sex with both peers and adults. In addition, online flirting and cybersex, whether based on real or role-played identities, are very common among young people. It is difficult to assess the extent or impact of these interactions because they often occur, not in the public space of MUDs, but in private chats. Again, we need research to understand the informative and social role of online interaction.

IMPACT OF COMPUTER USE ON VIOLENT BEHAVIOR

As computer games become more graphic, violent, and pervasive, and as the Internet puts an increasing amount of information at children's fingertips, questions surround their role in encouraging violent behavior. These questions have taken on an increasing urgency in the wake of violent incidents, such as the 1999 massacre at Columbine High School in Littleton, Colorado, in which children killed children. The Columbine case has particularly spotlighted the role of video games as the shooters, Eric Harris and Dylan Klebold, were later described as being "obsessed with the violent video game Doom—in which the players try to rack up the most kills—and played it every afternoon" (Anatomy of a massacre, 1999). In this section, we review the limited research on the links between computer games, access to the Internet, and violent behavior.

Although home education games encourage positive prosocial behaviors (when players cooperate or share, they are often rewarded), many popular entertainment software (action and adventure games) involve competition and aggression. Although violence is an integral part of computer games today (Provenzo, 1991), this was not always the case. The first game, Pong, was nonviolent. Aggression started in the second generation with Breakout, which involved destruction, but no human aggression. The next generation of popular games, such as The Empire Strikes Back, involved human aggression, and became more personal, with hand-to-hand combat, in games such as Mortal Kombat. Violence continues to reign in the current generation of action games that include titles such as Doom, Duke Nukem, Mace, and Mortal Kombat 2. A content analysis of recent popular Nintendo and Sega Genesis computer games found that nearly 80% of the games had aggression or violence as an objective (Dietz, 1998).

While many children are familiar with and even seem to prefer violent computer games, parents are generally ignorant of such games. In a survey of seventh- and eighth-grade students, Funk (1993) found that half of their favorite games had violent themes. Many parents are unaware of even the most popular violent titles; for example, a survey found that while 80% of junior high students said they were familiar with Duke Nukem, a violent computer game rated "mature," a survey of more than 500 parents found that fewer than 5% had ever heard of it (Oldberg, 1998).

Given the amount of violence in computer games, the amount of time children spend playing these games, and their liking for violent games, an important question is their deleterious impact on children. Central among these concerns is the fear that playing an aggressive or violent computer game could increase children's aggressive behavior in other situations. Based on the evidence that watching violent media (television and films) increases children's (Friedrich-Cofer & Huston, 1986) and adults' (Zillman & Weaver, 1999) aggression and hostility, it is plausible to hypothesize that playing violent computer games would have similar effects. Indeed, the limited research on the effects of playing violent computer games suggests that there may be an association between playing such games and increased aggression.

Several experimental studies suggest that playing a violent game, even for brief periods of time, can generate short-term transfer effects such as increased aggression in children's free play (Cooper & Mackie, 1986; Irwin & Gross, 1995; Schutte, Malouff, Post-Gorden, & Rodasta, 1988; Silvern & Williamson, 1987), increased aggressive/hostile responses on ambiguous, open-ended questions (Kirsh, 1998), and increased aggressive ideation (Graybill, Kirsh, & Esselman, 1985). For example, Kirsh reported that third- and fourth-grade children who played Mortal Kombat 2, a violent game, responded more violently to open ended questions than did children who played a nonviolent basketball game. Children who prefer and play aggressive computer games also demonstrate less prosocial behavior, such as donating money or helping someone (Chambers & Ascione, 1987; Wiegman & van Schie, 1998). Since the 1980s, the military in both the United States and Britain has used violent video games for military training (Kiddoo, 1982). Finally, virtual reality may be the best stand-in for increasing levels of graphic realism found in computer games. Calvert and Tan (1994), for example, found that playing (versus observing) a violent virtual reality game led to more aggressive thoughts and arousal in college student players. Virtual reality can potentially have stronger effects than computer games because the player is immersed in the simulation; the effects could also be stronger for younger children, who may have a weaker discrimination between fantasy and reality.

Self-reported research on the relation between the amount of computer game playing and aggressive behavior is somewhat ambiguous. For instance, Fling, Smith, Rodriguez, Thornton, Atkins, and Nixon (1992) report that the amount of computer game play (as measured by questionnaires) was positively correlated with self-reported aggression as well as teachers' ratings of aggression among sixth through twelfth graders. However, when van Schie and Wiegman (1997) had participants (10 to 14 years) record their out-of-school activities on a daily basis for a week, there was no relation between the amount of computer game playing and peer nominations of aggressive behavior. Van Schie and Wiegman suggest that the critical variable might be children's preference for aggressive computer games; in other words, those who liked aggressive computer games were rated as more aggressive by their peers.

Along with the possibility that playing violent computer games could increase aggressive behavior and decrease prosocial behavior, continued exposure to violence and aggression in computer games may also desensitize children to violence. Although this effect has been shown with television (Rule & Ferguson, 1986), it has not been explored with computer games. However, there have been reports in the popular press that the U.S. military has used video games for combat training to make recruits more willing to kill (Platoni, 1999). The military appears to have used violent video games to desensitize soldiers to the suffering of their targets. Similarly, few studies exist that examine the extent to which the increased availability of information over the Internet contributes to violent behavior. For instance, information about building bombs is freely available on the Internet and Columbine student Harris had detailed bomb-making instructions on his web site (Walsh, 1999).

In sum, while the research on the effects of playing violent computer games is limited, preliminary evidence suggests that playing such games may lead to increased aggressiveness and hostility. The training experience of the U.S. military also suggests that violent games may desensitize players of violent computer games to the suffering of their victims.

CONCLUSIONS AND FUTURE DIRECTIONS

Available estimates of time use vary and are mostly based on self-reports, suggesting the need for more reliable estimates. Teenagers use the computer more than younger children or adults. Use is also greater for boys compared to girls, for Whites compared to Black or Hispanic children, and for children in households with higher parental income and education. Children still seem to be spending more time watching television than using computers, although computer users watch less television than noncomputer users.

Although playing specific computer games has immediate positive effects on specific spatial, iconic, and attentional skills used by the game, we need more research to see if long-term computer and Internet use (both game and nongame) can lead to long-term improvements in cognitive skills and academic achievement. Also, we need research to understand the cognitive and social effects of the newer generation of video games and other software, especially the multiuser games now available on the Internet.

While much of the time on computers is spent alone, moderate computer use does not negatively impact children's social skills and activities. On the contrary, e-mail and the Internet may actually help maintain interpersonal communication and sustain social relationships. However, we need to determine the impact of excessive computer and Internet use on children and adolescents' loneliness, social relationships, and psychological well-being.

Our review suggests a need to explore more fully the relation between violent games and children's aggression, particularly whether repeated game playing can desensitize children to the impact of violent behavior. Finally, the increasing dominance of simulated worlds (versus real-world experiences) in children's daily experiences and their impact on children's and adolescents' developing identities and sense of reality are topics meriting serious attention.

ACKNOWLEDGMENT

Reprinted from *Applied Developmental Psychology*, Vol. 22 (1), Subrahmanyam, K., Greenfield, P., Kraut, R., & Gross, E., The impact of computer use on children's and adolescents' development, pp. 7–30, © 2001, with permission from Elsevier Science.

NOTES

1. These comparisons control for the greater number of hours per week that teens are online compared to adults.

2. Overall, boys reported slightly more time on computers in the past week compared to girls (4.7 versus 4.1 hours). This difference was due to a small number of boys who reported using the computer for more than 20 hours a week.

3. Controlling for parental income and education yielded a weaker but significant relationship such that computer ownership was related to less television viewing, suggesting that having a home computer does influence the amount of television watched by children.

4. Results show that social involvement and psychological well-being measured before respondents got their Internet connections did not predict how much they subsequently used the Internet. Thus, the direction of causation is more likely to run from use of the Internet to declines in social involvement and psychological well-being, rather than the reverse.

5. For an in-depth discussion of video game effects, please see *Journal of Applied Developmental Psychology* (1994). Special Issue: Effects of interactive entertainment technologies on development, Volume 15. Reprinted in P. M. Greenfield & R. R. Cocking (Eds.) (1996), *Interacting with video* (Norwood, NJ: Ablex).

6. These simulations/virtual toys should not be confused with the new "smart toys" for girls such as, "Friend.link," the electronic note-passing hand-held machine or "Password Journal," in which a voice-recognition feature replaces a lock and key. These toys are communication devices and are part of real life, the way paper

note passing and diaries are, and we do not expect them to raise the issue of confusion that the simulations/virtual pets might.

REFERENCES

Anatomy of a massacre (Columbine High School Shootings). *Newsweek*, May 3, p. 24.

Argote, L., & Epple, D. (1990). The learning curves in manufacturing. *Science, 247*, 920–924.

Blanton, W. E., Moorman, G. B., Hayes, B. A., & Warner, M. L. (n.d.). Effects of participation in the Fifth Dimension on far transfer. www.ced.appstate.edu/projects/5dClhse/pubs/tech/effects.html.

Brown, B. B., Mounts, N., Lamborn, S. D., & Steinberg, L. (1993). Parenting practices and peer group affiliation in adolescence. *Child Development, 64*, 467–482.

Calvert, S. L., & Tan, S. L. (1994). Impact of virtual reality on young adults' physiological arousal and aggressive thoughts: Interaction versus observation. *Journal of Applied Developmental Psychology, 15*, 125–139. Reprinted in P. M. Greenfield & R. R. Cocking (Eds.) (1996), *Interacting with video* (pp. 67–81). Norwood, NJ: Ablex.

Chambers, J. H., & Ascione, F. R. (1987). The effects of prosocial and aggressive videogames on children's donating and helping. *Journal of Genetic Psychology, 148*, 499–505.

Coffey, S., & Stipp, H. (1997). The interactions between computer and television usage. *Journal of Advertising Research, 37*, 61–67.

Cole, M. (1996). *Cultural psychology: A once and future discipline.* Cambridge, MA: Harvard University Press.

Colwell, J., Grady, C., & Rhaiti, S. (1995). Computer games, self esteem, and gratification of needs in adolescents. *Journal of Community and Applied Social Psychology, 5*, 195–206.

Cooper, J., & Mackie, D. (1986). Video games and aggression in children. *Journal of Applied Social Psychology, 16*, 726–744.

Dietz, T. L. (1998). An examination of violence and gender role portrayals in video games: Implications for gender socialization and aggressive behavior. *Sex Roles, 38*, 425–442.

Dworetzky, J. (1996). *Child development* (6th ed.) Saint Paul, MN: West Publishing Company.

Elmer-Dewitt, P. (1993). The amazing video game boom. *Time, 142*, September 27, 66–72.

Fling, S., Smith, L., Rodriguez, T., Thornton, D., Atkins, D., & Nixon, K. (1992). Videogames, aggression, and self-esteem: A survey. *Social Behavior & Personality, 20*, 39–45.

Flynn, J. R. (1994). IQ gains over time. In R. J. Sternberg (Ed.), *Encyclopaedia of human intelligence* (pp. 617–623). New York: Macmillan.

Friedrich-Cofer, L., & Huston, A. H. (1986). Television violence and aggression: The debate continues. *Psychological Bulletin, 100*, 364–371.

Funk, J. (1993). Reevaluating the impact of video games. *Clinical Pediatrics, 2*, 86–89.

Gallup Poll. U.S. Teens and Technology. (1997). http://www.nsf.gov/od/lpa/nstw/ teenov.html.

Granovetter, M. (1973). The strength of weak ties. *American Journal of Sociology*, 73, 1361–1380.

Graybill, D., Kirsch, J. R., & Esselman, E. D. (1985). Effects of playing violent versus nonviolent video games on the aggressive ideation of aggressive and nonaggressive children. *Child Study Journal*, 15, 199–205.

Greenfield, P. M. (1984). *Mind and media: The effects of television, video games, and computers.* Cambridge, MA: Harvard University Press.

Greenfield, P. M. (1994). Video games as cultural artifacts. *Journal of Applied Developmental Psychology*, 15, 3–12. Reprinted in P. M. Greenfield & R. R. Cocking (Eds.) (1996), *Interacting with video* (pp. 85–94). Norwood, NJ: Ablex.

Greenfield, P. M. (1998). The cultural evolution of IQ. In U. Neisser (Ed.), *The rising curve: Long-term gains in IQ and related measures.* Washington, DC: American Psychological Association.

Greenfield, P. M., Camaioni, L. E., Ercolani, P., Weiss, L., Lauber, B. A., & Perucchini, P. (1994). Cognitive socialization by computer games in two cultures: Inductive discovery or mastery of an iconic code? *Journal of Applied Developmental Psychology*, 15, 59–85. Reprinted in P. M. Greenfield & R. R. Cocking (Eds.) (1996), *Interacting with video* (pp. 141–168). Norwood, NJ: Ablex.

Greenfield, P. M., deWinstanley, P., Kilpatrick, H., & Kaye, D. (1994). Action video games and informal education: Effects on strategies for dividing visual attention. *Journal of Applied Developmental Psychology*, 15, 105–123. Reprinted in P. M. Greenfield & R. R. Cocking (Eds.) (1996), *Interacting with video* (pp. 187–205). Norwood, NJ: Ablex.

Griffiths, M. (1997). Friendship and social development in children and adolescents: The impact of electronic technology. *Educational and Child Psychology*, 14, 25–37.

Griffiths, M. D., & Hunt, N. (1995). Computer game playing in adolescence: Prevalence and demographic indicators. *Journal of Community & Applied Social Psychology*, 5, 189–193.

Gross, E. F., Juvonen, J., & Gable, S. L. (2002). Online communication and well-being in early adolescence. *Journal of Social Issues*, 58 (1), 75–90.

Harrell, J. S., Gansky, S. A., Bradley, C. B., & McMurray, R. G. (1997). Leisure time activities of elementary school children. *Nursing Research*, 46, 246–253.

Irwin, A. R., & Gross, A. M. (1995). Cognitive tempo, violent video games, and aggressive behavior in young boys. *Journal of Family Violence*, 10, 337–350.

Kiddoo, T. (1982). Pacman meets G. I. Joe? *Soldiers*, 37, 20–23.

Kiesler, S., Lundmark, V., Zdaniuk, B., Kraut, R. E., Scherlis, W., & Mukhopadhyay, T. (1998). Troubles with the Internet: The dynamic of help at home. Unpublished manuscript, Carnegie-Mellon University.

Kirsh, S. J. (1998). Seeing the world through Mortal Kombat–colored glasses: Violent video games and the development of a short-term hostile attribution bias. *Childhood: A Global Journal of Child Research*, 5, 177–184.

Krackhardt, D. (1994). The strength of strong ties: The importance of *Philos* in organizations. In N. Nohria & R. Eccles (Eds.), *Networks and organizations: Structure, form, and action.* Boston: Harvard Business School Press.

Kraut, R., Kiesler, S., Boneva, B., Cummings, J., Helgeson, V., & Crawford, A. (2002). Internet paradox revisited. *Journal of Social Issues, 58* (1), 49–74.

Kraut, R., Patterson, M., Lundmark, V., Kiesler, S., Mukhopadhyay, T., & Scherlis, W. (1998). Internet paradox: A social technology that reduces social involvement and psychological well-being? *American Psychologist, 53*, 1017–1031.

Kraut, R., Scherlis, W., Mukhopadhyay, T., Manning, J., & Kiesler, S. (1996). The HomeNet field trial of residential Internet services. *Communications of the ACM, 39*, 55–63.

Kubey, R., & Larson, R. (1990). The use and experience of the new video media among children and young adolescents. *Communication Research, 17*, 107–130.

Madden, D., Bruekman, J., & Littlejohn, K.V. (1997). *A contrast of amount and type of activity in elementary school years between academically successful and unsuccessful youth.* ERIC ED411067.

McClurg, P. A., & Chaille, C. (1987). Computer games: Environments for developing spatial cognition? *Journal of Educational Computing Research, 3*, 95–111.

McGarvey, L. (1986). Microcomputer use in kindergarten and at home: Design of the study and effects of computer use on school readiness. Presentation at the 67th Annual Meeting of the American Educational Research Association, San Francisco, CA, April 16–20.

McKenna, K.Y.A. (1999). *Can you see the real me? Formation and development of interpersonal relationships on the Internet.* Retrieved November 23 from http://www.geocities.com/ResearchTriangle/Facility/3308/realme.html (no longer accessible at this URL).

McKenna, K.Y.A., & Bargh, J. A. (1998). Coming out in the age of the Internet: Identity "de-marginalization" from virtual group participation. *Journal of Personality and Social Psychology, 75*, 681–694.

McMahon, T. A., & Duffy, T. M. (1993). Computers extending the learning environment: Connecting home and school. Paper presented at Proceedings of Selected Research and Development Presentations at the Convention of the Association for Educational Communications and Technology, New Orleans, LA, January 13–17.

Media Metrix. (1999) http://www.mediametrix.com/pressroom/mmxarchives/data 09_08_97.html.

Meyrowitz, J. (1985). *No sense of place: The impact of electronic media on social behavior.* New York: Oxford University Press.

Miller, M. D., & McInerney, W. D. (1995). Effects on achievement of a home/school computer project. *Journal of Research on Computing in Education, 2*, 198–210.

Mitchell, E. (1985). The dynamics of family interaction around home video games. Special Issue: Personal computers and the family. *Marriage & Family Review, 8*, 121–135.

Nielsen Media Research. (1998). http://www.nielsenmedia.com/reports.html/report ontv.html.

Okagaki, L., & Frensch, P. A. (1994). Effects of video game playing on measures of spatial performance: Gender effects in late adolescence. *Journal of Applied Developmental Psychology 15*, 33–58.

Oldberg, C. (1998). Children and violent video games: A warning. *New York Times*, December 15, p. A16.

Parks, M. R., & Roberts, L. D. (1997). Making MOOsic: The development of personal relationship on-line and a comparison to their office counterparts. Paper presented at the annual meeting of the Western Speech Association, Monterey, CA, February.

Pellegrino, J. W., & Kail, R. (1982). Process analyses of spatial aptitude. In R. J. Sternberg (Ed.), *Advances in the psychology of human intelligence* (Vol. 1, pp. 311–365). Hillsdale, NJ: Erlbaum.

Pew Internet and American Life Project. (2001). *Teenage life online: The rise of the instant message generation and the Internet's impact on friendships and family relationships*. Retrieved July 19 from http://www.pewinternet.org/reports/pdfs/PIP_Teens_Report.pdf.

Phillips, C. A., Rolls, S., Rouse, A., & Griffiths, M. (1995). Home video game playing in schoolchildren: A study of incidence and patterns of play. *Journal of Adolescence, 18*, 687–691.

Platoni, K. (1999). The Pentagon goes to the video arcade (video games used as military training). *Progressive, 63*, 27.

Provenzo, E. F., Jr. (1991). *Video kids: Making sense of Nintendo*. Cambridge, MA: Harvard University Press.

Richard, B. (1998). Digitaler grossangriff auf die seelen junger menschen (spiegel). Die sorge um ein virtuelles wesen (tamagotchi). Presentation in a conference "Self-socialization, Child Culture, and Media," University of Bielefeld, Germany.

Rideout, V. J., Foehr, U. G., Roberts, D. F., & Brodie, M. (1999). *Kids and media at the new millennium: Executive summary*. Menlo Park, CA: Kaiser Family Foundation, November.

Roberts, D. F., Foehr, U. G., Rideout, V. J., & Brodie, M. (1999). *Kids and media at the new millennium: A comprehensive national analysis of children's media use*. Menlo Park, CA: Kaiser Family Foundation, November.

Rocheleau, B. (1995). Computer use by school-age children: Trends, patterns and predictors. *Journal of Educational Computing Research, 1*, 1–17.

Rule, B. G., & Ferguson, T. J. (1986). The effects of media violence on attitudes, emotions, and cognitions. *Journal of Social Issues, 42*, 29–50.

Schiano, D. J., & White, S. (1998). The first noble truth of cyberspace: People are people (even when they MOO). In *Proceedings, CHI'98: Human factors in computing systems* (pp. 352–354). New York: Association of Computing Machinery.

Schutte, N. S., Malouff, J. M., Post-Gorden, J. C., & Rodasta, A. L. (1988). Effects of playing videogames on children's aggressive and other behaviors. *Journal of Applied Social Psychology, 18*, 454–460.

Shih, C-F., & Venkatesh, A. (1999). Intra-household diffusion of new technologies: Conceptual foundation and illustrative example. Working paper, Center for Research on Information Technology and Organizations, University of California, Irvine.

Silvern, S. B., & Williamson, P. A. (1987). The effects of video game play on young children's aggression, fantasy, and prosocial behavior. *Journal of Applied Developmental Psychology 8*, 453–462.

Sparks, J. A. (1986). The effect of microcomputers in the home on computer literacy test scores. Central Missouri State University, Warrensburg, MO, unpublished manuscript.

Stanger, J. D. (1998). *Television in the Home 1998: The third annual national survey of parents and children.* Philadelphia, PA: The Annenberg Public Policy Center of the University of Pennsylvania.

Stanger, J. D., & Gridina, N. (1999). *Media in the Home: The fourth annual survey of parents and children.* Philadelphia, PA: The Annenberg Public Policy Center of the University of Pennsylvania.

Subrahmanyam, K., & Greenfield, P. M. (1994). Effect of video game practice on spatial skills in girls and boys. *Journal of Applied Developmental Psychology, 15*, 13–32. Reprinted in P. M. Greenfield & R. R. Cocking (Eds.) (1996), *Interacting with video* (pp. 115–140). Norwood, NJ: Ablex.

Subrahmanyam, K., & Greenfield, P. M. (1998). Computer games for girls: What makes them play? In J. Cassell and H. Jenkins (Eds.), *From Barbie to Mortal Combat: Gender and computer games.* Cambridge, MA: MIT Press.

Summary of cognitive evaluation studies. (n.d.). www.ced.appstate.edu/projects/5d Clhse/pubs/tech/studies/studies/html.

Suzuki, H., Hashimoto, Y., & Ishii, K. (1997). Measuring information behavior: A time budget survey in Japan. *Social Indicators Research, 42*, 151–169.

Tizard, B., Philips, J., & Plewis, I. (1976). Play in preschool centers: Play measures and their relationship to age, sex, and I.Q. *Journal of Child Psychology and Psychiatry and Allied Disciplines, 17*, 252–264.

Turkle, S. (1984). *The second self: Computers and the human spirit.* New York: Simon and Schuster.

Turkle, S. (1995). *Life on the screen: Identity in the age of the Internet.* New York: Simon and Schuster.

Turkle, S. (1997). Constructions and reconstructions of self in virtual reality: Playing in the MUDs. In Sara Kiesler et al. (Eds.), *Culture of the Internet* (pp. 143–155). Mahwah, NJ: Lawrence Erlbaum.

Turow, J. (1999). *The Internet and the family: The view from the parents/The view from the press.* Philadelphia, PA: The Annenberg Public Policy Center of the University of Pennsylvania.

U.S. Teens and Technology. (1997). http://www.nsf.gov/od/lpa/nstw/teenov.html.

van Schie, E.G.M., & Wiegman, O. (1997). Children and videogames: Leisure activities, aggression, social integration, and school performance. *Journal of Applied Social Psychology, 27*, 1175–1194.

Walsh, T. (1999). Colorado school reaches out through the Internet (Littleton-based Columbine High School) (Internet/Web/Online Service Information). *Government Computer News, 18*, 1.

Waters, H. F. (1977). What TV does to kids. *Newsweek*, February 21, pp. 62–70.

Wellman, B., Salaff, J., Dimitrova, D., Garton, L., Gulia, M., & Haythornthwaite, C. (1996). Computer networks as social networks: Collaborative work, telework, and virtual community. *Annual Review of Sociology, 22*, 213–238.

Wiegman, O., & van Schie, E.G.M. (1998). Video game playing and its relations with aggressive and prosocial behavior. *British Journal of Social Psychology,* *37,* 367–378.

Zillman, D., & Weaver, J. B. III. (1999). Effects of prolonged exposure to gratuitous media violence on provoked and unprovoked hostile behavior. *Journal of Applied Social Psychology, 29,* 145–165.

Chapter 2

American Children's Use of Electronic Media in 1997: A National Survey

*John C. Wright, Aletha C. Huston, Elizabeth A. Vandewater,
David S. Bickham, Ronda M. Scantlin, Jennifer A. Kotler,
Allison Gilman Caplovitz, June H. Lee, Sandra Hofferth,
and Jonathan Finkelstein*

Over the course of the twentieth century, broadcast and electronic media became an increasingly important part of the environments in which children grew up. As the twenty-first century begins, the variety of options available on television and the range of other media activities available are increasing almost exponentially. In the majority of American homes, children have 50 to 100 television channels as well as video tape players; many also have video game equipment and computers that support interactive software and that provide access to the Internet (Rideout, Foehr, Roberts, & Brodie, 1999). Children spend an average of about three hours a day with television (Huston & Wright, 1997; Rideout et al., 1999), and video and computer games are rapidly becoming a frequent activity for many children. Both theory and popular speculation award these media an important role in children's development, but solid information about who uses them and what they use is scarce.

In this chapter, we describe age and gender differences and similarities in the patterns of electronic media use (television and video/computer games) in a large nationally representative sample of children ages 0 to 12. A core assumption in this research is that the genre and content of media used by children are critical to understanding their role in children's lives. This assumption is supported by a large body of evidence from television research indicating that educational programs can teach academic and pro-social skills, while viewing general entertainment is associated with lower levels of school readiness and academic performance (Huston & Wright, 1997; Anderson, Huston, Schmitt, Linebarger, & Wright, 2001; Huston, Anderson, Wright, Linebarger, & Schmitt, 2001). Moreover, viewing preferences for particular television genres are quite stable over time (Tangney & Feshbach, 1988).

Computers and video games allow interaction, problem solving, and challenge—all qualities that many people think make them more stimulating than the "passive" processes alleged to be involved in television viewing. Yet, because such games and software range from cognitively simple perceptual-motor activities to highly abstract, complex, and difficult problems, it is important to differentiate them by content. Despite the fact that interactive electronic media surround many American children from birth onward, there is relatively little information about very young children's patterns of use of media other than television, or about age differences in early and middle childhood use. However, the more extensive television literature may provide hints as to what will be learned about interactive media use.

AGE DIFFERENCES

Both cross-sectional and longitudinal studies show that television viewing time increases with age from infancy to around age 6, declines at school entry, then increases again into early adolescence, peaking around 10 to 12 (Comstock, 1991; Huston, Wright, Marquis, & Green, 1999; Timmer, Eccles, & O'Brien, 1985). In one investigation, 2- and 3-year-olds spent considerable time in "secondary" viewing (that is, viewing that accompanied another activity) of general audience programs, probably because they spent time near adults who were viewing, but such secondary viewing declined with age (Wright & Huston, 1995). Genres of programs viewed also change with age. Educational program viewing peaks around age 4; cartoon viewing increases to about age 5, then levels off (Funk, Germann, & Buchman, 1997; Huston, Wright, Rice, Kerkman, & St. Peters, 1990; Huston et al., 1999). By the early years of middle childhood, situation comedies are typically the most popular shows (Condry, 1989).

Children's use of computers and video games also changes as they mature. As with television, changes in media-use habits as children grow older appear to result from changes in use opportunities and from cognitive and social developmental changes (Huston et al., 1992). Analyses of longitudinal time-use data for children from ages 2 through 7 showed that video game play increased with age, particularly for boys (Huston et al., 1999). In a cross-sectional analysis of a nationally representative sample, Rideout et al. (1999) reported that 2- to 7-year-olds spent an average of 40 minutes a day using computers for games and other purposes; 8- to 18-year-olds averaged 1 hour and 40 minutes. Buchman and Funk (1996) found that total time playing interactive games decreased as a function of age for fourth through eighth graders. Unfortunately, most studies do not provide information about the content or type of game or activity. In one study of fourth through eighth graders, younger children were more likely to prefer educational games than were older children (Buchman & Funk, 1996). Among the 8- to 18-year-olds surveyed by Rideout et al. (1999), only about one-fourth of their computer time was devoted to games; the remainder was spent on Internet uses and work or study tasks.

GENDER DIFFERENCES

Previous research shows small, but fairly consistent, gender differences in total television viewing, although these change with age. During the preschool years, boys are more frequent viewers than girls, particularly of cartoons and action adventure programs (Huston et al., 1990; Singer & Singer, 1981; Wright & Huston, 1995). That difference continues at least until late childhood (McKenzie, Sallis, Nader, & Broyles, 1992; Ridley-Johnson, Chance, & Cooper, 1984; Timmer et al., 1985). Patterns of gender differences are less consistent for adolescents (Brown, Childers, Bauman, & Kotch, 1990; Timmer et al., 1985). On the whole, however, adolescent boys watch more cartoons, action adventure, and sports programs than girls (Comstock, 1991).

By contrast, there are large and consistent gender differences in computer use that begin as early as age 3 or 4 (Huston et al., 1999). Boys use computers more than girls do, particularly to play video and computer games (Funk et al., 1997; Greenfield, 1994; Huston et al., 1999; Rideout et al., 1999). Boys also tend to monopolize computer-use time in the classroom, particularly in periods of uncontrolled access (Cassell & Jenkins, 1998; Kinnear, 1995). Many explanations have been proposed, including the characteristics of boys' social networks, advertising, content of games, parental socialization practices, and classroom management strategies by teachers, as well as a growing general cultural expectation of gender-typed usage.

The few studies that have included information about game content demonstrate that boys and girls have different preferences. Gailey (1996) observed game playing in a small sample of urban children ($N = 21$) ages 6 to 12; boys preferred violent action games, and girls preferred spatial relations games. In a survey of 900 fourth through eighth grade children, girls preferred educational games or those containing cartoon fantasy violence, while boys preferred sports games and those containing realistic human violence (Buchman & Funk, 1996; Funk et al., 1997). Gender differences are probably influenced by the pervasive masculine themes of speed and fighting in many video games (Johnson & Swoope, 1987; Kinder, 1996; Kubey & Larson, 1990).

THE PRESENT STUDY

The goal of the present study was to describe children's patterns of television and interactive game use by age and gender in recently collected data. Despite the volume of literature on television use, available studies generally have one of two weaknesses: poor quality measures of viewing, or small, convenience samples (Huston & Wright, 1997). With the exception of the large-scale survey by Rideout et al. (1999), investigations of computer use suffer from these same weaknesses. The data used for this study suffer from neither of these problems. Our data come from the Child Development Supplement (CDS) to the Panel Study of Income Dynamics (PSID), a large-scale investigation designed to provide a range of assessments of a nationally representative sample of approximately 3,000 children ages 0 to 12 years old.

The method in our study is a detailed time-use diary in which respondents reported *all* of their activities; media are not given special emphasis over other activities, as they are in methods based on media-use diaries or other forms of self-reported media use. Most important for our purposes, respondents recorded titles of television programs and video games when either were used, permitting analyses by program genre and game type.

METHOD

The Panel Study of Income Dynamics

Begun in 1968, the PSID is an ongoing panel study focusing primarily on the transfer of social and economic capital within families. In 1997, additional data focusing on PSID children and their families were collected via the Child Development Supplement (CDS). All families participating in the PSID with children under 12 years old were asked to complete the CDS. A total of 2,380 families agreed to participate, yielding a sample of 3,562 children (Hofferth & Sandberg, 1999). The subsample used here includes all respondents who completed at least one time-use diary ($n = 2,902$). Because the PSID oversamples minorities, lower income groups, and less educated people, data are weighted to achieve national representation. Thus, all analyses presented here were conducted using weighted data (with weights recalibrated for our subsample), thus allowing us to make statements about children's television and video game use in the general population. The weighted subsample was 67.4% White, 15.4% Black, 12.3% Hispanic, and 4.9% "Other," with a median income of $38,000.

The CDS consists of a number of instruments completed by primary and secondary caregivers, teachers, and, occasionally, the older children. Among these instruments are two 24-hour time-use diaries that provided all the television and video game data reported in the present analysis. On one weekday and one weekend day, the primary caregiver of each child was asked to report all activities that the child engaged in that day. Older children participated in the completion of their own diaries. A primary activity and its duration were recorded to account for every minute of each 24-hour period, and, if appropriate, a secondary activity was also noted. For example, if a child was eating while watching television, eating would be coded as the primary activity and watching television as the secondary activity. For a more complete discussion of the diary procedure see Hofferth and Sandberg (in press). When "watching television" or "playing a video game" (including computer games on CD-ROM) was the child's primary activity, the title of the program or game was requested. No request for titles was made for media use when it was a secondary activity.

Television Subsamples

Total Minutes of Viewing

The analyses for television viewing were conducted on data from two subsamples of the PSID-CDS participants. The first subsample includes all respondents who returned at least one completed time-use diary ($n = 2,902$). Analyses regarding *total* television viewing were performed on this subsample. For respondents who returned only one diary ($n = 71$), television viewing for the missing day was imputed. Using respondents with two complete diaries, regression equations were created to predict the missing television time from known minutes viewed on the other day. Because gender and age are known to affect television viewing (Huston et al., 1999), different equations were created for boys and girls of each age category (0 to 2 years, 3 to 5 years, 6 to 8 years, and 9 to 12 years) to impute weekday from weekend viewing and weekend from weekday viewing.

Program Viewing by Genre

The second subsample ($n = 2,263$) consists of participants who completed two time-use diaries and whose TV entries were at least 70% codable for program type ($n = 1,994$). Participants' diaries that included no television viewing on either day were considered 100% codable ($n = 269$). Analyses of this sample's viewing were concerned with minutes of viewing by television program genre *only*.

Television Program Genre Coding System

Based upon viewing in the PSID-CDS sample, we developed a coding system comprised of nine genre categories: *educational, noneducational cartoon, comedy, action, relationship drama, fantasy/supernatural, reality based* (e.g., *COPS, America's Funniest Home Videos*), *sports* and *other* (including talk shows, game shows, variety shows, home videos, music videos, and commercials). In this system, educational and noneducational cartoon categories supersede all others. Educational programs were defined as those with an explicit intent to educate and inform children above and beyond entertainment value. Programs with this intent were coded as educational regardless of format (i.e., animated or live-action) and content (e.g., comedy, drama, etc.). Unless already determined to be educational, animated programs (including those containing some live-action footage or characters) were coded as noneducational cartoons.

The diary procedure resulted in 13,659 instances of television viewing consisting of 1,174 unique codable titles and 167 responses determined to be uncodable (e.g., "a show about a woman," "the midnight program," "don't know"). All television programs were coded by two coders with a Kappa estimate of interrater agreement of .81. Coding disagreements were resolved through discussion.

A number of the program titles (1,355) in the time-use diaries were ambiguous. Some were reported as the network or cable channel viewed (e.g., NBC, MTV) at a particular time, and others were titles of which multiple program versions had been produced (e.g., *101 Dalmatians, Batman*). In order to identify ambiguous programs on cable stations, we first ascertained exact time of viewing for participants in different local time zones using postal zip codes. Program title was then determined using television listings from the *New York Times* for the day of the reported viewing. Programs identified only by network or channel number were identified using Library of Congress newspaper files for the main city in the child's zip code to look up the TV schedule for the day and time of the time-use diary. When all of these methods failed to identify the program watched, the entry was designated as uncodable.

Video Game Subsamples

Analyses of total game play were performed on the subsample of children who reported any video game play (*n* = 730). Total game play was imputed for six children who returned one diary reporting game play using the method described above for television viewing. Game play by type was analyzed for the respondents who returned two complete time-use diaries at least one of which contained some game play (*n* = 724). Accordingly, subsamples used for total game play and type of game play differed slightly.

Video Game Type Coding System

Because of the interactive nature of video games, the coding system for game type was designed to reflect the cognitive demands of the game, as well as some content features. A total of 637 unique game titles were coded into one of five types: *educational/informative, sports, sensorimotor* (action/ arcade, fighting/shooting, driving/racing, other vehicular simulations), *strategy* (adventure/role playing, war, strategic simulations, puzzles/games), and *unknown* (other content, unspecified games, platform only). Using manufacturers' World Wide Web sites, published information available in stores, conversation with gaming experts, collaborative assistance from the Entertainment Software Ratings Board, and their own knowledge of the games, two coders classified each game. The Kappa estimate of interrater agreement was .89. All coding disagreements were resolved through discussion.

Calculation of Minutes of Time Use

All television viewing is reported in two ways: minutes per week and minutes per day type (weekday or weekend). Because games available for play do not change on weekends, only minutes per week are reported for game play. Minutes per week is a composite value comprising reported weekday and weekend minutes of television viewing or video game play loaded in the following manner: minutes per week = 5 × (weekday minutes) + 2 × (weekend minutes). Thus, minutes reported in the one weekday time-use diary are assumed to be representative of that subject's weekday viewing or game play habits. The same is true for weekend use.

RESULTS

Total Minutes of Primary Television Viewing

Because of the large sample size, an alpha level of .01 was used for all statistical tests. An alpha level of .05 was considered marginally significant.

Age Effects

An analysis of variance revealed a main effect of age on total minutes of television viewed per week, $F (3, 2378) = 13.67$, $p < .01$. The youngest children (age 0 to 2) watched significantly less television ($M = 644.56$, $SD = 528.19$) than the three older groups of children, who watched functionally equivalent amounts of television (age 3 to 5: $M = 828.63$, $SD = 562.34$; age 6 to 8: $M = 811.30$, $SD = 526.80$; age 9 to 12: $M = 846.72$, $SD = 592.40$).

Day Type Effects

A mixed-model ANOVA revealed a main effect of day type on the amount of television watched, $F (1, 2663) = 269.37$, $p < .01$. Children watch more television on a weekend day ($M = 130.61$, $SD = 119.14$) than on a weekday ($M = 91.62$, $SD = 91.54$).

There was a significant age by day type interaction, $F (3, 2663) = 45.67$,

$p < .01$. Weekend viewing increases as a function of age between the 0 to 2-year-olds ($M = 67.60$, $SD = 86.89$), the 3- to 5-year-olds ($M = 131.57$, $SD = 101.43$) and the 6- to 8-year-olds ($M = 160.69$, $SD = 117.26$). The 9- to 12-year-olds ($M = 157.01$, $SD = 134.76$) do not differ from 6- to 8-year-olds in the amount of time spent viewing television on the weekend. Thus, weekend television viewing peaked among the 6- to 8-year-olds and then leveled off. In contrast, weekday viewing's relationship with age is best described as an inverted "U" pattern, with weekday viewing peaking among the 3- to 5-year-olds ($M = 111.32$, $SD = 97.97$). Children ages 0 to 2 view the smallest amount of weekday television ($M = 64.63$, $SD = 83.36$), followed by children in the oldest two age groups who watch functionally equal amounts (6- to 8-year-olds: $M = 92.16$, $SD = 86.27$; 9- to 12-year-olds: $M = 98.12$, $SD = 91.91$).

Gender Effects

Although there were no significant effects for gender or gender by age interactions, there was a marginally significant three-way interaction of age-by-gender by day type, $F (3, 2087) = 3.46$, $p < .05$. Post-hoc analyses revealed that 9- to 12-year-old girls ($M = 106.68$, $SD = 91.63$) watched more weekday television than 6- to 8-year-old girls ($M = 82.24$, $SD = 70.15$). This pattern was reversed for boys, with 9- to 12-year-olds ($M = 87.89$, $SD = 91.31$) watching less weekday television than 6- to 8-year-olds ($M = 100.49$, $SD = 97.09$).

Total Minutes of Secondary Television Viewing

Analysis of variance was employed to determine if secondary television viewing varied as a function of age, gender, and day type. A main effect of age was found, $F (3, 2663) = 7.46$, $p < .01$; and post-hoc analyses revealed that differences in secondary viewing occur between the oldest and the two youngest age groups. Children ages 9 to 12 years old spend fewer minutes per week viewing television as a secondary activity ($M = 98.06$, $SD = 176.55$) than do children ages 0 to 2 ($M = 132.31$, $SD = 267.95$) and 3 to 5 ($M = 152.61$, $SD = 249.07$).

The main effect for gender approached significance, $F (1, 2663) = 4.24$, $p < .05$), with boys ($M = 130.16$, $SD = 245.68$) watching more television as a secondary activity than girls ($M = 113.80$, $SD = 207.91$). The age-by-gender interaction was also significant, $F (3, 2663) = 4.32$, $p < .01$. Boys show an inverted "U"-shaped pattern of secondary television usage with a peak among boys ages 3 to 5 and a large decline in use among 9- to 12-year-old boys. Girls, on the other hand, display a steady amount of secondary viewing across three age groups with a slight dip in the 6- to 8-year-old group.

A main effect of day type was found, $F (1, 2663) = 7.64$, $p < .01$. Children use television as a secondary activity more during a weekend day (M = 19.30, SD = 41.82) than a weekday (M = 16.68, SD = 37.87). There were no significant interactions for secondary television viewing.

Minutes of Television Viewing by Program Genre

An age-by-gender (4 × 2) Multivariate Analysis of Variance (MANOVA) was conducted to examine minutes spent watching programs in each of the nine genre categories using the subsample comprised by children whose reported program titles were at least 70% codable (n = 2263). Table 2.1 shows the weighted means and standard deviations for number of minutes viewed per week in each genre category by age and gender.

Age Effects

The MANOVA revealed a significant main effect for age: Pillais' F (27, 6243) = 29.93, $p < .001$, with age groups differing in every genre category (*educational*, F = 43.54; *noneducational cartoon*, F = 51.75; *action*, F = 13.09; *comedy*, F = 85.91, *reality based*, F = 7.45; *relationship drama*, F = 9.80; *fantasy/supernatural*, F = 20.87; *other*, F = 27.78; for all, Fs, df = 3, 2087, $p < .001$). The two most watched categories are educational programs and noneducational cartoons (see Figure 2.1). Both show an inverted "U" pattern with viewing peaking among the 3- to 5-year-olds. Immediately following the peak, use of noneducational cartoons drops by 19%. Educational television viewing drops more severely after its peak: 6- to 8-year-olds watch 47% less educational television than do 3- to 5-year-olds. While 6- to 8-year-olds begin to move away from programs designed primarily for children, they do so more rapidly for educational programs than for non-educational cartoons.

Gender Effects

There was also a main effect for gender: Pillais' F (9, 2079) = 12.61, $p < .001$. Boys and girls differed in four of the nine genre categories: Boys were higher viewers of *noneducational cartoons*, F (1, 2087) = 14.72, $p < .01$; *fantasy/supernatural*, F (1, 2087) = 9.38, $p < .01$; and *sports*, F (1, 2087) = 62.87, $p < .01$. Girls were higher viewers of *comedy*, F (1, 2087) = 16.28, $p < .01$; and "*other*," F (1, 2086) = 7.36, $p < .05$. Educational viewing did not differ by gender.

Age-by-Gender Interactions

The MANOVA revealed significant interactions of age-by-gender in four genres: *comedy*, F (3, 2087) = 12.78, $p < .01$; *sports*, F (3, 2087) = 12.11, $p < .01$; *relationship dramas*, F (3, 2087) = 4.23, $p < .01$; and *cartoons*, F (3, 2087) = 3.98, $p < .01$ (see Table 2.1 for means and standard deviations).

Table 2.1
Number of Minutes Viewed per Week in Each Program Type by Age and Gender

	0 to 2-Year-Olds (n = 598)		3- to 5-Year-Olds (n = 524)		6- to 8-Year-Olds (n = 465)		9- to 12-Year-Olds (n = 676)		All Ages (n = 2263)	
	M	SD	M	SD	M	SD	M	SD	M	SD
Educational Programs:										
All children	199.17[abc]	298.70	240.44[ac]	281.42	113.70[bc]	181.63	96.42[a]	162.68	158.48	243.17
Boys	189.17	309.35	236.35	285.41	98.23	176.15	91.57	166.05	151.87	248.28
Girls	208.78	288.33	245.59	276.93	133.13	186.90	100.71	159.76	165.45	237.59
Noneducational Cartoons:										
All children	126.94[a]	230.33	320.05[ab]	339.54	260.95[ab]	301.11	162.33[b]	223.48	209.74	282.36
Boys	114.09	201.87	330.68	340.57	306.19	348.57	187.00	236.46	231.96	299.37
Girls	139.27	254.45	306.67	338.60	204.17	215.78	140.53	209.28	186.31	261.35
Action Programs:										
All children	14.68[a]	77.77	23.46[b]	89.46	34.51[c]	108.55	61.58[abc]	200.94	35.14	135.79
Boys	15.32	66.09	17.09	70.48	29.94	84.60	57.55	162.93	30.89	107.59
Girls	14.06	87.64	31.49	108.41	40.25	132.64	65.13	229.54	39.62	160.15
Comedy Programs:										
All children	26.39[a]	104.97	67.42[a]	141.87	131.68[a]	208.90	199.83[a]	264.45	110.98	206.61
Boys	33.66	128.08	71.47	145.21	118.71	200.71	141.60	208.48	92.81	179.99
Girls	19.41	76.09	62.32	137.74	147.95	218.15	251.29	296.42	130.13	229.91
Reality-Based Programs:										
All children	2.58[a]	18.71	4.45[b]	26.66	7.60	34.21	11.89[ab]	52.43	6.91	36.70
Boys	2.54	20.73	4.26	26.21	10.30	40.88	15.23	59.00	8.31	40.65
Girls	2.61	16.58	4.69	27.28	4.22	22.93	8.95	45.73	5.44	31.97

44

Relationship Drama Programs:

All children	18.59[ab]	84.58	25.92[cd]	88.10	44.81[ac]	116.97	49.16[bd]	127.23	35.20	107.72
Boys	25.44	107.50	28.28	91.75	47.77	125.78	34.97	111.22	34.07	109.91
Girls	12.02	53.53	22.95	83.42	41.10	105.06	61.70	138.82	36.40	105.41

Fantasy Programs:

All children	7.43[abc]	30.71	43.25[a]	130.52	61.68[b]	153.19	51.97[c]	122.15	40.72	118.61
Boys	8.58	33.99	57.07	153.87	72.24	163.31	54.22	123.52	46.99	130.53
Girls	6.33	27.21	25.85	90.59	48.42	138.71	49.99	121.08	33.05	104.11

Sports Programs:

All children	7.88[a]	44.90	23.11[b]	94.45	33.51[a]	121.81	63.03[ab]	187.69	33.54	129.72
Boys	12.59	60.08	33.78	119.66	54.05	154.60	110.91	254.18	54.71	170.90
Girls	3.36	21.26	9.67	42.90	7.75	48.27	20.71	74.45	11.22	53.16

Other Programs:

All children	6.82[a]	35.89	14.05[b]	62.55	25.53a	74.27	50.91[ab]	133.24	25.85	89.86
Boys	7.22	39.84	15.59	64.34	12.73	42.84	43.42	140.79	20.54	86.53
Girls	6.44	31.70	12.11	60.33	41.59	98.49	57.53	126.02	31.44	92.96

Note: Gender group *n*s within age for all program types: Ages 0–2 (Boys *n* = 297, Girls *n* = 301); Ages 3–5 (Boys *n* = 300, Girls *n* = 301); Ages 6–8 (Boys *n* = 247, Girls *n* = 218; Ages 9–12 (Boys *n* = 335, Girls *n* = 341). For age group main effects, values marked with the same superscript in the same row significantly differ at $p < .05$. Means and standard deviations for all ages are included for descriptive purposes.

Figure 2.1
Minutes per Week of Educational Program and Noneducational Cartoon Viewing
by Age and Gender

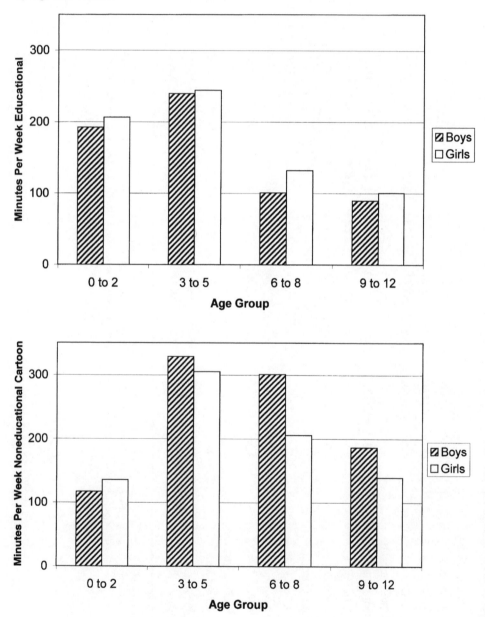

Significant age-by-gender interactions indicated that among 9- to 12-year-olds, girls watch more comedy and relationship dramas than boys. Among boys, viewing of sports programs increases dramatically with each successive age group. Boys in the 9- to 12-year-old group watch almost twice as much sports programming as do boys ages 6 to 12.

For both genders the pattern of minutes of noneducational cartoons viewed peaks among 3- to 5-year-olds and then declines as a function of age. This decline, however, occurs more quickly among girls than among boys. The 6- to 8-year-old girls spend much less time viewing noneducational cartoons than do 3- to 5-year-old girls. This is not true for boys; their major movement away from noneducational cartoons appears in the 9- to 12-year-old group. Among the 9 to 12-year-olds, girls watch fewer minutes of noneducational cartoons than do boys.

Age-by-Gender by Program Genre Interactions

Noneducational cartoons and educational programs were a major focus throughout the analyses, in part because they have important implications for school readiness (Wright & Huston, 1995) and to subsequent scholastic achievement (Anderson et al., 2001). In order to explore the relationship among watching these types of programs and children's age and gender, a mixed-model MANOVA was employed. A marginally significant three-way interaction was found, $F (3, 2087) = 3.12$, $p = .05$ (see Figure 2.2 for graphical depiction of differences in educational and noneducational cartoon program viewing by age and gender). The figure shows that 9- to 12-year-old boys spend more time watching noneducational cartoons than do 9- to 12-year-old girls. Boys apparently lose interest in these noneducational cartoons at an older age than do girls. The reverse is true for educational programming. For both genders, 6- to 8-year-olds watch considerably fewer minutes of educational programming than do 3- to 5-year-olds. Girls' viewing, however, does not decline as dramatically as boys' between these two age groups.

Video Game Play in Sample

Among the entire sample used in this study ($n = 2,902$), 25% reported playing games at least once in their time use diaries, while 75% reported no game use. Chi-square tests by age and sex for game play versus no game play within each age group indicated no differences in the number of 0 to 2-year-old boys and girls who played (Boys $n = 16$, Girls $n = 13$) than those who did not (Boys $n = 334$, Girls $n = 332$). However, all chi-square tests for the three remaining age groups were significant (Ages 3 to 5, χ^2 [1] = 8.33, p < .01; Ages 6 to 8, χ^2 [1] = 22.81, p < .001; Ages 9 to 12, χ^2 [1] = 46.75, p < .001). Taken together, these chi-squares indicated that the number of children playing video games increased with each increasing

Figure 2.2
Minutes of Video Game Play of Each Type by Age and Gender

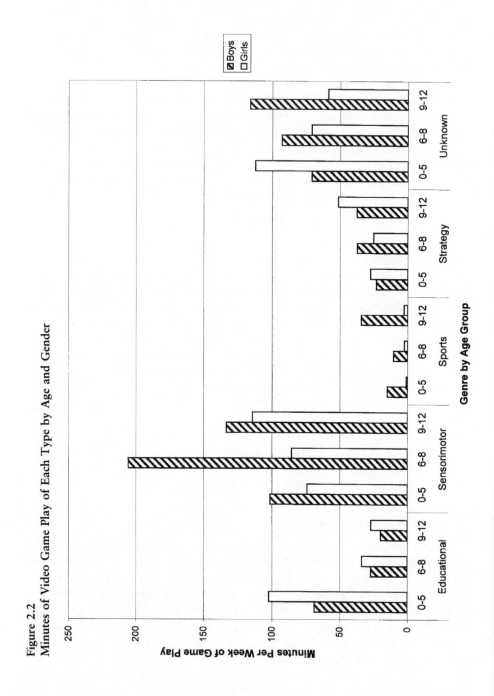

age group, and that boys played more games than girls in each age group (Players Ages 3 to 5, Boys n = 90, Girls n = 46; Nonplayers Ages 3 to 5, Boys n = 290, Girls n = 263; Players Ages 6 to 8, Boys n = 141, Girls n = 80; Nonplayers Ages 6 to 8, Boys n = 178, Girls n = 228; Players Ages 9 to 12, Boys n = 218, Girls n = 126; Nonplayers Ages 9 to 12, Boys n = 218, Girls n = 329).

Total Minutes of Video Game Play

Due to the large proportion of nonplayers, parametric analyses of total video game play were conducted for players only (n = 730). This sample included the six participants for whom total game play minutes for their second diary were imputed from their first. Because the 0 to 2-year-old age group contained only 29 children, it was combined with the 3- to 5-year-old age group. Boys (M = 374.77, SD = 417.41) spent significantly more minutes per week playing video games than did girls (M = 264.85, SD = 255.61), F (1, 669) = 9.78, $p < .01$. There were no significant age effects on total minutes of game play.

Video Game Play by Game Type

The sample used for the categorical analyses included only those who completed two diaries (n = 724). Figure 2.2 shows means for age-by-gender-by-game-type use.

Age Effects

Significant main effects were found for *educational* games, F (2, 666) = 20.42, $p < .01$, and *sports* games, F (2, 666) = 5.57, $p < .01$. For *educational* games, 0 to 5-year-olds (M = 81.65, SD = 126.79) played more than did 6- to 8-year-olds (M = 29.21, SD = 83.88) and 9- to 12-year-olds (M = 22.73, SD = 89.11). For *sports* games, 9- to 12-year-olds (M = 22.02, SD = 67.18) played more than did 6- to 8-year-olds (M = 8.06, SD = 24.69). There were no significant age effects for the sensorimotor, strategy, and "unknown" game types.

Gender Effects

A significant gender effect was found only for *sports* games, F (1, 666) = 24.62, $p < .01$. Boys (M = 22.66, SD = 64.97) played more sports games than did girls (M = 2.33, SD = 9.94). The gender effects for *sensorimotor* games reached marginal significance, F (1, 666) = 4.11, $p < .043$. There were no gender differences for educational, strategy, and "unknown" game types. Analyses revealed only marginally significant age-by-gender interactions for two game type categories: *sports*, F (2, 666) = 3.41, $p < .05$, and *"unknown,"* F (2, 666) = 3.69, $p < .05$ (see Figure 2.2).

DISCUSSION

With respect to television use, the present data support the general findings in the existing literature. Previous studies of television use have found that preschool children (3- to 5-year-olds) and older elementary school children (9- to 12-year-olds) spend more time with television than do young school-aged children (6- to 8-year-olds) and very young children (0 to 2-year-olds; Timmer et al., 1985). This pattern is also evident in the present data. Very young children watch whatever their adult caregiver is watching and do a lot of secondary viewing. Correspondingly, the drop in total weekday television viewing at 6 to 8 years of age corresponds to the age at which most children begin regular attendance at a full-day school program. The concurrent rise in weekend viewing may represent a "compensatory" adjustment for loss of weekday viewing time to school demands. It is also in part a function of the fact that many school-age children are permitted to watch later in the evening on Saturday nights. Thus, it is likely that these changes are due to changes in contextual demands on children's time.

The gender differences clearly indicate the diverging interests of girls and boys, and are best understood at the level of analysis involving age-by-gender interactions in individual genres of programming. This is because as children's tastes become differentiated in consistent ways, the nonhomogeneity of the medium becomes apparent. *How much* you watch becomes less critical than *what* you watch, and global statements about use of a monolithic medium become less and less meaningful. Specifically, the older girls' attraction to the relationship dramas offered during weekday, primetime broadcasts could account for part of the three-way observed interaction between gender, age, and genre. Another part of the increase in weekday viewing for 9- to 12-year-old girls corresponds with the rise in viewing comedy programs. It is probable that these girls are beginning to become interested in weekday evening situation comedies that generally target teenagers and adults.

With respect to the two most viewed program categories, which are also the two with most nearly opposite relations to outcomes in the longitudinal literature, apparently boys maintain their interest in noneducational cartoons into the older age groups more readily than do girls, whereas girls remain interested in educational programs longer than do boys (Anderson et al., 2001). There is a quality of maturity and serious social concern among the girls that is not evident among most boys, and an attraction to action, confrontation, and probably violence among boys that is not shared by girls.

With respect to video games, it is no surprise to find boys spending about three times as many minutes per week in engagement with games as girls. Just as previous research has shown for the initial advent of television, new media tend to fill time previously devoted to functionally equivalent media.

That is, television displaced the use of radio, records, telephones, and comic books rather than taking time previously devoted to high-level educational activities or serious leisure reading. In the present study we find that the drop in TV viewing for older boys has occurred at the same time that sensorimotor and later sports games were captivating their attention. It is, therefore, of serious concern that there is no comparably attractive route from viewing educational TV programs to interactive media use for girls.

For girls, the future may be more optimistic. New games, both computer- and video-based, are being developed to engage the involvement of girls. Many involve some serious relationships, social knowledge, or "people-sense" (like the SimFamily game). The same emerging effort toward interesting girls in interactive play and learning is evident in new protected and monitored web sites and chat rooms for girls on the Internet. Clearly such efforts are needed if we are to give girls a headstart in the cyber world comparable to that now enjoyed by boys.

Most of the games reported are played on Sega, Nintendo, or Play Station platforms. While there is a growing overlap of software across platform boundaries, it is still true that there are many more educational interactive games marketed as CD-ROMs for computers than are made for the popular video game platforms. Conversely there is a very high proportion of sensorimotor, sports, shooting, and fighting games made for the video game platforms, but a larger share of the adventure and strategy games are made for use on computers. The fact of a disproportionate share of the less educational, more violent games being used by low-income and minority children in the PSID-CDS has been noted by Scantlin (1999), and gives cause for concern. It is not simply the higher cost of computer hardware and software that produces ethnic and socioeconomic inequities in children's electronic play. Research on television use shows similar discrepancies which are not due to differences in access. Poor and minority children in America, especially boys, watch more violent and other commercial entertainment television programming, and less educational and informative programming than do majority and middle-class youngsters (Comstock, 1991; Huston & Wright, 1997).

While there are few surprises in the outcomes, they serve as "snapshot" population estimates for the nation as of 1997, and provide a baseline for longitudinal comparison when the next Child Supplement diaries are collected. These new data on the same sample are expected to be collected in 2002 and to be available in 2004. We believe there is an urgent need for developmentally organized research of the same depth and variety for children's use of interactive electronic media as has been devoted over the past 20 years to the effects of various kinds of television. We need studies of different ages and different contexts, experiments and surveys, and especially longitudinal studies in order to converge on valid conclusions, analogous to those we have already reached about television outcomes, in the domains of interactive media. It is our hope that this study establishes a few of the anchor points necessary for such a program of applied research.

ACKNOWLEDGMENTS

Reprinted from *Applied Developmental Psychology*, Vol. 22 (1), Wright, J. C., Huston, A. C., Vandewater, E. A., Bickham, D. S., Scantlin, R. M., Kotler, J. A., Caplovitz, A. G., Lee, J. H., Hofferth, S., & Finkelstein, J., American children's use of electronic media in 1997: A national survey, pp. 31–47, © 2001, with permission from Elsevier Science.

Funding for this research was provided by grant No. R01HD33474 from the National Institute of Child Health and Human Development to the University of Michigan's Institute for Social Research, by grant No. 3797 from the Hogg Foundation for Mental Health to the first author, and by grant No. 98–1911–98 from the William T. Grant Foundation to the first three authors. This research was conducted at the Center for Research on the Influences of Television on Children (CRITC), University of Texas at Austin. We would like to thank the Entertainment Software Ratings Board, an industry-sponsored advisory group, for graciously supplying many game descriptions and ESRB ratings for games reported in the diaries.

REFERENCES

Anderson, D. R., Huston, A. C., Schmitt, K., Linebarger, D., & Wright, J. C. (2001). Early childhood television viewing and adolescent behavior. *Monographs of the Society for Research in Child Development, 66* (1, Serial No. 264).

Brown, J. D., Childers, K. W., Bauman, K. E., & Koch, G. G. (1990). The influence of new media and family structure on young adolescents' television and radio use. *Communication Research—An International Quarterly, 17* (1), 65–82.

Buchman, D. D., & Funk, J. B. (1996). Video and computer games in the '90s: Children's time commitment and game preference. *Children Today, 24,* 12–15.

Cassell, J., & Jenkins, H. (1998). Chess for girls? Feminism and computer games. In J. Cassell & H. Jenkins (Eds.), *From Barbie to Mortal Kombat: Gender and computer games* (pp. 2–45). Cambridge, MA: MIT Press.

Comstock, G. (1991). *Television and the American child.* Orlando, FL: Academic Press.

Condry, J. (1989). *The psychology of television.* Hillsdale, NJ: Erlbaum.

Funk, J. B., Germann, J. N., & Buchman, D. D. (1997). Children and electronic games in the United States. *Trends in Communication, 2,* 111–126.

Gailey, C. W. (1996). Mediated messages: Gender, class, and cosmos in home video games. In I. E. Sigel (Series Ed.) & P. M. Greenfield & R. R. Cocking (Vol. Eds.), *Interacting with video, Vol. 11: Advances in applied developmental psychology* (pp. 9–23). Norwood, NJ: Ablex.

Greenfield, P. M. (1994). Video games as cultural artifacts. *Journal of Applied Developmental Psychology, 15,* 3–11.

Hofferth, S., & Sandberg, J. (1999). *American children's use of time in 1997.* Unpublished paper. Ann Arbor: Institute for Social Research, University of Michigan.

Hofferth, S., & Sandberg, J. (in press). How American children use their time. *Journal of Marriage and the Family, 63* (2).

Huston, A. C., Anderson, D. R., Wright, J. C., Linebarger, D. L., & Schmitt, K. (2001). *Sesame Street* viewers as adolescents: The recontact study. In S. Fisch & R. Truglio (Eds.), *"G" is for "growing": Thirty years of research on Sesame Street.* Mahwah, NJ: Erlbaum.

Huston, A. C., Donnerstein, E., Fairchild, H., Feshbach, N., Katz, P., Murray, J., Rubinstein, E., Wilcox, B., & Zuckerman, D. (1992). *Big world, small screen: The role of television in American society.* Lincoln: University of Nebraska Press.

Huston, A. C., & Wright, J. C. (1997). Mass media and children's development. In W. Damon (Series Ed.), I. Sigel, & A. Renninger (Vol. Eds.), *Handbook of child psychology, Vol. 4: Child psychology in practice* (5th ed., pp. 999–1058). New York: Wiley.

Huston, A. C., Wright, J. C., Marquis, J., & Green, S. B. (1999). How young children spend their time: Television and other activities. *Developmental Psychology, 35,* 912–925.

Huston, A. C., Wright, J. C., Rice, M. L., Kerkman, D., & St. Peters, M. (1990). Development of television viewing patterns in early childhood: A longitudinal investigation. *Developmental Psychology, 26,* 409–420.

Johnson, C. S., & Swoope, K. F. (1987). Boys' and girls' interest in using computers: Implications for the classroom. *Arithmetic Teacher, 35* (1), 14–16.

Kinder, M. (1996). Contextualizing video game violence: From Teenage Mutant Ninja Turtles 1 to Mortal Kombat 2. In I. E. Sigel (Series Ed.) & P. M. Greenfield & R. R. Cocking (Eds.), *Interacting with video: Advances in applied developmental psychology: Vol. 11* (pp. 25–37). Norwood, NJ: Ablex.

Kinnear, A. (1995). Introduction of microcomputers: A case study of patterns of use and children's perceptions. *Journal of Educational Computing Research, 13,* 27–40.

Kubey, R., & Larson, R. (1990). The use and experience of the new video media among children and young adolescents. *Communication Research, 17,* 107–130.

McKenzie, T. L., Sallis, J. F., Nader, P. R., & Broyles, S. L. (1992). Anglo- and Mexican-American preschoolers at home and at recess: Activity patterns and environmental influences. *Journal of Developmental and Behavioral Pediatrics, 13,* 173–180.

Rideout, V. J., Foehr, U. G., Roberts, D. F., & Brodie, M. (1999). *Kids and media at the new millenium: Executive summary.* Menlo Park, CA: Kaiser Family Foundation.

Ridley-Johnson, R., Chance, J. E., & Cooper, H. (1984). Correlates of children's television viewing: Expectancies, age, and sex. *Journal of Applied Developmental Psychology, 5,* 225–235.

Scantlin, R. M. (1999). *Interactive media: An analysis of children's computer and video game use.* Unpublished doctoral dissertation, University of Texas, Austin.

Singer, J. L., & Singer, D. G. (1981). *Television, imagination and aggression: A study of preschoolers.* Hillsdale, NJ: Erlbaum.

Tangney, J. P., & Feshbach, S. (1988). Children's television viewing frequency: Individual differences and demographic correlates. *Personality and Social Psychology Bulletin, 14,* 145–158.

Timmer, S. G., Eccles, J., & O'Brien, K. (1985). How children use time. In F. T. Juster & F. P. Stafford (Eds.), *Time, goods, and well-being* (pp. 353–382). Ann Arbor, MI: Survey Research Center, Institute for Social Research.

Wright, J. C., & Huston, A. C. (1995). *Effects of educational TV viewing of lower income preschoolers on academic skills, school readiness, and school adjustment one to three years later.* Report to Children's Television Workshop, Center for Research on the Influences of Television on Children, University of Kansas, Lawrence, June.

Part II

Behavioral Effects of Media

Chapter 3

Identity Construction on the Internet

Sandra L. Calvert

Who am I? Although this question has long been of interest to humans, philosophers, and psychologists, it has been a particularly strong preoccupation of the developing adolescent. For the first time, adolescents can think about who they are from an abstract perspective, allowing them to consider the possibilities of who they are, who they have been, and who they will be.

Living within a body impacts the construction of identity (Harre, 1983). People have a biological sex, an age, a race, and other physical features that affect how people perceive themselves and how others perceive and treat them. They also have a name, given to them at birth. But what if individuals were no longer constrained by their physical body or their real-life name in presenting themselves to others? How would they choose to present themselves? Who would they be? These questions are now being examined as people spend time and create online characters, or personae, on the Internet, particularly in the context of Multi-User Domains (MUDs) which are online fantasy worlds and adventure games where people interact online. Currently, hundreds of thousands of players, primarily adolescent males (Turkle, 1995), are engaged in role-playing activities on MUDs during the stage of their lives when they should be in the most active phase of identity construction (Erikson, 1968).

WHAT IS IDENTITY?

Although identity can refer to how cultures, groups, or individuals are characterized, in developmental psychology the focus is on (1) personality characteristics that define the self by the individual and by others; and (2) the internal sense of continuity in self-images over time (Grotevant, 1998). Identity includes an interpersonal aspect, consisting of roles and relationships; a potentiality aspect, consisting of who a person may become; and a values aspect, consisting of moral beliefs (Baumeister, 1997). There are also those who do not believe in identity or a unitary sense of self (Harter, 1998); rather, they believe that there are multiple "selves" that are presented to others depending upon the situation (Turkle, 1995).

Identity is an important developmental milestone during adolescence because it serves as the foundation for adult psychosexual development and relationships, as an anchor for self-definition, and as a predictor of behavioral problems (Grotevant, 1998). An optimal sense of identity is achieved when a person feels comfortable within his or her own body, when a person knows where they are going, and when a person feels support from significant others (Erikson, 1968).

The literature about identity has focused on areas that the individual can control, such as work and occupational roles, ideological values, and social relationships. However, there are many other dimensions that individuals have little control over, such as age, gender, race, and sexual orientation, that are also important in identity construction (Grotevant, 1998). These areas can be controlled on the Internet, making the exploration of identity far more flexible in cyberspace. For instance, virtual bodies, made possible on the Internet, allow adolescents to create any kind of body that they want to present to others. The fat can be thin, the short can be tall, the weak can be strong. The anonymity provided by the Internet even allows gender changes, ethnic changes, and experiments in sexual orientation without ever leaving the safety of one's home.

Identity has been conceived as a unitary construct that is developed across the life-span (Erikson, 1968), and as a meeting place where archetypal images are integrated into the personality (Jung, 1959). By contrast, social interactionists focus on linguistic constructions where multiple "selves" are role-played depending upon the situation (Mead, 1925). Each perspective contributes to our understanding of how the Internet impacts identity construction.

Erikson's Perspective: The Quest for Identity

The belief in a single, unitary identity that is forged after a period of exploration and search is best expressed by Erikson (1968). The construction of identity is achieved throughout the life-span as individuals explore and then consolidate changes in how they define themselves (Grotevant, 1998). This kind of exploration takes on a new character during adolescence because the person is experiencing simultaneous changes in physical, social, and cognitive development. Cognitive changes allow the adolescent to reflect on who he or she is at an abstract level that was not possible earlier in development.

Erikson (1968) theorized that identity versus role confusion was the psychosocial conflict that adolescents must resolve. Identity achievement occurred only after a search in which adolescents explored different facets of their personality. This search, which takes place during a moratorium on making a firm commitment to an identity, allows the adolescent to try out different roles and to determine which ones best suit him or her. The Internet has become a new context in which adolescent identity exploration and construction is taking place (Calvert, 1999a).

Jung's Perspective: The Archetypes and the Formation of the Self

Like Erikson, Jung (1959) believed in a unitary self, but he viewed the construction of that self somewhat differently. For Jung, the self was a meeting place where archetypal images were explored and integrated into the personality (Hall & Nordby, 1973). Archetypal images, which reside in our shared collective unconscious, include mother, father, hero, king, queen, sorcerer, witch, and healer (Calvert, 2002). Humans are predisposed to construct archetypal images. Expanding on Jung's work, it is the thesis of this chapter that role-play activities are one mechanism by which those archetypal images are developed and integrated into our sense of self.

Any archetypal image that is acted on will be developed, but there are key images that are needed for the formation of personality (Hall & Nordby, 1973). These are the persona (the public mask representing how people display the self to others), the animus and the anima (the masculine principle of females and the feminine principle of males, respectively), the shadow (the life-preserving, but potentially destructive dark side of the personality), and the self (the meeting place where all archetypal images are integrated into a coherent identity).

In many Internet MUDs, adolescents role play archetypal personae such as wizards and heroes who engage in adventures where they attempt to vanquish their enemies. Thus, Internet MUDs can provide a setting where a significant number of adolescents can explore and construct their identity by enacting archetypal roles including various personae, the anima or animus, and the shadow.

Social Interactionists: We Are Only the Roles That We Say or Play

Social interactionists believe that individuals have multiple "selves" rather than a unitary self-construct (Harter, 1998). These selves are public images, not unlike Jung's personae. However, the self only exists in the realm of social discourse, not in real life. Specific situations determine which "self" will be shown. There is considerable evidence that adolescents enact numerous roles and display multiple selves depending on the social context (Harter, 1998). The Internet is one place where these multiple selves are being enacted (Turkle, 1995).

Social interaction allows a social mirror through which individuals can see themselves through the eyes of others. In this way, individuals learn to take on the role of others toward themselves. To do so, children initially play at adult roles via imitation, taking on the stance of mother, father, or teacher. Therefore, role play allows children to understand and to adopt the attitude of other people in relation to the self (Mead, 1925).

Social interactionists view the self as a social construction, created through linguistic exchanges with others (Harter, 1998). Using one's voice in telling online stories and narratives is one way for an adolescent to explore and to construct his or her sense of self (see Chapter 7 in this volume). Expanding on the ideas of Mead and Cassell, the thesis of this chapter is that multiple "selves" are role played to construct a unified sense of self, or identity. While some of these exchanges are only textual in nature, others involve symbolically enacted behaviors through avatars.

Summary

Theories vary with respect to their use of basic concepts such as a "core identity" versus "multiple selves." From the perspective of Erikson, the exploration of identity that is now taking place on the Internet in spaces such as MUDs may be a search for a unitary construct about the self. Creating and acting on various personae should take place during the identity search, or moratorium, as adolescents actively construct their identity. From the perspective of Jung, adolescents are using their MUD personae to enact various archetypal images that should be integrated into the personality. From the perspective of Mead and other social interactionists, adolescents may be constructing multiple selves by using both language and role play in Internet MUD interactions. Building on the ideas of Jung, Mead, and Erikson, the perspective taken in this chapter is that adolescents are using role-play activities on the Internet to try out and construct a coherent, unified identity.

MULTI-USER DOMAINS OR MULTI-USER DUNGEONS OR DRAGONS

Internet users have many choices about where they interact and how they present themselves in social interactions. User names, or handles, are often abbreviations of a person's real name, particularly in work settings. When given choices, however, many users create their own handle, often bringing an element of fantasy into those selections.

Adventure-type MUDs are a space on the Internet that was originally modeled after a board game called Dungeons and Dragons (Calvert, 2002). In this game, players assumed the personae (i.e., the actor's masks) of various characters and then proceeded to slay beasts and dragons in a fantasy adventure setting (Turkle, 1995). This type of game was adapted to the Internet, and there are numerous games where players don their masks and assume various archetypal roles such as hero, elf, healer, and wizard. Such games are goal-directed and players win or lose.

Social MUDs are a more-open, less-constrained space where players assume various personae and create whatever type of MUD interests them (Turkle, 1995). In social MUDs, objects and places are constructed, sometimes by all players and sometimes only by wizards, who are the master players (Turkle, 1995). The point of social MUDs is social interaction with the other people in these virtual spaces (Turkle, 1995).

Initially, MUDs were only textual in nature. That is, players described who they were and interacted with each other only by textual commands on the screen. These solely textual interactions are now being enhanced with the use of visually-presented avatars, cartoon-like representations of a character's persona. Put another way, text-based personae are becoming embodied (Calvert, 1999a). The visual addition of an embodied character changes the nature of Internet interactions. For example, a textual argument becomes a fight between two avatars and textual vows of marriage become a marriage between two avatars (Schroeder, 1997).

Numerous opportunities are available for players to become involved in MUD experiences, some of which can impact their real-life identity. These include (1) the players' initial choices about their personae, or online identity; and (2) the role playing and social interactions that occur as they play out these personae. Case studies, where detailed descriptions are made about individual players, and participant observation, where the researcher dons a mask and participates in the MUD while he or she observes the other players, are the two primary types of methodologies used to study Internet identity construction, role playing, and social interaction (Schroeder, 1997; Turkle, 1995, 1997).

The Construction of Personae

When people initially join a MUD, they must make decisions about how they want to present themselves to others. This persona functions as an onscreen identity. The term "persona," or onscreen identity, is derived from Jung's archetypal image of persona, or public mask. In MUDs, text provides the mask of a player (Danet, 1998).

Choices are made involving the construction of a persona with a: (1)

name, (2) gender, and (3) self-description (Curtis, 1997). Since there is no way to check the accuracy of these self-presentations, players are free to be anyone they want to be (Calvert, 1999a). In other words, players are anonymous.

What's in a Name?

The names of people have life-long implications for how others treat them, yet people have little control of their name. Parents select them. Some names, such as Mary, Tommy, and Suzie, carry little social risk, but names like Hugo and Hilda do. For instance, children with popular names are better liked, and teachers gave better grades to essays that were randomly paired with popular rather than unpopular names of children (Asher, Oden, & Gottman, 1977).

One of the first activities MUD players decide is a name for their persona. In LambdaMOO, Curtis (1997) found considerable variability in player names though there were some common styles. These styles included names that come from myth, fantasy, and literature (e.g., Merlin, Arthur), names that come from real life (e.g., Amy, Bruce), and names of concepts, animals, and everyday objects (e.g., Coyote, Ford). On our Internet site, children from ages 7 to 12 created pretend names as Georgetown Hoya TV Reporters (see Chapter 9, this volume, for a full description of the project). Most children chose real-life names such as Jen, Jill, and Andy, but many names, such as Pikachu, Tigger, Eyeore, Tweety, LALA, and Kermit D Frog, were taken from children's television characters (Calvert, 1999a).

Characters in MUDs can become possessive of their names. For instance, *ZigZag* complained when *ZigZag!* and *Zig* appeared on the LambdaMOO site (Curtis, 1997). Such complaints suggest that players invest in and identify with the names of their personae. They want a unique online identity just as they want a unique real-life identity.

Internet players can change names readily if they select an unpopular name for themselves, or if they act in socially inappropriate ways that require a fresh start and a new identity (Curtis, 1997). Such alterations of identity are far more difficult in real life. Because there are few consequences for mistakes, players can experiment more with who they are online than they can in real life.

Gender Identity and Gender Stability

Biological sex plays a key role in most people's constructions of identity (Calvert, 1999b). Kohlberg (1966) theorized that children acquire gender identity, the knowledge that they are a boy or a girl, by about age 3. Gender constancy, the knowledge that one's biological sex is an immutable person characteristic, is understood by about age 7.

Martin and Halverson (1981) believe that knowledge of one's gender is important, in part, because children use that construct to define who they are. Being a boy or a girl has cultural implications for personal interests, for personal conduct, and for personality traits (Ruble & Martin, 1998). Because the male role is more valued in most cultures, girls are given far more latitude to act in masculine ways than boys are given to act in feminine ways (Calvert, 1999b).

Biological rules about gender can change on the Internet. Unconstrained by a physical body, males and females are allowed unlimited freedom to explore being the other sex. Many of them do. Some males, for instance, present themselves as female personae and some females present themselves as male personae. Men, who as a group experience the most real-life constraints in gender-defined behaviors, are more likely to explore being a woman than women are to explore being a man. For instance, there is a ratio of 4 real men to every real woman on the MUD Habitat, but within that MUD the ratio is 3 male personae to every female persona (Turkle, 1997). In real numbers, at least 120,000 men present themselves as women on this MUD alone.

Although there is more flexibility in selecting one's gender on the Internet, gender still remains the most constrained choice that people make about their online identity (Curtis, 1997). Players can create a male or a female persona, though some choose gender-neutral names or even create their own genders. Other players, however, typically try to find out the gender of any player by asking that player if they are male or female, presumably because gender frames the stance we take and how we interact with others (Danet, 1998).

Why do people engage in gender-bending? In Erikson's theory, the search for a mature sexual identity is a key developmental task. The Internet provides a safe haven to explore sexual identity by participating in sexual fantasies, including homosexual ones (Curtis, 1997). One male became concerned that his female partner was experimenting with women in Internet chat rooms. He ended their relationship because she often played a male-presenting persona who had sex with a female-presenting persona. This kind of experimentation about sexual identity would be far more difficult without the Internet where a player's true biological sex is unknown (Turkle, 1995).

Knowledge of another's gender also impacts how that player will be treated in a MUD, just as it impacts how people are treated in real life. For this reason, many females present themselves as males so they will not be sexually harassed online (Danet, 1998). Male-presenting personae, for instance, offer more assistance to new female-presenting personae; in return, they often request an online sexual interaction with them, known as "TinySex" (i.e., textually based sexual interactions on the Internet) (Turkle, 1997). By contrast, new male-presenting personae are often left to their own resources to figure out how the MUD works. Because male-presenting females are left alone, they discover that they don't really need help from others, thereby becoming more independent and autonomous online (Turkle, 1995)—traits that are traditionally considered to be masculine.

Another reason for gender-bending may result from an interest in finding out what it is like to be a male or a female (Danet, 1998). By being the other gender, both gender roles can be better understood, thereby helping the individual construct a mature sex role identity. Some males try out and explore feminine aspects of their personalities while females try out and explore masculine aspects of their personalities. In Jung's theory, this would be the exploration of the animus or the anima. In feminist theory, it is called androgyny, a blending of traditionally masculine and feminine personality characteristics (Calvert, 1999b). For instance, one woman, who thought that she was too passive in real life, began to act more assertively online. She became a wizard (an archetypal image) named Ulysses and practiced being firm in her online persona. Her online firmness also carried over into real life. After she reached her desired level of real-life firmness, she abandoned her male online persona lest she become too aggressive (Turkle, 1995).

In some instances, experimentation with gender bending results in deceptions that can damage relationships. For instance, one female-presenting male, "Joan," joined a female group and became their close friend and confidante. As a female, he shared in intimate female confidences until he was discovered to be a male. In one version of the story, he "introduced" some of his online friends to a man named Alex (his true self), who then in real life had sex with some of them. Many of the women who interacted with the "female" Alex, known as Joan, felt upset and violated by his online deception (Turkle, 1995).

On our Georgetown Hoya TV Reporter site, boys occasionally presented themselves as girls. Our interpretation of this behavior was that boys thought it was funny or that they were playing with "being a girl" in an anonymous space. For instance, one fifth-grade boy's pretend name was Goldylocks while another chose to be Spice Girls (Calvert, 1999a).

Self-Description

When people meet a new person in real life, they often ask questions to find out more about him or her. The same is true on MUDs, except it is done in text rather than in speech.

When first entering a MUD, new players define their characters with textual passages about themselves. These passages can be lengthy or brief, depending on how much information the player wants to provide. As soon as past MUD players discover a new player in a common space, they often read these passages and then use them to create their first impression of that new persona (Curtis, 1997).

The initial perception of characters impacts how the newcomer will be treated. As noted above, female-presenting characters are offered more help than male-presenting characters, but nonthreatening descriptions of male characters also elicit help. For instance, a female who created a male character named Argyle described him as a fellow who was short, squatty, and always in search of his socks. Other male characters gave Argyle weapons and showed him where the most vulnerable "monsters" on the site were rather than leaving him to his own devices. The woman who created him thought the reaction would have been quite different had Argyle been a large, broad-shouldered, burly character who might have challenged the power lines of the male hierarchy (Turkle, 1997).

Role Playing and Social Interactions on the Internet

Once an online identity is constructed, players can enact various social roles. A unique part of online role-playing experiences is that we can bring others into our fantasies, and those people do not know how truthful our public online identities are (Huntemann & Morgan, 2001).

As a participant observer, Schroeder (1997) visited two MUDs, known as Alphaworld and Cybergate, where he examined the social roles of participants and the structure of the virtual world. In both worlds, Schroeder donned personae himself as he role played a human and a cartoon avatar.

Schroeder (1997) found evidence of social stratification in these virtual worlds, broken along the lines of novice and experienced players. Novice players often stayed in common spaces where there were many users. They were observers far more so than participants in social interactions. In fact, novice players in one world had to wear a camera around their neck, indicating that they had to assume the role of a tourist.

By contrast, experienced players visited the far reaches of these virtual worlds. They were more likely to construct virtual spaces with others and to actively pursue certain relationships. Experienced players assumed personae such as guides, pranksters, or bullies. Put another way, experienced players were more likely to create distinctive identities than were novice players. Moreover, they had more social status in a world where there is social stratification and power based on identity, experience, and expertise.

How do these online social interactions affect people's real-life social relationships? In Erikson's theory, the psychosocial conflict in early adulthood shifts to intimacy versus isolation. Examinations of Internet interactions on people's real-life intimate relationships initially yielded mixed results (Calvert, 2002), but those effects now seem to be less negative than originally thought. For instance, increased Internet interaction initially seemed to result in feelings of isolation, less family interaction, more depression, and more loneliness (Kraut, Patterson, Lundmark, Kiesler, Mukophalhya, & Scherlis, 1998), but three years later, depression had declined and loneliness was no longer associated with Internet use for that same sample of individuals (Kraut, Kiesler, Boneva, Cummings, Helgeson, &

Crawford, 2002). Internet interactions can lead to real-life intimate interactions when people meet their online friends, and those new relationships can complement, rather than disrupt, family interaction and community involvement (Katz & Aspden, 1997; Parks & Roberts, 1998). Social benefits of Internet use seem greatest for extroverts, and social problems seem greatest for introverts (Kraut et al., 2002).

Intimate social interactions also occur online. While some players are looking only for sex, others seek more enduring relationships and get "married" online. Some of these online interactions turn into real-life meetings and partnerships whereas for others, the online relationship is an end in itself (Calvert, 1999a). In either case, players gain practice in developing a close intimate relationship with another person. Players learn to take turns, to please another person, to ask for a commitment to a relationship. In so doing, they may be preparing themselves for a real-life relationship, even if it is with someone other than the virtual partner.

ONLINE IDENTITY ISSUES

While role play and social interactions on Internet MUDs seem like harmless entertainment, there are potential issues that can occur for players, particularly young ones. These issues include deception, mistaking "bots" (intelligent robots) for real people, identity confusion, and constructing a negative identity by acting out antisocial activities in cyberspace (Calvert, 2002).

Deception occurs when a player constructs personae that mislead the other players about who that player is. By its very nature, fantasy involves distortions of reality. Even so, some distortions appear to be more salient to players than others. Problems of deception are reported by Internet users most frequently when characters engage in gender-bending, particularly when they are personally in search of sex, but deceptions are also harmful when friendships are violated, as in the case of "Joan." The difficulty in determining another person's true gender, due to the anonymous nature of Internet interactions, mean that there are few, if any, consequences for deceiving others.

When men pretend to be women, and other men have online sex with them, should their real sex be disclosed? Do other players care? It seems there is considerable variation in how players feel about such deceptions. While some could care less about the real identity of that person, others do, reporting that they feel angry and used (Curtis, 1997). There is even the danger that adolescents and children may be sexually exploited by adults, a common fear of parents with youngsters on the Internet (Turow, 1999).

For adolescents and adults who have an ongoing relationship with a significant other, TinySex can undermine real-life relationships. Some consider TinySex to be infidelity while others allow their partner to explore other sexual partners online. Some feel they have no control over their partner's trysts (Turkle, 1995), which can lead to decreased feelings of trust in the relationship. For young people who are just learning to trust others in romantic relationships, these violations could be particularly unsettling and undermine intimacy feelings that are developing with real people.

Although TinySex can be an end in itself, some players get emotionally involved. If the players meet in real life and the age or physical appearance of that person is not what is expected, then those meetings can be rather disappointing (Turkle, 1995). As one person explained, real life (RL) can simply provide too much information (Turkle, 1995). Adolescents who are in search of the perfect other person may well be disillusioned if they put too much stock in what people tell them about themselves online.

Questions about the real identity of an online character is complicated by the inclusion of "bots" who inhabit MUDs (Calvert, 1999a). "Bots" are often available on MUDs all of the time. A male persona, who did not realize that he was interacting with an intelligent robot named "Julia," invited "her" to have sex on repeated occasions (Turkle, 1995). Some players believe that "bots" should immediately identify themselves as computer agents so that real people understand that they are interacting with a robot, not a person (Curtis, 1997). Will adolescents know they are interacting with a robot? Will they care, or will that just become a part of their cyber-reality?

Identity confusion or diffusion, a concept developed by Erikson (1968), occurs when people are unclear about who they are. The Internet offers adolescents diverse opportunities to experiment with different roles. Gergen (1991), a social interactionist, argues that rapidly changing information technologies place demands on people to be socially connected. The demands to be many different people in many different situations can result in multiple presentations of the self that may not be in harmony. Because adolescents want to fit in with their peer groups, they may be especially vulnerable to presenting themselves in multiple, and sometimes incompatible, ways. The social chameleon being played online may make it difficult for some adolescents to coordinate these multiple images into a singular self, or in Erikson's view, a coherent identity.

Players may also choose negative roles, and then participate in antisocial role-playing activities (Calvert, 1999a). The shadow, Jung's potentially dark side of the personality, can emerge with impunity. For instance, the persona "Mr. Bungle" raped other players on LambdaMoo (MacKinnon, 1997). Even though the site wizard destroyed "Mr. Bungle," he returned as a new persona. The potential reconstruction of self makes antisocial acts difficult to control in cyberspace. Because there are no serious negative consequences for online antisocial behavior in MUDs, there is a danger that some of these acts will be acted on in real-life situations, particularly by youngsters who are just learning the rules about social interactions with the other gender.

Fantasy identities also offer the potential for less popular adolescents to assume personae where they become important to others and to themselves (Calvert, 2002). In cyberspace, a player can become a Walter Mitty—a fictional literary character who lived a mundane life until he entered the world of daydreams—who has more social opportunities online than in real life. If fantasy is better than reality, a person may increasingly choose to escape into a fantasy world, just as Walter Mitty did.

CONCLUSIONS

Online Internet interactions, in which players pretend to be someone else or at least stretch their own self-presentations, are common experiences of adolescents. Online interactions allow adolescents to experiment with facets of themselves that they are not always comfortable expressing in real life. By having their personae role play and interact with others, MUDs allow an unprecedented opportunity for adolescents to experiment with any kind of information in ways that can enhance or undermine their personal development and identity construction. Sexual identity and intimacy—key developmental issues in Erikson's psychosocial theory—are two areas that players are exploring and experimenting with online. Various archetypal images are also being role played and explored online—personae that according to Jung would potentially impact identity development.

From Turkle's work (1995, 1997) we know that adolescents are extensive users of MUDs and that they experiment with different online identities. Just as Erikson's theory would predict, adolescents often explore issues of identity and intimacy online (Turkle, 1995, 1997). It would be particularly interesting to see if adolescents who create online personae are more likely to be in the moratorium phase of identity development, in which they are searching for information about themselves through experimentation, than to have a prematurely foreclosed identity, in which they decide who they want to be early on and are relatively rigid about new options.

As children and adolescents construct their identities in the information age, it is becoming clear that part of that construction is occurring and will continue to occur online. As a society, our challenge is to help young people navigate their real life and their online "selves" to forge a constructive, unified personal identity.

REFERENCES

Asher, S., Oden, S., & Gottman, J. (1977). Children's friendships in school settings. In E. M. Hetherington & R. Parke (Eds.), *Contemporary readings in child psychology*. New York: McGraw-Hill.

Baumeister, R. (1997). Identity, self-concept, and self-esteem. In R. Hogan, J. Johnson, & S. Briggs (Eds.), *Handbook of personality psychology*. San Diego: Academic Press.

Calvert, S. L. (1999a). Identity on the Internet. Paper presented at the Annenberg Public Policy Center Conference on the Internet and the Family, Washington, DC, May.

Calvert, S. L. (1999b). *Children's journeys through the information age*. Boston: McGraw Hill.

Calvert, S. L. (2002). The social impact of virtual environments technology. In K. M. Stanney (Ed.), *Handbook of virtual environments technology*. Hillsdale, NJ: Erlbaum.

Curtis, P. (1997). Mudding: Social phenomena in text-based virtual realities. In S. Kiesler (Ed.), *Culture of the Internet*. Mahwah, NJ: Erlbaum.

Danet, B. (1998). Text as mask: Gender, play, and performance on the Internet. In S. Jones (Ed.), *CyberSociety 2.0: Revisiting computer-mediated communication and community*. Thousand Oaks, CA: Sage.

Erikson, E. (1968). *Identity: Youth and crisis*. New York: Norton.

Gergen, K. (1991). *The saturated self*. New York: Basic Books.

Grotevant, H. D. (1998). Adolescent development in family contexts. In W. Damon (Ed.) & N. Eisenberg (Vol. Ed.), *Handbook of Child Psychology, Vol. 3: Social, emotional and personality development* (5th ed.). New York: John Wiley.

Hall, C., & Nordby, V. (1973). *A primer of Jungian psychology*. New York: Mentor Books.

Harre, R. (1983). *Personal being*. Oxford: Blackwell.

Harter, S. (1998). The development of self-representations. In W. Damon (Ed.) & N. Eisenberg (Vol. Ed.), *Handbook of Child Psychology, Vol. 3: Social, emotional and personality development* (5th ed.). New York: John Wiley.

Huntemann, N., & Morgan, M. (2001). Mass media and identity development. In D. Singer & J. Singer (Eds.), *Handbook of children and the media*. Thousand Oaks, CA: Sage.

Jung, C. (1959). *The basic writings of C.G. Jung*. New York: The Modern Library.

Katz, J., & Aspden, P. (1997). A nation of strangers? *Communications of the ACM, 40*, 81–87.

Kohlberg, L. (1966). A cognitive-developmental analysis of children's sex-role concepts and attitudes. In E. E. Maccoby (Ed.), *The development of sex differences*. Stanford, CA: Stanford University Press.

Kraut, R., Kiesler, S., Boneva, B., Cummings, J., Helgeson, V., & Crawford, A. (2002). Online communication and well-being in adolescence. *Journal of Social Issues, 58*, 49–74.

Kraut, R., Patterson, M., Lundmark, V., Kiesler, S., Mukophadhya, T., & Scherlis, W. (1998). Internet paradox: A social technology that reduces social involvement and psychological well-being. *American Psychologist, 53*, 1017–1031.

MacKinnon, R. (1997). Punishing the persona: Correctional strategies for the virtual offender. In S. Jones (Ed.), *Virtual culture: Identity and communication in cybersociety*. London: Sage.

Martin, C., & Halverson, C. (1981). A schematic processing model of sextyping and stereotyping in children. *Child Development, 52*, 1119–1134.

Mead, G. (1925). The genesis of the self and social control. *International Journal of Ethics, 35,* 251–273.

Parks, M., & Roberts, L. (1998). Making MOOsic: The development of personal relationships online and a comparison to their offline counterparts. *Journal of Social and Personal Relationships, 15,* 517–537.

Ruble, D., & Martin, C. (1998). Gender development. In W. Damon (Ed.) & N. Eisenberg (Vol. Ed.), *Handbook of Child Psychology, Vol. 3: Social, emotional and personality development* (5th ed.). New York: John Wiley.

Schroeder, R. (1997). Networked worlds: Social aspects of multi-user virtual reality technology. *Sociological Research Online, 2.* http://www/socresonline.org.uk.swocresonline/2/3/5.html.

Turkle, S. (1995). *Life on the screen.* New York: Simon and Schuster.

Turkle, S. (1997). Constructions and reconstructions of self in Virtual Reality: Playing in MUDs. In S. Kiesler (Ed.), *Culture of the Internet.* Mahwah, NJ: Erlbaum.

Turow, J. (1999). The Internet and the family: The view from parents, the view from the press. Paper presented at the Annenberg Public Policy Center Conference on the Internet and the Family, Washington, DC, May.

Chapter 4

Adolescents, the Internet, and Health: Issues of Access and Content

Dina L. G. Borzekowski and Vaughn I. Rickert

Unlike other mass media, the Internet can reach narrowly targeted audiences with countless insights on a range of personal and social concerns. Young people, who are familiar and comfortable with this medium, may access important content that can improve their physical and psychological health. Little nonproprietary data, however, are available on whether and how adolescents actually use the Internet to learn more about and improve their health.

In this chapter, we begin by describing issues around access to the Internet. Then, we discuss the range of content that can be found through this medium regarding health information. As part of this section on content, we critique three examples of current Internet health web sites. We then present a preliminary study on Internet use, drawing from data collected from two distinct samples of New York City adolescents. After discussing the results of this study, we conclude by providing recommendations for improving health-related web sites targeting adolescents.

ADOLESCENT ACCESS TO THE INTERNET

For adolescents to obtain health information from the Internet, they must first gain access to this technology. Concerns regarding access are particularly acute for disenfranchised and minority groups who may be less able to afford the necessary hardware and software. The Internet access issue might be remedied in part, though, through public access from locations such as schools and libraries. In fact, efforts made in the 1990s to improve public Internet access have been quite successful (NTIA, 1998). This bipartisan agenda received public and private support and, by 1996, 65% of public high schools and 77% of public libraries had Internet links (Heaviside, Riggins, & Farris, 1997). In 1998, 84% of public libraries were connected to the Internet in some capacity with 73% offering public access to the Internet (Bertot & McClure, 1998).

Public points of access can serve as an equalizer, providing individuals with Internet connections regardless of income and education. Continued public and private support allow economically disadvantaged and geographically remote communities necessary and affordable services and upgrades. Throughout the United States, some 80,000 schools and libraries have employed the E-rate program to secure discounted rates for telecommunication services (NTIA, 1999). The computer industry and less-advantaged community groups have been forging partnerships as well. "Plugged In" represents one such partnership. This group facilitates the training of poor minority youth to create web pages and it is located in downtown East Palo Alto, California, a city known for its high crime and poverty rates despite its proximity to affluent communities in Silicon Valley (Lacey, 2000).

Besides public access, the increasing affordability of computers has allowed Internet use levels to climb at steady rates across ethnic groups (NTIA, 1999). The number of Black and Hispanic households that owned home computers doubled from 1994 to 1998. Internet use (as defined by owning a modem) also increased steadily in the past few years. In 1989, less than 2% of Black and Hispanic (as compared to an overall national percentage of 3%) households had Internet access. By 1997, the number of connected households increased to 12% (compared to an overall national percentage of 26%) (NTIA, 1999). What separates users from nonusers, though, appears to be income and education (Hoffman & Kalsbeek, 1996). In households with an average annual income greater than $75,000, there were no significant differences between White, Black, and Hispanic families with regard to computer ownership (NTIA, 1999). A "digital divide" between ethnic groups becomes apparent at lower income levels. According to a recent Federal study, among households with annual incomes between $15,000 and $35,000, a third of White families compared to a fifth of Black and Hispanic families owned computers (NTIC, 1999).

HEALTH-RELATED CONTENT ON THE INTERNET

The majority of U.S. adults agree that "people should take primary responsibility for their own health and not rely so much on doctors" (Yankelovic MONITOR survey cited in Miller & Reents, 1999). The Internet allows consumers to educate themselves on a variety of health-related topics from diseases to prescription drugs, before and after they go to a doctor's office. It lets Internet users ask targeted questions of their doctors and obtain additional opinions and links to online support groups and individuals.

During 1998, over 17 million U.S. adults searched this medium for health and medical information (Miller & Reents, 1999), a 43% increase compared to the prior 12 months (Cyberdialogue, 2000). In 2000, more than 33.5 million adults are expected to seek health information online (Cyberdialogue, 2000). This report also indicates that 35% of all U.S. adults are online and, of these, 38% have used the Internet for health and medical information over the last year (Cyberdialogue, 2000). Other sources concur that approximately 40% of adult Internet users have researched health information (Miller & Reents, 1999). Of those receiving health and medical information, 52% retrieved information on diseases, 36% on diet and nutrition, 33% on pharmaceuticals, 32% on online health newsletters, 31% on women's health, 29% on fitness, 15% on children's health, and 13% on illness support groups (Miller & Reents, 1999). Reviewing these statistics, we wondered whether and what types of Internet health information adolescents would try to obtain. A search of both the academic and marketing literature, however, revealed no current data on such adolescent use of the Internet.

HEALTH-RELATED WEB SITES: THREE ILLUSTRATIONS

Although data on use patterns are unavailable, there are Internet health information sites that target adolescents and teens with health information. In Spring 2000, colleagues involved in either health communication or adolescent medicine provided the authors with the names and URLs of health sites that could serve as examples of existing Internet resources. From two dozen suggestions, we found three that clearly illustrated the range of qualities and further the current dialogue on adolescent Internet health sites: zaphealth.com, cyberisle.org, and not-2-late.com. In the following paragraphs, we provide qualitative descriptions of these three sites, evaluating features that include: perceived purpose, intended audience, ease of use, interactivity, use of advertisements, and links. These evaluation criteria derived from a sample of urban adolescents (from 2 multi-grade classes with 20 students each) with whom we discussed the features that could be used to judge adolescent health web sites.

Zaphealth

Zaphealth is a health site for adolescents with the byline "when you can't ask mom." Designed to "help young people deal with health problems and make informed decisions about their own health and lifestyles" (http://www.zaphealth.com, Spring 2000), the information appears in a nonjudgmental, unbiased, and informative style, clearly aimed at a young audience. Included is a comprehensive list of topics that adolescents might be interested in, such as eating disorders, relationships, sexually transmitted diseases, and even a section called "bad smells." The site is easy to navigate with opportunities to write in questions or search by topics. Additionally, chat rooms and topic-specific bulletin boards are available.

Though this site is commendable in creating a health specific site for adolescents, the advertising banners at the top and bottom of the page may be problematic (even though the advertising policy indicates that site content and advertisements will be separate). Zaphealth also mentions that site content will not be dictated by advertising relationships, that they do not endorse any product or service advertised on the site, and viewers should use their own discretion when reading these advertisements and buying related products. Nevertheless, such an advertising policy seems contradictory, since accepting certain advertisers (and not others) sets up a situation where the average adolescent would and should not believe that the host site is indifferent to the included advertisements.

CyberIsle

CyberIsle.org, created by TeenNet, is a "network of collaborating partners directly involved in education and health promotion with youth" (www.cyberisle.org, Spring 2000). The site is guided by five principles: (1) participation, (2) relevance, (3) support of adolescent autonomy, (4) active learning, and (5) accessibility. Designed with adolescents' assistance, the site feels like an adolescent's room, disorganized and hard to understand but with some recognizable parts. Within CyberIsle are seven rooms, including men's and women's washrooms, a beach, and a Cyberia (a hangout place).

Few words direct CyberIsle visitors to any specific room or links within a room. Navigating through the site, clicks on various icons (ashtrays, people, table tops) will transport the user to new web pages. This makes for a complicated navigation system. It is unclear, unless attention is directly paid to Internet URL addresses, where one will wind up after a mouse click. Sometimes it is a health-prevention page within the CyberIsle domain, other times, one has left CyberIsle and has been transferred to another host's web site. This is disorienting and requires a very competent web surfer to know how to get particular information without getting launched to other web sites (some that are health focused, others that are not).

Internal and external links are of serious concern with regard to health web sites for adolescents. Though there are no advertisements on the CyberIsle pages, direct links can bring a user to a commercial music or movie (i.e., music.com or movie.com) web site outside of the TeenNet network. Additionally, some CyberIsle links seem tailored to a Canadian youth audience (the site originates out of the Department of Public Health Sciences at the University of Toronto) and this makes some links less relevant to a broader adolescent audience. This site would benefit from clearer principles organizing links and a reduction in the numerous commercial links that may be inappropriate for a health web site targeting youth.

Not-2-Late

The Not-2-Late site run by the Office of Population Research at Princeton University is a web site about emergency contraception. It is part of a national campaign to inform people about emergency contraception methods, where to find them, and how to get them. This straightforward site contains few graphics and a substantial amount of text, which can be read in English or in Spanish. We felt that the most valuable part of this site was the searchable database, where a visitor could enter geographical information and obtain a list of nearby sites and providers who supply emergency contraception. Though the site is not specifically designed for an adolescent audience, it concerns an issue that might attract young visitors. There is a "frequently asked questions" page that answers adolescent focused questions such as "Is it possible to obtain emergency contraception without parents' knowledge or consent for minors?" No advertisements appear on the Not-2-Late site and it is explicitly stated that there is "no connection whatsoever with any companies that manufacture or sell emergency contraceptives" (www.not-2-late.com, Spring 2000).

While the site is informative and interactive, its sophistication and text-based material may be too difficult for an adolescent to understand. There are opportunities to ask questions, however, and the search engine is easy to use. The information within the site is targeted and useful, but it does not go beyond emergency contraception to other realms of health information. In this sense it serves only a limited role in acting as a health site aimed at adolescents. This web site can act as a model for other health sites, because of its simple but dynamic design, easy navigation, lack of advertisements and endorsements, and lack of ambiguous links.

A PRELIMINARY STUDY: ADOLESCENT INTERNET USE AND HEALTH INFORMATION

After reviewing the adult literature and many existing adolescent Internet sites, we designed an exploratory study to assess whether and how adolescents use the Internet to gather health information. To this end, we identified two samples of New York City adolescents: one from a health center, the other from an elite high school. Respondents were asked to complete a pencil-and-paper survey to describe their access, frequency of use, and comfort levels regarding general Internet use. In addition, we asked whether they had ever used the Internet to get health information and, if so, what types of information had they tried to obtain. Last, we asked about the value they placed on using the Internet as an information source on a range of topics.

Given "digital divide" concerns, we assumed that adolescents from the health center would access the Internet with much lower frequency than those from the elite high school. Beyond this no other hypotheses were made.

Sample and Methods

To understand how and if adolescents use the Internet, especially for health information, we collected data in the fall of 1999. The first sample came from a health center serving ethnically diverse and disadvantaged youth from Central and East Harlem. This group consisted of 145 adolescents, aged 13 to 21 years (mean 17.3 years, $SD = 1.9$), where 81% were either Latino American or African American. The second sample consisted of a randomly selected group of high school students (ninth through twelfth grade) from an elite Upper East Side independent high school. There were 173 boys and girls in this group. The mean age was 15.7 years ($SD = 1.2$) and 82% were White.

For this study, we used a 50-item, pencil-and-paper survey. We created media-use measures (modeled after existing media-use surveys) and found reliability to be high for question batteries about Internet use and perceived value of Internet information across health content areas (alpha coefficients ranged .71 to .86). This allowed us to assess the overall reliability of the measures since they were adaptations of other batteries). At the health center, all adolescents, other than those coming for urgent care/sick visits, were asked to complete our anonymous and voluntary survey while they waited for their appointments. At the high school, randomly selected homerooms were chosen and all students were invited to participate. In both locations, few adolescents declined to do the survey; however, specific refusal statistics were not recorded. On average, adolescents completed the survey in 8 to 10 minutes.

Results

We expected that health center adolescents' Internet use rates would be much lower than those of the elite high school students. While use rates differed significantly ($\chi^2 = 26.1$, $df = 1$, $p < .001$), we found that Internet use was widespread among these urban adolescents. Practically all (99%) of the elite high school students and 83% of the health center adolescents said that they used this medium. On frequency of Internet use, 39% of elite high school students in comparison to 20% of health center adolescents said that they used the Internet 6 to 7 days a week ($\chi^2 = 59.0$, $df = 5$, $p < .001$). Among the elite high school students, a quarter of the sample

(26%) indicated that they used the Internet for a half-hour or less per week and another 17% reported using the Internet five or more hours a week. For the health center adolescents, around half (51%) used the Internet for a half-hour or less per week, while 12% reported five or more hours of use per week. Of the elite high school students, 34% said they were "extremely" comfortable with the Internet compared to 17% of the health center adolescents who reported these levels of comfort. Over half (56%) of the health center adolescents, however, said that they were "pretty" or "extremely" comfortable using the Internet. Differences existed between the groups with students indicating higher comfort than center adolescents (χ^2 = 34.2, df = 4, p < .001), but few adolescents from either group were uncomfortable with this medium.

Adolescent Internet users reported accessing the Web from multiple locales. Among all adolescent Internet users, 20% accessed the Internet from one place, 33% from two, 24% from three, 14% from four, and 9% from five or more places. Elite high school students differed significantly from health center adolescents in the number of places they accessed the Internet (χ^2 = 58.4, df = 5, p < .001). While twice the percentage of elite high school students (70%) accessed from two or three places compared to the percentage of health center adolescents (39%), similar percentages of elite high school students (24%) and health center adolescents (21%) accessed from four or more locales. Only 6% of elite high school students accessed from just one locale in contrast to 41% of health center adolescents.

Almost all (97%) the elite high school students reported home use of the Internet. This was significantly different than the 52% of health center adolescents who said that they used the Internet from home (χ^2 = 84.8, df = 1, p < .001). Most elite high school students (90%) reported Internet use at school compared to 66% of the health center adolescents who were currently in school (χ^2 = 34.4, df = 1, p < .001). Compared to the elite high school students, more health center adolescents used the Internet at another family member's house (32% versus 14%, χ^2 = 13.9, df = 1, p < .001) or a community center (6% versus 1%, χ^2 = 5.1, df = 1, p < .05). Similar percentages of elite high school students and health center adolescents used the Internet at the library (overall 36%) or at a friend's house (overall 40%).

When asked, "Have you ever tried to get health information from the Internet?" 42% of the health center adolescents responded "yes" and, interestingly, this was not significantly different from the 43% of elite high school students, who also responded "yes." Examining the sample by gender and ethnicity, we observed no significant associations for trying to get health information from the Internet. Among those who had tried to get health information from the Internet (N = 126) from both groups, 50% said that they had tried to get information on different diseases (i.e., cancer, heart disease, STDs, etc.), 37% on diet and nutrition, 33% on fitness and exercise, 27% on sex (i.e., sexual activity, contraception, pregnancy, etc.), 25% on alcohol and drug abuse, 18% on mental health issues, 19% on medicines and pharmaceuticals, 13% on violence among peers/gangs, 8% on tobacco and smoking, 7% on parenting and children's health, 6% on emotional or physical abuse, 5% on sexual abuse, and 3% on illness support groups. Comparing health center adolescents to high school students, significantly higher percentages had tried to obtain information on sexually transmitted diseases (50% versus 16%), on sexual behaviors (50% versus 11%), on peer/gang violence (23% versus 5%), on dating violence (14% versus 3%), on parenting (17% versus 0%), on emotional abuse (12% versus 1%), and on sexual abuse (10% versus 1%).

Adolescents reported that they thought the health information on the Internet to be reliable, with only a quarter suggesting that available information was "not at all" or "a little" reliable. There was an overall consensus from both groups that general health information on the Internet was valuable; 55% responded it was "very" or "extremely" worthwhile. When asked about specific health topics, 77% of the adolescents indicated that it was "very" or "extremely" worthwhile to have Internet information on emotional and sexual abuse. Seventy percent thought it "very" or "extremely" worthwhile to have antiviolence information, 62% for contraception information, 56% for diet and nutrition information, and 31% for antismoking information.

Discussion

The first area we examined was Internet use and access, particularly as it relates to adolescent groups characterized by their socioeconomic status and ethnic differences. As expected, we found the elite high school students to be technologically savvy, having high levels of both Internet access and comfort with the medium. These adolescents attend a school that costs close to $21,000 a year and e-mail accounts are provided to each student through a school server. We were, however, surprised by the access and comfort levels reported by the health center adolescents. Health center adolescents, of whom 70% report having no health insurance, were using the Internet at rates higher than predicted. During the Internet's early emergence, many voiced concern over whether and how underserved populations might be a part of the Information Revolution. This study offers promising data suggesting that less-privileged youth manage to get Internet access. These findings reflect initiatives to provide Internet links through public schools and libraries, and should encourage continued support of facilitated access for users regardless of gender, age, ethnicity, geography, and socioeconomic status.

This preliminary study, indicates that among the elite high school students, the few non-Whites did not differ from the Whites with regard to

Internet access and use. In the health center sample, non-Whites and Whites also exhibited similar Internet patterns. Most of the significant differences between the two samples would appear to be the result of differences in socioeconomic status. Although efforts were made by less-advantaged adolescents to access and use the Internet, a "digital divide" along income lines was apparent.

The second area we examined was whether adolescents sought out health information from the Internet. This study suggests that a substantial proportion of adolescent Internet users, like adult Internet users (for whom, there are some published statistics), access the Internet to find health information. Furthermore, percentages from this study indicate that adolescents seek similar health information as that which is sought by adults. Interestingly though, when one compares topics singled out by the two different groups, variations emerge. Health risk behaviors, such as engaging in unprotected sexual activity or physical and sexual victimization, which have urgent short-term consequences, were the topics more often chosen by health center adolescents. One qualification with these results is that the adolescents from the health center may have been more inclined to seek out health information than their peers who do not use a health center.

The final area we considered was how valuable urban adolescents felt it was to be able to access Internet health information. Overwhelmingly, adolescents of all socioeconomic and ethnic groups indicated that having general and targeted health information available through this medium was worthwhile. Few thought that Internet health information was unreliable.

The results from this preliminary study are promising, suggesting the continued support of adolescents accessing and using the Internet for health information may be beneficial. Additional research conducted by our group and others ought to investigate the areas and issues raised by this work—specifically, the access and use of Web-related health information by youth from different racial and ethnic groups and different social strata and the most efficacious ways of conveying this information to specific youth populations.

To benefit current and future adolescent users, we urge that Internet health information be interesting, understandable, relevant, and secure. Raised on television, video games, and computers, most adolescents come to expect well-produced appealing media. Other media options are a remote control or mouse click away; therefore, it is vital to capture the users' attention. Similar to television, which combines macro features (action and pace), visual micro features (pans, zooms, and fades), and auditory micro features (dialogue, sound effects, and music) (Calvert, 1999), Internet sites must include and merge attention-keeping qualities. Additionally, Internet sites ought to take advantage of this medium's interactive nature. The case sites described earlier all benefit from having interactive components. We believe that electronic pamphlets, which characterize many existing sites, are less likely to entice the adolescent user to seek information, regardless of his or her involvement and information needs. Specific to this medium, Internet sites can engage the user by providing tailored information, a feature often used in effective health communication (Slater, 1995). For example, an antismoking web site might be more appealing (and constructive) if it obtains data on the adolescent's likes and dislikes, personal and interpersonal experiences, habits regarding number of cigarettes smoked per week, and readiness to change before it offers personalized advice on smoking cessation.

Health information provided through the Internet must be made understandable to the adolescent user. Web sites should explain technical terminology and avoid confusing medical jargon. Taking advantage of the layered aspects of Internet sites, additional explanations can be linked to provided information. Furthermore, these explanations can be directed at the user's cognitive strengths. As an illustration, the ways that a web site provides information on the daily challenges of living with asthma might vary if the adolescent indicates preferences for video rather than text. The Internet is one medium that can effectively alter the presentation of information in relation to young peoples' intelligence, which can include skills in linguistic, logical-mathematical, spatial, musical, bodily-kinesthetic, interpersonal, and intrapersonal areas (Gardner, 1993). Using formative evaluations, web designers should examine if and how adolescents understand given sites. Finally, it is important that web sites offer information in languages other than English to serve the growing population of non-English speaking adolescents in the United States.

General health web sites can serve as an entry point, but to better serve the adolescent, sites should provide targeted information. While adults and adolescents share common health problems such as alcohol/drug abuse, depression, nutrition and weight control, physical exercise, and depression (Jinks & Daniels, 1999; Waters, Wake, Toumbourou, Wright, & Salmon, 1999), unique concerns reflect the different generational experiences. For adults, concerns include cancer, diabetes, and lung and/or heart disease (Cowley, 1999); and for adolescents, concerns include depression, social stressors, and unsafe sexual practices (Hampton, 2000). Even if health concerns are similar, the resources and viable treatment approaches might differ. If an adult wanted to use birth control pills, she might schedule an appointment with her primary care physician and that exam (and even the prescription) might be covered by her health insurance. In contrast, an adolescent who is uncomfortable or unwilling to approach this need with her pediatrician or family care provider might have to locate a subsidized adolescent health clinic and consult with the health center staff. It is vital that health web sites for adolescents provide current, relevant, and realistic information to address an individual adolescent's health needs.

Most important, health web sites for adolescents must be safe, secure, and confidential environments. Proposed by the American Medical Association, "health Web sites must adhere to strict personal privacy codes to prevent individual's personal medical information, including patterns of use and interests, from involuntarily entering the hands of marketers, employers, and insurers" (Winker, Flanagin, Chi-Lum, White, Andrews, Kennett, DeAngelis, & Musacchio, 2000). In April 2000, the Children's Online Privacy Protection Act (COPPA) became law. This law, enforced by the Federal Trade Commission (FTC), protects children under the age of 13 from being asked to provide personal information that would facilitate direct marketing. We believe that when any individual, regardless of age, attempts to access a health information web site, such protection should be in place as well. Health information is personal and sensitive and should not be linked directly to the individual.

As previously discussed when evaluating the sample health sites, advertising and links to commercial sites undermine a health site's credibility and security. Public health and educational organizations might sponsor adolescent health sites, ensuring that vulnerable youth can retrieve content without serving as a captive market. In addition, the potential biases that may result from funding and competing interests should be obvious and offered upon site entry.

CONCLUSION

In conclusion, few published studies consider the adolescent user of the Internet and we are aware of no peer-reviewed studies that focus on adolescents, the Internet, and health. There is a tremendous need to examine existing sites and to better understand whether and how adolescents use the Internet for health information. Currently, we are collecting survey data from a representative sample of 3,000 urban, suburban, and rural New York State tenth graders on media use and health information sources. Results from this research should inform the discussion of how youth use traditional and new media. Similar to the television and children research, Internet research should include content analyses along with cross-sectional, longitudinal, and experimental studies. Further information should be gathered on messages conveyed through the Internet as well as how those messages impact youth. Through such research, we will be able to maximize the potential of this new health communication medium.

ACKNOWLEDGMENT

Reprinted from *Applied Developmental Psychology*, Vol. 22 (1), Borzekowski, D.L.G., & Rickert, V. I., Adolescents, the Internet, and health: Issues of access and content, pp. 49–59, © 2001, with permission from Elsevier Science.

REFERENCES

Bertot, J. C., & McClure, C. R. (1998). The 1998 National Survey of Public Library Outlet Internet Connectivity. American Library Association Office of Information Technology Policy. http://www.ala.org/library/fact26.html.

Calvert, S. L. (1999). *Children's journeys through the information age.* Boston: McGraw-Hill.

Cowley, G. (1999). So, how's your health? *Newsweek,* August 2.

Cyberdialogue. (2000). http://www.cyberdialogue.com/resource/data/cch/index.html#data.

Ervin, S., & Gilmore, G. (1999). Traveling the superinformation highway: African Americans' perceptions and use of cyberspace technology. *Journal of Black Studies, 29* (3), 398–407.

Gardner, H. (1993). *Multiple intelligences: The theory in practice.* New York: Basic Books.

Hampton, H. L. (2000). Adolescent gynecology: Examination of the adolescent patient. *Obstetrics Gynecology Clinics of North America, 27* (1), 1–18.

Heaviside, S., Riggins, T., & Farris, E. (1997). *Advanced telecommunications in U.S. public elementary and secondary schools, Fall 1996.* U.S. Department of Education, Office of Educational Research Improvement. National Center for Education Statistics, March.

Hoffman, D. L., & Kalsbeek, T. P. (1996). Internet and Web use in the U.S. *Communication of the Association for Computing Machinery, 39* (12), 36–46.

Jinks, A. M., & Daniels, R. (1999). Workplace health concerns: A focus group study. *Journal of Management in Medicine, 13* (2–3), 95–104.

Lacey, M. (2000). Clinton hopes to raise Indian Internet use. *New York Times,* April 18.

Miller, T. E., & Reents, S. (1999). [online]. The health care industry in transition: The online mandate to change. http://www.cyberdialogue.com.

National Telecommunications and Information Administration and U.S. Department of Commerce (NTIA). (1998). *Falling through the Net II: New data on the digital divide.* Washington, DC.

National Telecommunications and Information Administration and U.S. Department of Commerce (NTIA). (1999). *Falling through the Net III: Defining the digital divide.* Washington, DC.

Slater, M. (1995). Roles of media in community-based health promotion. In E. Maibach & R. L. Parrott (Eds.), *Designing health messages* (pp. 186–198). Thousand Oaks, CA: Sage.

Waters, E., Wake, M., Toumbourou, J., Wright, M., & Salmon, L. (1999). Prevalence of emotional and physical health concerns amongst young people in Victoria. *Journal of Pediatrics and Child Health, 35* (1), 28–33.

Winker, M. A., Flanagin, A., Chi-Lum, B., White, J., Andrews, K., Kennett, R. L., DeAngelis, C. D., & Musacchio, R. A. (2000). Guidelines for medical and health information sites on the Internet. *Journal of the American Medical Association, 283,* 1600–1606.

Chapter 5

Political Socialization in the Digital Age: The "Student Voices" Program

Emory H. Woodard IV and Kelly L. Schmitt

It was in 1838, well before the mind-boggling data processing and distribution capabilities of the digital age, that James Fenimore Cooper wrote, "[T]he success of democracies is mainly dependent on the intelligence of the people. . . . [Democracies] prosper as a consequence of general information" (1989, pp. 121–122). Today this statement seems ironic. The proportion of Americans with at least a high school diploma has risen from 13.5% in 1910 to 82.8% in 1998 (Snyder & Hoffman, 2000). Americans can obtain unlimited civics information from home through television, a newspaper subscription, access to the Internet, or some combination of all three. However, voter turnout for the presidential election of 1996 tied for an all-time low at 48.9% (*Statistical Abstract*, 1999), almost half the proportion of eligible voters in the election of 1840 when Cooper penned his remarks (U.S. Bureau of the Census, 1975).

Today's young citizens appear to be part of this trend of decreased voting. Lewis (2001) notes that the number of eligible voters between the ages of 18 and 29 who cast their ballots has dropped from one in two in 1972 to less than one in five in 2000. Young citizens are not only less likely to participate in political elections than older Americans, but they are also less trusting of their fellow citizens, less interested in politics or public affairs, less knowledgeable about the substance or process of politics, less likely to watch or read the news, and less likely to engage in other political behaviors (Delli Carpini, 2000). This pattern occurs even though youth are involved with the Internet, a medium that can provide them with a wealth of information to engage them in the political process.

Though fraught with formidable technical, social, and ethical challenges (see Naughton, 2000), early indications suggest that the Internet may hold some promise for connecting young voters to the political process. In what was termed the first Internet voting experiment, citizens of Arizona could vote online in the state's Democratic Party primary election during the spring of 2000. Nearly 86,000 Democrats cast ballots, 40,000 of which were submitted through the Internet. Importantly, three-quarters of the Internet voters were between the ages of 18 and 35 (Lefort, 2000).

This chapter presents an evaluation of a program called "Student Voices," developed in 1999 as a joint effort by the Annenberg Public Policy Center and the Pew Charitable Trusts. "Student Voices" was an in-school intervention aimed at engaging high school seniors in the discourse and political activity surrounding the Philadelphia mayoral election. A key component of this program was providing students with access to the Internet and web-based information about politics, candidates, and the issues surrounding the campaign. Working within the school setting, students were encouraged to get to know the candidates, explore the issues, form opinions, find their voices, and ultimately participate in the voting process.

BACKGROUND

Understanding how youth come to participate as citizens means focusing on the political socialization process that occurs in the early years. Specifically, "political socialization" refers to the "learning process by which the political norms and behaviors acceptable to an ongoing political system are transmitted from generation to generation" (Sigel, 1965, p. 1). Beck (1977) indicates that there are four primary agents of socialization: parents, peers, school, and the mass media. According to this framework, the ability of agents to influence the learning of political norms and behavior or the process of becoming a citizen is preconditioned by three factors: exposure, communication, and receptivity.

Clearly, political socialization can be a lifelong process. However, socializing agents may be at their most powerful during the teenage years—a time in life when youth begin to develop opinions independent from their parents' and anticipate a time when they will have an opportunity to vote (Beck, 1977; Jennings & Niemi, 1974; Krampen, 2000). The "Student Voices" project was designed to engage students in the political process through two of the primary socialization agents—schools and the media (Beck, 1977).

Citizenship Education in the School Setting

One of the early goals of public education was to create good citizens (Brickman, 1978; Flanagan & Faison, 2001). Nevertheless, questions remain about the effectiveness of political socialization in the classroom. In one of the rare evaluations of civic education within schools, Tolo (1999) found that although many states have standards, statutes, course requirements, and constitutional provisions that explicitly address civic education in the classroom, civic education programs are poorly implemented. His report spells out an overly simplistic emphasis on mere civic facts and figures, inadequate instructional materials, the absence of sufficient testing, and a lack of initial and ongoing teacher training in civics. Often, civic education programs tend to emphasize lower-order thinking skills (e.g., identifying and describing positions) rather than higher-order thinking skills (e.g., evaluation, taking and defending positions).

Tolo notes that preservice certification and ongoing professional development programs often do not include civic educator training. In the face of school districts' failure to provide adequate civics instructional materials and the lack of emphasis in degree-granting schools, teachers who are self-motivated to teach civics report that they turn to supplemental materials, particularly the Internet, for guidance and materials.

What are America's youth learning about civic life in school? Niemi and Junn's recent (1998) survey of high school seniors indicates that students have a general grasp of the criminal justice system, individual rights, and divisions of power among various levels of government. However, they are hazy on the details of governance, and know considerably less about political parties and lobbying, have challenges working with civics materials (e.g., making political inferences from short government documents), and struggle with theoretical concepts concerning government (e.g., representative governance).

Niemi and Junn argue that the timing of enrollment in civic courses can be a contributing factor in the knowledge gap. In their view, taking courses later in high school seems to be more effective. In addition, students may have difficulty seeing the relevance of civics-related information as many classes deal sparsely with contemporary events, problems, and controversies. Their research indicates that students are more likely to retain civic information that is already familiar to them from other contexts or that are meaningful to them in some direct way. The implication is that students might better learn about government at all levels if greater attention is paid to local politics.

One approach to meeting the challenges to school-based civic education outlined by Tolo (1999) and Niemi and Junn (1998) has been to bring in external agencies, funded by private sources, to run tailored programs to stimulate interest and teach civics. The outside funding source has eliminated many of the fiscal constraints that have faced school-funded programs and have introduced the notion of outcome-based evaluations.

One such example is "Kids Voting USA," launched in 1988 and expanded to 20 states plus the District of Columbia (Simon & Merrill, 1998). The two primary objectives of "Kids Voting USA" are: (1) to elicit higher-order thinking about the electoral process (to instill in students a sense of the value of voting); and (2) to encourage students to discuss political issues with their parents or adults within their household environment (to both reinforce classroom learning and also increase parents' interest in political participation).

Though an evaluation of "Kids Voting USA" has been conducted (1998), methodological shortcomings of the research (specifically, no pretest data and no control groups) make it difficult to assess the impact of the program on youth knowledge, parental participation, and voter turnout among the young. Nevertheless, the researchers collected postelection survey data from 24,976 students and 1,084 teachers. Most of the students in the program took part in political debates at school (76%), asked questions about the election at home (71%), were exposed to news coverage of the campaign on television (73%), and the radio (73%), and felt that it was very important to vote on election day (76%). Teachers rated the program favorably (89–98 %), thought the program increased student knowledge (99%), and sensed greater student enthusiasm (99%). Finally, the geographic areas using "Kids Voting USA" in 1994 experienced a small but consistent increase in voter turnout compared to similar matched areas.

Tolo (1999) and Niemi and Junn (1998) also highlight the importance of information that is useful and that resonates with civics information that youth are already familiar with. An important consideration is the overall context of information flow in youths' lives and, in particular, finding ways to increase the take-away value of in-school content by connecting youth with information in the media that are already a ubiquitous part of their lives.

Mass Media and Political Socialization

Much of the recent research on the political socialization of youth has focused on the role the mass media play in creating citizens (Eveland, McLeod, & Horowitz, 1999; Rahn & Hirshorn, 1999). Media can be quite important as socialization agents, most notably because of their heavy daily use of media (Woodard, 2000), but also because there is an increasing amount of political information directed at youth, such as MTV's "Rock the Vote" or youth-oriented political web sites.

Studies on mass communication and political socialization have found a strong relationship between exposure to the media—particularly television news—and political knowledge (Atkin, 1977; Chaffee, Ward, & Tipton, 1970; Rubin, 1978). Older children are more influenced by media sources than are younger children (Eveland, McLeod, & Horowitz, 1999). Media use and the political knowledge of students are also reciprocally related to one another and jointly are *better* predictors of political attitudes and behaviors than school grade, gender, parental influence, and school curriculum (Conway, Wyckoff, Feldbaum, & Ahern, 1981). It is, therefore, timely to examine the potential of new media on our youths' introduction to the political world.

THE "STUDENT VOICES" PROGRAM

"Student Voices" began as part of the Philadelphia Compact, a joint project of the Annenberg Public Policy Center at the University of Pennsylvania and the Pew Charitable Trusts. The main objective of the Philadelphia Compact, the larger project from which "Student Voices" emerged, was to actively engage candidates for the city's mayoral primaries (spring of 1999) and the general election (fall of 1999) on substantive issues relevant to all city residents. "Student Voices" sought to generate interest in the substantive issues of the campaign among high school seniors who were either eligible to participate in the election themselves or who could influence adults within their households to vote.

Implemented in one classroom in each of 33 high schools across the School District of Philadelphia, the program officially began in January 1999 with a day-long training session for teachers just before candidates began campaigning. American government, social studies, and history teachers from the school districts' service learning program were asked to participate in the program as the "Student Voices" project was thought to be most easily integrated into their subject areas. Altogether, approximately 1,000 students and 33 teachers participated in the project.

The "Student Voices" approach was developed to counter general trends of youth political apathy. It was informed by communication and political science theory and research that indicated the best practices for reaching youth with information about how and why they should participate in the political life of the city. Yet there were additional challenges in reaching Philadelphia area youth that reflect challenges facing most inner-city schools.

The School District of Philadelphia serves a racially and ethnically diverse student population from low-income families (School District of Philadelphia, 2001). The District routinely has difficulty meeting its operating budget (Snyder & Benson, 2001) and struggles to keep updated textbooks. Although many surrounding suburban school districts enjoy new technologies (Snyder, 2000), this is not typical within the District.

To overcome the general challenge of turning youth on to politics and the specific challenge of doing it within a low-income, urban setting, the "Student Voices" approach had seven key features for promoting civic knowledge, interest, and participation. These features were developed based on the lessons learned from previous evaluations.

Catch 'Em Young

The program purposefully targeted high school seniors. Typically seniors are of voting age or on the verge of being able to vote. As Niemi and Junn (1998) argue, high school seniors are developmentally prepared to handle the abstract reasoning required for processing complex political issues and may also be more motivated to attend to the civic lessons conveyed as entry into civic life is upon them or just around the corner. Moreover, there is some evidence that self-perceptions of political competence and knowledge during adolescence leads to political activity and voting in early adulthood (Krampen, 2000).

Reintroduce Civics

As Niemi and Junn (1998) observed, many civics courses deal primarily with historical facts as opposed to contemporary events, problems, and controversies. As a consequence, students frequently lack motivation and fail to make connections between course content and their everyday lives. The "Student Voices" approach encouraged teachers to help students identify issues in their communities that needed redressing by public officials. Once relevant issues were identified, students researched candidate positions on the issues, investigated opposing views, debated proposed solutions to problems, and developed questions that could be posed to campaign candidates.

Study a Local Campaign

To keep the subject matter germane to the lives of students, it was important that the "Student Voices" approach be centered on a local campaign. This ensured that aspects of government that students could directly observe and immediately understand were the consistent object of course lessons. Students could see how their involvement could, in fact, make a difference. Most textbook approaches, by contrast, emphasize the federal government, where the complexities of governance make it more challenging for students to understand and see their role.

Use the Internet

Each classroom in the project was equipped with a new personal computer and Internet access. With their computers and online access, students and teachers could browse a web site developed specifically for the project. Designed by the local newspaper company, the web site offered daily campaign news coverage, the ability to search local newspaper archives, access to research databases, links to candidates' web sites and profiles, an online discussion forum, and regular click polls (online opinion surveys) developed by students. There were a number of advantages to using the Web for civic pedagogy. Practically speaking, the Internet is a cost-effective medium for distributing information in terms of ease of daily updates and lower printing costs. In addition, students enjoy using the Internet and are increasingly likely to turn to it as a primary political information source (Delli Carpini, 2000), or as a means of participating in political forums (Lefort, 2000).

Interact with Candidates

Students were shown how they could easily communicate with candidates via e-mail. This allowed classroom discussions to be more than academic exercises, as students could actually solicit candidate input on debates surrounding pertinent issues. Face-to-face interactions were encouraged as well. Public forums in the town-meeting style were staged where students could voice their informed opinions directly to candidates and get feedback on their views. On some occasions, candidates actually responded to invitations to address classes about their stances on controversial issues, allowing students the opportunity to have their voices heard on their "own turf."

Get Media Coverage

A common complaint of students, particularly minority students, is that they do not feel that their views are accurately represented in the media (Entman, 1994). If the media are the only windows into the political world for young citizens and they do not see themselves represented in that world, there is a great likelihood that they will not participate in that world. One of the explicit goals of the "Student Voices" approach was to get the local news to cover the students' involvement in the project. This, in turn, had the potential to provide students with a sense that the media was representing them, increase their attention to the media (as they sought to see themselves), and raise the general public's attention to the issues in the political campaign.

Service Learning

"Student Voices" emphasized community service. Each classroom received a mini-grant to engage in some form of outreach to educate their communities about the issues of the election campaign and encourage community members to vote. Classrooms developed voters' guides that they distributed to their surrounding communities, engaged in voter registration drives, developed web sites, and conducted neighborhood public opinion polls on the issues most pertinent to a particular community.

THE "STUDENT VOICES" EVALUATION

Would the "Student Voices" approach be sufficient to promote civic knowledge, interest, and participation? Four questions were posed: (1) Does the project increase students' pursuit of civics knowledge in the media? (2) Does the project increase civics knowledge? (3) Does the project influence civic behaviors such as voting and political communications? (4) Does the project impact civic attitudes? To answer these questions, an evaluation of the effect of the "Student Voices" project was conducted.

Method

A quasi-experiment was designed to evaluate the project. Implementing "Student Voices" resulted in a naturally occurring "treatment" group, but no natural control group. A control group was created by having teachers nominate a peer teacher with a group of students similar to their own in every respect except for participation in the project. Initially, we created a Salomon's 4 groups design, which consists of two experimental and two control groups; one experimental and one control group received a pretest and a posttest while the other experimental and control group received a posttest only. However, because the matching procedure for creating control groups failed to yield comparable groups, we retained only the two groups who had been pretested.

Participants

Two classrooms (one control and one experimental) from each of 15 remaining schools in the School District of Philadelphia participated in the evaluation. A total of 419 students completed both the pretest and posttest questionnaires. The average age of students was 16.8 years. Sixty-two percent of the students were Black, 30% were White, 5% were Asian, and 3% classified themselves as "other." Fifteen percent of the sample classified itself as having a Spanish background. The sample was 57% female. Students reported a median grade point average of "B." The average number of years of education obtained by the mothers of participants was 13, or one year beyond high school.

Procedure

To ensure the equivalency of groups in every respect except for the manipulation, every classroom (experimental and control) received a new computer with Internet access. In addition to receiving a computer, participants in experimental classrooms completed the "Student Voices" project. To control for differences in literacy skills, the teachers in the classrooms administered questionnaires orally. While teachers read questionnaire items, students recorded their individual responses. For applicable classrooms, pretests were administered in February 1999. All posttests were administered in May 1999, after Philadelphia's mayoral primary election.

Instruments

A 76-item pretest questionnaire and an 87-item posttest questionnaire were administered to program participants. New questions about voting behavior and civic involvement in the mayor's election were added to the posttest. The pursuit of civics information was operationalized through measures of both media consumption and media attention. A goal of the "Student Voices" project was to influence the quantity of participants' media experiences (media consumption), the quality of media experiences (media attention), or both. Definitions of the measures were as follows:

Media Consumption

Several items were used to assess media use. The frequency of newspaper reading was measured through the question, "How often do you read the newspaper?" Response choices included, "Every day," "A few times a week," "Once or twice a week," "Once or twice a month," "Less than once a month, but at least once a year," and "Never." These response categories were annualized to create a continuous variable of days during the year on which a newspaper is read (e.g., every day = 365; a few times a week = 150; once or twice a week = 52; once or twice a month = 12; less than once a month but at least once a year = 5; and never = 0). Browsing the Internet for news or political information was measured through the open-ended question, "How many days in the past week did you use a computer to go online to get information about current events, public issues, or politics?" Listening to radio news broadcasts dealing with local issues was measured through the open-ended question, "How many days in the past week did you listen to a radio news broadcast dealing with local issues for at least five to ten minutes?" Listening to talk radio shows dealing with local issues was measured through the open-ended question, "How many days in the past week did you listen to talk radio shows that invite listeners to call in to discuss local events, issues, or city politics?" Watching network television news was measured through the open-ended question, "How many days in the past week did you watch the national nightly network news on ABC, CBS, or NBC—as you know, this is different from the local news and comes on at 6:30 P.M. in Philadelphia?" Watching local television news broadcasts was measured through the open-ended question, "How many days in the past week did you watch the local news about Philadelphia—this comes on before the national news and then again at either 10 P.M. or 11 P.M.?"

Media Attention

Media attention items included attention paid to newspaper stories about the mayoral election (How much attention have you paid to newspaper stories about the upcoming mayoral election?) and attention paid to local TV news stories about the mayoral election (How much attention have you paid to local TV news stories about the upcoming mayoral election?). These two self-report items were measured on a four-point scale where 0 = None, 1 = A little, 2 = Some, 3 = A lot. Following public affairs and interest in the mayoral election were also used to assess the general interest and motivation for following civics. Following of public affairs was measured with the item, "Some people seem to follow what's going on in government and public affairs most of the time, whether there's an election going on or not. Others aren't that interested. Would you say you follow what's going on in government and public affairs most of the time, some of the time, only now and then, or hardly at all?" Following of the mayoralty was measured with the subsequent item, "What about local affairs? Some people are interested in city government and the upcoming race for mayor, while others are not that interested. Would you say you are very interested in the upcoming race for mayor, somewhat interested, not too interested, or not at all interested?" These items were measured on four-point scales similar to the one used for the other media attention items.

Civics Knowledge

Learning civic knowledge was evaluated through a standard eight-item civics knowledge test (combination of multiple choice and fill-in-the blank items) and a 10-item mayoral candidate and local civic leader recognition test. Typical items on the standard civics knowledge test included: "Who is Janet Reno?" "Who is William Rehnquist?" "What is the name of the city council person who represents your neighborhood?" One point was given for each correct answer. The candidate/local civic leader familiarity index was a local civic leader recognition test that had participants rate their feelings on a scale from 1 to 100 toward a list of 10 mayoral candidates, public officials, and community leaders. Participants were instructed to indicate a "DK" for persons on the list that they did not recognize. Participants received a point for each leader that they could recognize and rate.

Political Talk

The impact of "Student Voices" on civic behaviors was evaluated through the project's impact on political communication. Political talk measured the frequency of communications with family ("How often, if ever, do you discuss problems affecting Philadelphia and its neighborhoods with your family?"); acquaintances and classmates ("Outside of your family and close friends, how often, if ever, do you discuss problems affecting Philadelphia and its neighborhoods?"); and about the mayor's race ("Now thinking about the upcoming election for mayor, how often in the past week have you talked with other people about the election?"). Each of these items had the following response categories, "Everyday," "3 or 4 times a week," "Once or twice a week," "Never." The measures were recoded to represent days in the course of the week in which participants discussed civics (everyday = 7, 3 or 4 times a week = 3, once or twice a week = 1, and never = 0).

Voting Behavior

The "Student Voices" project was also evaluated in terms of voting behavior among participants eligible to vote (18 years of age). Two voting behaviors were evaluated: voter registration and voting in the primary election. Both were measured on dichotomous, yes (1)—no (0) scales. Voter registration information was gathered on both the pretest and the posttest. Intention to vote in the primary was asked in the pretest and voting in the primary was only assessed in the posttest.

Cynicism

Participants were asked to respond to the following six items on a five-point agree/disagree Likert scale (adapted from Cappella & Jamieson, 1997): (1) The city government is generally run for the benefit of all the people. (2) When the city government runs something, it is usually inefficient and wasteful. (3) Most city public officials are trustworthy. (4) City officials don't care much about what people like me think. (5) Sometimes city politics and government seem so complicated that a person like me can't understand what is going on. (6) People like me don't have any say about what the city government does.

RESULTS

A one-way analysis of covariance (ANCOVA) examined differences between treatment and control groups for media consumption, media attention, civic knowledge, political talk, voting behaviors, and voting attitudes, respectively, while controlling for prior knowledge of these particular topics.

Pursuit of Civic Knowledge: Media Consumption and Media Attention

As seen in Table 5.1, the ANCOVA revealed that after controlling for pretest levels of media consumption, participants in "Student Voices" spent significantly more time browsing the Web and listening to radio news pro-

Table 5.1

Adjusted Posttest Means Comparing Outcomes for Treatment versus Control Groups

	Groups			
Outcome	Treatment	Control	df	F
Media Consumption				
Newspaper Reading	133.51	132.94	(1, 412)	.00
Web Browsing	1.44	1.09	(1, 412)	4.24*
Radio News	2.04	1.57	(1, 412)	5.43*
Local TV News	3.58	3.33	(1, 412)	1.51
Network TV News	2.25	2.08	(1, 412)	.79
Talk Radio	1.09	1.09	(1, 412)	.00
Media Attention				
Newspaper Attention	2.05	1.42	(1, 412)	58.91***
Local TV News Attention	2.17	1.69	(1, 412)	51.36***
Follow Mayoralty	1.91	1.45	(1, 412)	30.08***
Follow Public Affairs	1.52	1.29	(1, 412)	6.79**
Civic Knowledge				
Candidate Familiarity	8.89	8.44	(1, 412)	5.19*
General Civics Knowledge	3.05	2.80	(1, 412)	2.76+
Political Talk				
Political Affairs	2.47	1.59	(1, 412)	15.95***
Mayoralty Discussions	2.72	1.73	(1, 412)	17.12***
Family Discussions	1.98	1.70	(1, 412)	1.93
Voting Behaviors				
Voter Registration	.72	.47	(1, 105)	5.73*
Voting in Primary[1]	.41	.21	(1, 105)	5.66*
Civic Attitude				
Cynicism	17.63	17.59	(1, 412)	.02

Note: Individual means were adjusted by the pretest score of the corresponding posttest score (e.g., posttest newspaper reading was adjusted by the pretest newspaper reading score).
[1] Adjusted by pretest intention to vote in the mayoral primary.
+ $p < .10$; * $p < .05$; ** $p < .01$ *** $p < .001$.

grams for civic information than their control group counterparts. Specifically, program participants spent 24% more time browsing the Internet for civics and 23% more time listening to civics information on the radio. There were no significant differences in the consumption of other media for political material.

Program participants paid significantly more attention to civics information in the media than the control group members in every area evaluated. Program participants in "Student Voices" paid more attention to political information in newspaper stories and in local television news programs than the control. Students in the civics intervention were more likely to follow public affairs generally and were more interested in following the mayor's primary race than were students in control classrooms.

Civic Knowledge

The ANCOVA revealed that the "Student Voices" program can be attributed with modest but statistically significant gains in civics knowledge (see Table 5.1). Participants were 5% more familiar with local civic leaders and mayoral primary candidates than their control group counterparts. Participants also scored 8% better than the control on the general civics knowledge test; however, this difference was only marginally significant.

Civic Behaviors: Political Talk and Voting Behaviors

The ANCOVA revealed that general political communications with acquaintances and communications about the mayor's race were significantly greater among project participants than among control group members. Program participants spent 36% more time talking with acquaintances about politics than the control group did and 36% more time talking about the mayor's race than students not in the project (see Table 5.1). There were no significant differences in political discussions with family members.

Significantly more students in "Student Voices" registered to vote in the primary and actually voted in the primary than did students not in the project. Twenty-five percent more students in the project registered to vote in the treatment group than in the control, and 20% more students in the project voted in the primary than in the control.

Civic Attitudes

The final area evaluated was civic attitudes, operationalized as cynicism. Alhough the experimental group has a slightly higher cynicism level than the control, there were no statistically significant differences in cynicism as a function of participation in the project.

DISCUSSION

The "Student Voices" program was successful in achieving many of its goals. In terms of student pursuit of civics knowledge, project participants spent more time browsing the World Wide Web and listening to the radio for civics information. More importantly, project participants spent more time attending to political information in the media. However, the knowledge gains that resulted from this increased pursuit of civics knowledge were somewhat limited. Knowledge of local and national leaders and familiarity with laws and events that impact local civic life among "Student

Voices" participants was statistically, but not necessarily substantially, greater than knowledge of the control group members.

"Student Voices" did have a more substantive influence on civic behaviors. Political talk outside of the home increased over time; voting in the primary was more than twice the average youth participation in national elections for program participants. The project was unable to reduce cynicism levels among the young, however. Perhaps such attitudes are so entrenched that a mere semester-long intervention was insufficient to make a difference.

There were a number of lessons learned from the "Student Voices" evaluation. The first is that youth can be politically activated within the classroom in general and through the medium of the Internet in particular. If civics is made relevant to their experience, students will pursue and attend to civics information in the media, they will learn more about civics, and get more involved in the political process. As suggested by Niemi and Junn (1998), the usefulness of studying local politics within a civics framework in the school setting was supported by this project. The relevance of civics may have been enhanced through the media attention paid to the project, the interaction students had with candidates, the accessibility of issue-based campaign information over the Internet, or the hands-on opportunity to extend what was learned to the community through the service projects.

Though this chapter has as its primary title, "Political Socialization in the Digital Age," it appears that technology alone is insufficient to address the complex phenomenon of political apathy. Content matters. Although both the experimental conditions and the control conditions received computers with Internet access, it was primarily those who also received curricular support who were affected. Technology is not a panacea for youth political apathy, but a tool that, with directed use, may help overcome it.

The results of this evaluation also suggest that schools and the media may have an important symbiotic relationship in the political socialization of youth. It appears that the "Student Voices" curriculum encourages youth to spend more time gathering civics information through the media. As a result, participants' exposure to the political information important for political socialization was magnified. The exposure likely influenced the increased conversations, even if only in the school setting, and heightened interest in processing information. While there is no direct evidence for this process, the findings from the "Student Voices" evaluation indicates that this may be fertile ground for further exploration.

Finally, motivated adult or peer mentors may be necessary to turn youth on to civics. Family discussions about civics did not change over the course of the project. In the absence of family involvement, teachers engaging students and students engaging others may make the program work.

There are some important next steps to be taken if the "Student Voices" model is to be expanded to other settings. The first step is to acknowledge limitations of this evaluation and plan better ones. A future evaluation would ensure the relative equivalency of treatment and control groups. Testing items may be more varied to reduce sensitization to the variables—particularly knowledge items—under study. Power analyses would assure sufficient statistical power to detect differences among important subgroups.

A more sensitive analysis of civic learning may be appropriate in future evaluations of the "Student Voices" model. Bias may have been introduced into evaluation results if students provided questionnaire responses that coincided with what the experimenters wanted rather than what actually occurred. Items may be expanded to move beyond simple fact gathering to the effect the program has on higher-order thought processes such as political reasoning. The durability of the program on student civic interest and involvement should also be tracked as well as the specific program components that made it effective.

Given the results of this project, what are the prospects for political socialization and youth development in the digital age? It appears that digital media, like their analog predecessors, may be important educational resources for youth in the classroom, home, and community. In the "Student Voices" project, teachers were able to use the Internet to amplify civics lessons taught in class, stimulate interest in collecting political information in other sources, and provide richer and more tailored information about local issues not included in textbooks in order to enhance political participation among their students. The challenge is that like analog media, the potential of digital media will go unrealized unless other agents, like parents or teachers, become involved in directing its use.

NOTE

"Student Voices" was a part of the Philadelphia Compact, a joint project of the Annenberg Public Policy Center at the University of Pennsylvania and the Pew Charitable Trusts.

REFERENCES

Atkin, C. (1977). Effects of campaign advertising and newscasts on children. *Journalism Quarterly, 54*, 503–508.

Beck, P. A. (1977). The role of agents in political socialization. In S. A. Renshon (Ed.), *Handbook of political socialization: Theory and research* (pp. 115–141). New York: Free Press.

Brickman, W. W. (1978). *Ideas and issues in educational thought, past and recent.* Norwood, PA: Norwood Editions.

Cappella, J. N., & Jamieson, K. H. (1997). *Spiral of cynicism: The press and the public good.* New York: Oxford University Press.

Chaffee, S. H., Ward, L. S., & Tipton, L. P. (1970). Mass communication and political socialization. *Journalism Quarterly, 47,* 647–659.

Conway, M. M., Wyckoff, M. L., Feldbaum, E., & Ahern, D. (1981). The news media in children's political socialization. *Public Opinion Quarterly, 45* (2), 164–178.

Cooper, J. F. (1989). *The American Democrat* (G. Dekker & L. Johnston, Eds.). New York: Penguin Books.

Delli Carpini, M. X. (2000). Gen.com: Youth, civic engagement, and the new information environment. *Political Communication, 17,* 341–349.

Entman, R. M. (1994). Representation and reality in the portrayal of blacks on network television news. *Journalism Quarterly, 71* (3), 509–521.

Eveland, W. P., McLeod, J. M., & Horowitz, E. M. (1999). Communication and age in childhood political socialization: An interactive model of political development. *Journalism & Mass Communication Quarterly, 75* (4), 699–718.

Flanagan, C. A., & Faison, N. (2001). Youth civic development: Implications of research for social policy and programs. *Social Policy Report, 15* (1), 3–14.

Jennings, M. K., & Niemi, R. G. (1974). *The political character of adolescence.* Princeton, NJ: Princeton University Press.

Krampen, G. (2000). Transition of adolescent political action orientations to voting behaviors in early adulthood in view of a social-cognitive action theory model of personality. *Political Psychology, 21* (2), 277–297.

Lefort, R. (2000). Internet to the rescue of democracy? *UNESCO Courier,* June, 44–46.

Lewis, A. C. (2001). Washington commentary: Political participation and the young. *Phi Delta Kappan, 82* (5), 344–345.

Naughton, J. (2000). Click your mouse and vote. *New Statesman, 129* (July), 29–30.

Niemi, R. G., & Junn, J. (1998). *Civic education: What makes students learn.* New Haven, CT: Yale University Press.

Rahn, W., & Hirshorn, R. M. (1999). Political advertising and public mood: A study of children's political orientations. *Political Communication, 16* (4), 387–407.

Rubin, A. (1978). Child and adolescent television use and political socialization. *Journalism Quarterly, 55,* 125–129.

School District of Philadelphia. (2001). School District of Philadelphia— Snapshot. http://www.philsch.k12.pa.us/executiveoffices/communications/snapshot.htm. Accessed February 13, 2001.

Sigel, R. S. (1965). Assumptions about the learning of political values. *Annals of the American Academy of Social and Political Science, 361* (165), 1–9.

Simon, J., & Merrill, B. D. (1998). Political socialization in the classroom revisited: The kids voting program. *The Social Science Journal, 35* (1), 29–43.

Snyder, S. (2000). Survey finds textbook access improving in schools. *Philadelphia Inquirer, SF ed.,* sec. Local, p. B02, April 5.

Snyder, S., & Benson, C. (2001). City schools may be short $189 million despite more proposed state aid: The 2001–2002 projection is more than twice this year's deficit. *Philadelphia Inquirer, SF ed.,* sec. City & Region, p. B01, February 9.

Snyder, T. D., & Hoffman, C. M. (2000). *Digest of Education Statistics, 1999, NCES 2000–031.* Washington, DC: U.S. Department of Education, National Center for Education Statistics.

Statistical abstract of the United States, 1999. (1999). Washington, DC: United States Government Printing Office.

Tolo, K. W. (1999). *The civic education of American youth: From state policies to school district practices.* Austin, TX: Lyndon B. Johnson School of Public Affairs.

U.S. Bureau of the Census. (1975). *Historical statitistics of the United States, colonial times to 1970.* Washington, DC: United States Government Printing Office.

Woodard, E. H. (2000). *Media in the home 2000: The fifth annual survey of parents and children.* Philadelphia, PA: The Annenberg Public Policy Center of the University of Pennsylvania.

Chapter 6

Violent Video Games and Aggressive Thoughts, Feelings, and Behaviors

Craig A. Anderson

A tranquil Alaskan night.
So quiet, you can barely hear a neck snap.
—Advertisement for Metal Gear Solid
(*PC Gamer*, February 2001, p. 91)

Media violence is big business. Youth between the ages of 8 and 18 spend over 40 hours per week using some type of media, not counting school or homework assignments (Rideout, Foehr, Roberts, & Brodie, 1999). Television is most frequently used, but electronic video games are rapidly growing in popularity. In the United States, the *average* 2- to 17-year-old child plays console and computer video games seven hours per week (Gentile & Walsh, 2001). In 1999, 2.5% of entering college men reported playing video games over 20 hours per week (CIRP, 1999). More than 191 million video games were sold in 2000, worth $6.5 billion (Video Game Sales, 2001).

A BRIEF HISTORY OF VIOLENT VIDEO GAMES

The first video games emerged in the late 1970s and contained relatively little violence. The violence that did exist in the early games was largely abstract, involving the "shooting" of alien spaceships. But as time passed, and graphics became better, and profits became larger, more frequent and more graphic violence began to appear, even in children's games. For example, the seemingly innocuous Super Mario Brothers games included the capacity to destroy harmful creatures that got in the way of the main characters by jumping on top of them or by throwing fireballs at them.

Truly violent video games came of age in the 1990s with the killing games Mortal Kombat, Street Fighter, and Wolfenstein 3D. In all three games, the main task is to maim, wound, or kill opponents. The graphics (e.g., blood) and sounds (e.g., screams) of these games were cutting edge at the time of their introduction. The 1993 Mortal Kombat, and its later versions, entails a series of fights to the death between the game player and various opponents. The game includes a variety of "fatal" moves that the player can use to finish off an opponent, such as ripping out a beating heart or popping off the head and spine. By the end of the twentieth century even more graphically violent games became available to players of all ages (FTC, 2000; Walsh, 2001). For example, Soldier of Fortune (released in 2000) features 26 different killing zones in the human body. Game characters react realistically to shots to different parts of the body, by different types of weapons. A shot to the arm at close range by a shotgun rips the arm from the socket, leaving exposed bone and sinew. Unfortunately, a recent "mystery shopper"–study conducted by the U.S. Federal Trade Commission (FTC, 2000) found that underage children (13 to 16) unaccompanied by an adult were able to purchase "M" rated games (mature, must be 17 or older to purchase or rent) in 85% of the 380 stores sampled. Similar results have been obtained by others (e.g., Walsh, 2001).

YOUTH ACCESS TO VIOLENT VIDEO GAMES

Although numerous educational, nonviolent strategy, and sports games exist, a significant majority of the most popular video games are extremely violent in nature, involving brutal mass killings as the primary goal in winning the game (e.g., Buchman & Funk, 1996; Dietz, 1998; Funk, Flores, Buchman, & Germann, 1999; Provenzo, 1991). For example, D. D. Buchman and J. B. Funk (1996) found that fourth-grade girls (59%) and boys (73%) report that the majority of their favorite video games are violent ones.

Video games are now subject to voluntary ratings, but there are numerous problems associated with the rating system. The ratings differ by outlet (video arcade versus console and home computer), are not well understood, are not reliably followed by retail outlets (FTC, 2000; Walsh, 2001), and apparently have little impact on the marketing efforts of the companies that produce them. Indeed, at least 70% of "M" rated games are marketed to children under 17 years of age, some as young as age 6 (FTC, 2000). Furthermore, this same FTC report found that over 90% of the surveyed companies producing "M" rated games market at least some of these rated games to children under 17. Finally, the video game ratings provided by the video game industry do not match those provided by other adults and game-playing youngsters. Many games involving violence by cartoon-like characters are classified by the industry as appropriate for general audiences, a classification with which adults and youngsters disagree (Funk et al., 1999).

The rating system itself may contribute to consumer confusion. For instance, games rated "E" (Everyone) can contain any of the following descriptor categories: Mild Animated Violence, Mild Realistic Violence, Animated Violence, Realistic Violence, Animated Blood, and Realistic Blood. Indeed, only two categories of violence are prohibited in "E" games: Animated Blood and Gore, and Realistic Blood and Gore (FTC, 2000). Teen games (age 13 and older) can contain any of these types of violence. So, when the video game industry violates it own standards, as has been found repeatedly, it is violating standards that are already seen by many as unreasonably lax.

A related problem involves the lack of parental oversight. Ninety percent of teens in grades 8 to 12 report that their parents never check the ratings of video games before allowing their purchase, and only 1% of the teens' parents had ever prevented a purchase based on its rating (Walsh, 2000). Also, 89% reported that their parents never limited time spent playing video games.

POTENTIAL NEGATIVE EFFECTS OF VIOLENT VIDEO GAMES

The concern over media violence in general, and violent video games in particular, is driven by the belief that exposure to such violence has negative consequences. School shootings in recent years at Paducah, Kentucky; Jonesboro, Arkansas; and Littleton, Colorado, played a major role in bringing the potential harmfulness of violent video games to the attention of the general U.S. public. In all three cases, the shooters were students who habitually played violent video games. Eric Harris and Dylan Klebold, the Columbine High School students who murdered 13 and wounded 23 in Littleton before killing themselves, enjoyed playing the bloody video game Doom (Glick & Keene-Osborn, 1999). Harris created a customized version of Doom with two shooters, extra weapons, unlimited ammunition, and victims who couldn't fight back—features that are eerily similar to the actual shootings.

As might be expected, the video game industry denies any link between playing violent video games and aggression. For example, in a May 12, 2000 CNN interview, Doug Lowenstein, president of the Interactive Digital Software Association, said, "I think the issue has been vastly overblown and overstated, often by politicians and others who don't fully understand, frankly, this industry. There is absolutely no evidence, none, that playing a violent video game leads to aggressive behavior" (*The World Today*, 2000).

In actuality, the research literature on media violence effects in general (including television and movie violence studies) is quite large, and by 1975 80 relevant studies had been published. A meta-analysis of those studies clearly showed that by 1975, there was no room for doubt about the significance of media violence exposure to childhood aggression; both experimental and correlational studies demonstrated significant positive relations between media violence and aggression. Of course, the literature is much larger and even more definitive now (Bushman & Anderson, 2001).

Furthermore, research specifically focussing on the effects of exposure to violent video games has been slowly accumulating since the 1980s. The first comprehensive meta-analysis of these studies has only recently been completed (Anderson & Bushman, 2001). Before examining these results, however, it is important to place these concerns in a larger theoretical context.

MEDIA VIOLENCE EFFECTS

Theory

Why does exposure to violent media increase aggression and violence? The General Aggression Model (GAM, Anderson & Bushman, 2002), which is based on several earlier models of human aggression (e.g., Anderson & Dill, 2000; Bandura, 1971, 1973; Berkowitz, 1993; Crick & Dodge, 1994; Geen, 1990; Huesmann, 1986; Lindsay & Anderson, 2000; Zillmann, 1983), is a useful framework for understanding violent media effects. The enactment of aggression is largely based on the activation and application of aggression-related knowledge structures stored in memory (e.g., scripts, schemas). Of course, central to any such model is the social learning process, by which the individual acquires these various knowledge structures. Because social learning processes are so well understood, they will not be discussed in detail in this chapter. Briefly, children learn much about their world by observing social events around them, real ones (e.g., interactions with and among family members) as well as media-based events (e.g., television, movies, video games). Of particular relevance to this chapter is the fact that children readily learn how to aggress, when to aggress, and the expected consequences of aggressing from media sources.

Figure 6.1 displays a simplified version of the single episode portion of GAM. This portion of GAM illustrates how recent exposure to violent media can cause short-term increases in aggression and other related effects. For example, playing a violent video game can increase aggressive behavior through its impact on the person's present internal state, represented by cognitive, affective, and arousal variables. Violent media can increase aggression by priming aggressive cognitions (including aggressive scripts and aggressive perceptual schemata), by increasing arousal, or by creating an aggressive affective state. Although not explicitly illustrated in Figure 6.1,

Figure 6.1
Single-Episode General Aggression Model

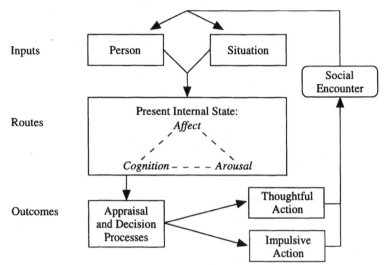

Source: Anderson & Bushman, 2002.

it seems likely that increasing aggressive thoughts, feelings, and behavioral tendencies must also decrease the accessibility of factors underlying other incompatible behaviors, such as prosocial ones, and thereby decreases the likelihood of those behaviors.

Long-term effects of media violence also involve learning processes, such as learning how to perceive, interpret, judge, and respond to events in the physical and social environment. Various types of knowledge structures (e.g., perception, interpretation, judgment, and action) develop over time, and are based on day-to-day observations of and interactions with other people, real (as in the family) and imagined (as in the media). Each violent media episode, as outlined in Figure 6.1, is essentially one more learning trial. Over time and with repeated exposure these knowledge structures become more complex, differentiated, and difficult to change. In a very real sense, a person's set of chronically accessible knowledge structures defines that person's *personality*.

Figure 6.2 illustrates this long-term learning process and identifies five types of relevant knowledge structures changed by repeated exposure to violent media. It also links these long term changes in aggressive personality to aggressive behavior in the immediate situation through both types of input variables described in the General Aggression Model: personological and situational variables. The link to person variables is obvious; less obvious is how long-term effects of repeated exposure to violent media can change situational variables. Briefly, as people become more aggressive,

Figure 6.2
Multiple-Episode General Aggression Model: Long-Term Effects of Video Game Violence

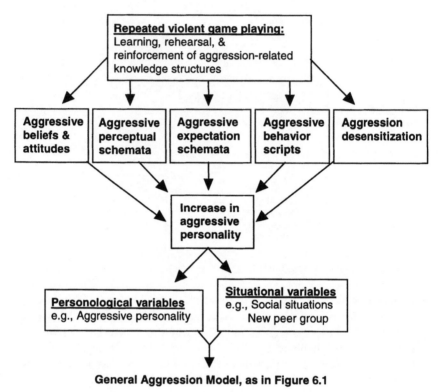

General Aggression Model, as in Figure 6.1

Source: Adapted from Anderson and Dill, 2000.

their social environments respond. The types of people who are willing to interact with them, the types of interactions that occur, and the types of situations made available to them all change. For example, interactions with teachers, parents, and nonaggressive peers are likely to decrease in frequency and quality, whereas interactions with other "deviant" peers are likely to increase.

Figure 6.2 also reveals that short-term effects of violent media on aggressive cognition are especially important. Of the five types of variables identified as contributing to the long-term increase in aggressive personality, four involve aggressive cognitions. Temporary mood states and arousal dissipate over time, but rehearsal of aggressive cognitions can lead to long-term changes in multiple aspects of aggressive personality. Furthermore, the literature on the development of behavioral scripts suggests that even a few rehearsals can change a person's expectations and intentions involving important social behaviors (Anderson, 1983; Anderson & Godfrey, 1987; Marsh, Hicks, & Bink, 1998).

A Recent Meta-analysis

As noted earlier, there is one recent comprehensive meta-analysis (Anderson & Bushman, 2001). Because the new analyses presented later in this chapter are based on this meta-analysis, a few methodological details will be presented here before summarizing the findings of that meta-analysis. Note that changes in methods used for the new analyses presented later in this chapter will be explained in that later section.

Methods

We searched the *PsycINFO* computer database for all entries through the year 2000 using the following terms: (*video** or *computer* or *arcade*) and (*game**) and (*attack** or *fight** or *aggress** or *violen** or *hostil** or *ang** or *arous** or *prosocial* or *help**). This search retrieved 32 research reports that included 46 independent samples of participants.[1] A total of 3,838 participants were included in the studies; over half (57%) were children under 18 years old. Studies were excluded if participants merely watched someone else play a video game. In several studies, half of the participants played the game while the other half watched, and the author(s) collapsed across this play/watch manipulation in their report. In such cases the collapsed results were used in the meta-analysis, but we divided the sample size in half.[2]

We coded the following characteristics for each study: (a) sex of participants, (b) age of participants (adults $\geq$ 18 years old or children < 18 years old), (c) type of study (experimental or correlational), and (d) publication status (published or unpublished). Correlational studies varied in how violent video game exposure was measured. The most direct measure (and the least frequently used) is some type of indicator of amount of time spent playing violent video games (e.g., hours per week). Less direct were measures of video game preferences (e.g., percentage of favorite games that have violent content) and hours per week spent playing any type of video games. We used the most direct measure available for each study, but included all studies even if only the less direct type of measure was used. For experimental studies, we also coded level of violence in the "violent" and "nonviolent" video game conditions.

We used the correlation coefficient as the effect size estimate for all studies, correlational as well as experimental, denoted by r. According to Cohen (1988), a "small" r is $\pm$ .10, a "medium" r is $\pm$ .30, and a "large" r is $\pm$ .50. Fisher's z transformation was applied to the correlations before they were averaged. Each Fisher's z was weighted by the inverse of its variance (i.e., $n - 3$). Once a 95% confidence interval was obtained for the pooled

z score, it was transformed back to a 95% confidence interval for the pooled r, denoted by r_+ (Hedges & Olkin, 1985).

Results

Moderator analyses revealed that there were no significant effects for age (adult versus child), sex of participant, publication status, or study type (experimental versus correlational). Furthermore, all of the average effect sizes were significantly different from zero, all $ps < .001$. Overall, the results indicated that exposure to violent video games significantly increases aggressive behavior ($r_+ = .19$, $k = 33$, $N = 3,033$), aggressive affect ($r_+ = .18$, $k = 17$, $N = 1,151$), physiological arousal ($r_+ = .22$, $k = 7$, $N = 395$), and aggressive cognition ($r_+ = .27$, $k = 20$, $N = 1,495$). Furthermore, exposure to violent video games significantly decreases prosocial behavior ($r_+ = -.18$, $k = 8$, $N = 676$) (k is the number of independent effect sizes in the average; N is the total number of participants in the average).

Discussion

The fact that neither age nor sex of participant moderated the effects suggests that these negative effects of exposure to violent video games occur to males and females at both young (< 18) and older ages. Furthermore, the fact that type of study (experimental versus correlational) didn't moderate the effects demonstrates that the effects are causal (i.e., the experimental studies) and apply to more real-world behaviors (e.g., aggressive delinquency) as well as to laboratory measures of aggression (e.g., the experimental studies). Indeed, if one merely considers the experimental studies, which provide the strongest tests of causality, we find that exposure to violent video games *caused* increases in aggressive behavior and aggressive thoughts, and decreases in prosocial behavior (Anderson & Bushman, 2001). More detailed results can be found in the Anderson and Bushman (2001) article.

These results appear pretty conclusive. Nonetheless, there are several more specific questions that can be addressed with these data, questions that were not directly addressed in the original article (mainly because of space limits). For instance, even though the age variable was not a significant moderator, one could argue that we need to test the effects separately for children under age 18.

In addition, in traditional meta-analyses, an attempt is made to include all possible studies, despite potential methodological shortcomings. If the research domain being examined is sufficiently large, one can code for specific shortcomings and do the appropriate moderator analyses to see which (if any) of the shortcomings reliably influences the estimated effect sizes. Unfortunately, the violent video game literature is not yet sufficiently large to allow such detailed comparisons. Therefore, the Anderson and Bushman

(2001) analyses did not attempt such methodological examinations, except for a comparison of correlational effect sizes as a function of the directness of the violent video game exposure measure (which yielded a nonsignificant effect of type of measure). The new analyses in the next section attend to these issues.

A New Meta-analysis

Method

The same data set used in the Anderson and Bushman (2001) article was used in these new analyses. The following changes were implemented: (a) effect sizes were collapsed across sex rather than averaged, where possible;[3] (b) for studies in which the "low violence" video game condition actually contained some violent content and the "no game" control condition was not particularly boring or frustrating, the control condition was used as the comparison group; (c) for studies in which the "no game" control condition was judged by participants as being particularly boring or frustrating, the "low violence" video game condition was used as the comparison group;[4] (d) studies which reported only combined video game player/observer results were dropped; (e) averaged self and observer reports of aggressive behavior; (f) included as aggressive behavior only measures in which aggression was targeted toward another person; (g) dropped one experimental study because the only control condition was rated by participants as significantly less entertaining and exciting than the comparison violent video game.

Results: Adults and Children Combined

Figure 6.3 presents the average effect sizes for each of the five dependent variables, along with the 95% confidence intervals, for the combined adult/children analyses. The results are very similar to those reported by Anderson and Bushman (2001). Exposure to violent video games increases aggressive behavior, aggressive thoughts, aggressive affect, and physiological arousal, and decreases prosocial behavior. The two behavioral measures yielded slightly larger effect sizes than in Anderson and Bushman (2001), the affect and arousal measures yielded slightly smaller effect sizes, and the aggressive cognition results were almost identical. For each dependent variable, the new analyses yielded effect sizes that are significantly different from zero and are small to moderate in size.

Results: Children Only

There were only two independent effects of aggressive affect in children, and only two involving physiological measures of arousal, too few for a meta-analytic study. The remaining three dependent variables had sufficient

Figure 6.3
Average Effects of Violent Video Games (r_+), Adults and Children Combined

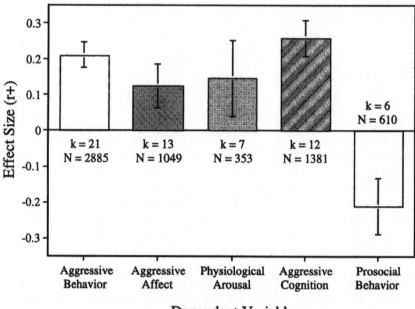

Vertical capped bars indicate 95% confidence intervals; k = number of independent tests; N = number of participants. *Note:* All effects were significantly different from zero, all ps < .001, except for physiological arousal, which was p < .01.

numbers of independent effects and of participants to warrant calculating effect size estimates separately from adults. Figure 6.4 presents the results. As can be seen, exposure to violent video games significantly increases aggressive behavior and aggressive cognition in children, and significantly decreases their prosocial behavior. Once again, all three effect sizes are small to moderate in size.

Results: Manipulation Size and Effect Size

One problem that became apparent while examining this literature is the vast difference in types of video games used within the violent and nonviolent conditions of various studies. Part of the difference results from the vast changes in video games themselves over the years. In the early days of video games, Pac-Man, in which the player controlled a circular object that "chomped" dots in a maze while trying to avoid being killed by ghosts (who could be killed by Pac-Man under some circumstances), had some parents concerned about potential consequences of playing this "violent" game. So it should come as no surprise that the violence of the "high vi-

Figure 6.4
Average Effects of Violent Video Games (r_+), Children Only

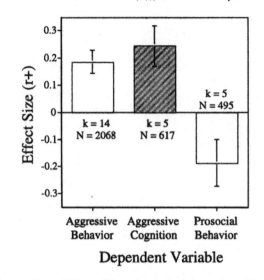

Dependent Variable

Vertical capped bars indicate 95% confidence intervals; k = number of independent tests; N = number of participants. *Note:* All effects were significantly different from zero, all ps < .001.

olence" conditions in early studies is very different from the high violence games in more recent studies. In addition, it appears that researchers using younger children often select fairly tame games for their "violent" conditions. But the problem is actually more than a time- or age-based phenomenon. Several experimental studies have used games with violent content in their "nonviolent" conditions. For example, several studies have used Sonic the Hedgehog games in the nonviolent condition. But Sonic can be hurt by his enemies, and can in turn kill them (e.g., by throwing fireballs at them). Thus, some of the apparent failures to find significant effects of violent content could be the result of poor operationalization of the violent and nonviolent experimental manipulations.

To test this idea, we rated the violent content of the video games used in the experimental studies. For a variety of reasons, this was possible for only 11 of the experimental studies. Each game was rated by two independent raters on a feature-anchored scale ranging from 0–10. For each study, then, one can subtract the violence rating of the nonviolent condition from the violence rating of the violent condition. Fortunately, none of the studies produced reversals, with the nonviolent game conditions actually being more violent than the violent game conditions. There was, however, one study in which the violent and nonviolent game conditions differed only by 2.5 points out of a possible 10. Figure 6.5 presents the scatterplot of the difference between the violent and nonviolent conditions (possible range of 0–10) and the aggressive behavior effect size (r) obtained for each study. As can be seen, the correlation is large and positive ($r = .60$). Studies with stronger manipulations (i.e., bigger differences between the violent and nonviolent game conditions) tended to produce bigger effect sizes on aggressive behavior.

There are too few studies to do this analysis separately for child and adult effects, and too few for reliable inferential statistics. Nonetheless, the point should be clear. Future studies need to be sure that their manipulations of violent and nonviolent games are appropriate, and as different in amount of violent content as is ethically feasible. Otherwise, the study is likely to produce results that are irrelevant at best, and misleading at worst.

DISCUSSION

Research Designs

There are several important lessons to be learned from the careful examination of existing violent video game literature. In hindsight, some of these lessons seem obvious. However, the initial studies in new domains frequently look weak when viewed from the perspective of later research and researchers who have benefited from the pioneers' difficulties.

Nonetheless, the field can and should learn and benefit from these early difficulties, and for this reason five key lessons will be highlighted. One has already been mentioned: More attention needs to be paid to the violent content in the selection of violent and nonviolent comparison games in experimental studies. It is imperative that there be a sizable difference in the amount of violent content in the violent and nonviolent conditions, else there is no reason to conduct the study. In recent years the level of violence in video games has increased, making it easier for researchers to create high and low violence conditions that differ appreciably in amount of violent content. Of course, this shift also increases the need for careful consideration of ethical issues in experimental research, especially with younger participants.

A second lesson arises from consideration of the average effect sizes obtained in recent meta-analyses of this literature: Sample sizes have generally been too small to reliably detect violent video game effects. The result of consistently too-small sample sizes is a set of studies that seem to have contradictory results (e.g., some "work" and others do not), but that is actually not contradictory when viewed from the meta-analytic perspective. The too-small sample phenomenon creates problems in any area of research, but it is particularly problematic in areas of direct relevance to

Figure 6.5
Relation between the Violent Content Difference between the Violent and
Nonviolent Video Game Conditions and the Effect on Aggressive Behavior,
Experimental Studies

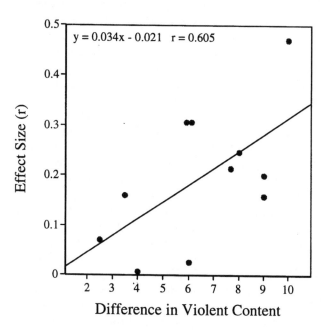

controversial public policy issues. In the video game case, the too-small
sample size problem provides a motivated industry with ammunition that
they can (and do) use to obfuscate the true overall (average) empirical
findings and thereby keep consumers, public policy officials, and politicians
confused and ineffective in attempts to address the issue.

We now know that the effect size of typical experimental manipulations
of video game violence and of correlational studies of video game violence
effects are likely to be about 0.18 to 0.20 (Anderson & Bushman, 2001;
see Figure 6.3). How big a sample is needed to find a "true" effect of this
size at the standard $p < .05$ level, assuming equal variances in the two
comparison conditions? If power is set to .80, one would need a sample
size of 236, half in each of the two conditions (violent and nonviolent). In
other words, one would get a "significant" effect only 80% of the time
researchers conduct studies with this sample size if the true effect size is r
= 0.18. Only one of the existing studies of video game effects has this large
a sample size, and that is a study that was not originally conducted with
video games as a primary concern (Hagell & Newburn, 1994). Several
others had sample sizes almost that large (e.g., Anderson & Dill, 2000).

To increase the probability of finding this true effect to 90% (i.e., power = .90), a sample size of 316 would be needed.

Two additional lessons to be learned have already been hinted at in the section describing methodological changes in the new meta-analysis presented in this chapter. The third lesson concerns the importance of the nonviolent or control comparison condition on dimensions other than violent content. Specifically, if the comparison condition in experimental studies is particularly boring, annoying, or frustrating, it is not an appropriate comparison for the violent condition. As any aggression textbook will note (e.g., Berkowitz, 1993; Geen, 1990), boring, annoying, and frustrating conditions themselves can increase aggressive tendencies. Therefore, using such "control" conditions may lead to an underestimation of the true effect of video game violence. Ideally, the nonviolent game(s) should be equated with the violent game(s) on dimensions that might be related to aggressive behavior but that are not part of the key processes under investigation (see Anderson & Dill, 2000; Panee & Ballard, in press, for two different ways of addressing this issue).

The fourth lesson has to do with reporting results. Meta-analyses are only as good as the data going into them. When research reports do not contain sufficient information to enable accurate calculation of effect sizes, then they cannot be included in future meta-analyses. This is particularly a problem with nonsignificant findings, which many scholars (including the present author, on occasion) simply report as nonsignificant without presenting relevant means, standard deviations, or inferential statistics (e.g., t or F tests). A similar problem in several of the video game studies was the reporting of means collapsed across the very important distinction of whether the participant actually played the assigned game or merely watched another play the game. Without separate means, one cannot accurately estimate the effect of playing the games.

The fifth lesson concerns the violent video game exposure measure to be used in correlational studies. If one wants to test the hypothesis that violent content in video games is associated with heightened aggression, then one should measure exposure to violent content, not exposure to video games in general. Anderson and Bushman (2001) found no significant moderator effects of type of exposure measure, but that may well change as the number of such studies (and hence, total participants) available for such a moderator analysis increases. The pattern of effect sizes across the three main types suggests that the more directly exposure to violent video games is assessed, the higher the correlation between exposure and aggressive behavior (r_+s = .26, .16, and .16 for time on violent content, violent content preference, and time on all video games, respectively).

Magnitude of Effects

Using Cohen's conventional descriptive labels, the average effects of violent video games all fall between "small" and "moderate" in size. Does this mean that concerns about exposing children (or young adults) are overblown? The various media representatives (from TV, movie, music, and video game industries) would certainly like to believe so (*The World Today*, 2000), and frankly, it would be comforting to believe that such effects are not big enough to be troublesome. But such a belief is simply not accurate.

One way to think about the effect size issue is to compare video game violence effects to other effects that U.S. society and U.S. public policy consider large. Interestingly, the effects of violent video games on aggressive and prosocial behavior found in our meta-analyses are larger than effects of several important medical effects: passive smoke on lung cancer (Wells, 1998); exposure to lead and IQ scores in children (Needleman & Gatsonis, 1990); nicotine patches and smoking cessation (Fiore, Smith, Jorenby, & Baker, 1994); calcium intake and bone mass (Welten, Kemper, Post, & van Staveren, 1995); exposure to asbestos and laryngeal cancer (Smith, Handley, & Wood, 1990). Thus, if you believe that any of these medical effects are important, then the video game violence effects should not be dismissed as being too small.

A second way to think about the effect size issue is to consider the "dosage" administered, and whether it is likely to be increasing with time. As Abelson (1985) and Rosenthal (1990) have pointed out, small effect sizes can yield large effects, especially when they accumulate across repeated occasions. Thus, differences in batting skills of major league baseball players account for a trivially small effect size on any given at-bat outcome, but over the course of a season teams with slightly better batters win considerably more games, and across seasons they win more championships. Similarly, the effect of smoking a single cigarette or even a pack of cigarettes on lung cancer is probably unmeasurably small, but the accumulated effects of years of smoking are quite large. As noted at the beginning of this chapter, young people are being exposed to violent video games at a high rate already, and the rate is increasing across time. Therefore, the cumulative long-term impact of exposure to violent video games may be sufficiently large to warrant considerable social concern.

NEW DIRECTIONS

The evidence is now clear that playing violent video games increases aggressive behavior and decreases prosocial behavior in children and in young adults. There is much more work needed, however. What follows is a list of research needs in this domain.

1. Does explicitly gory violence desensitize video game players more so than less gory violence? If so, does this desensitization increase subsequent aggression? Does it decrease helping behavior?

2. What features increase the game player's identification with an aggressive character in video games? Prior research and theory in the media violence domain suggest that the impact of exposure to violent video games is likely to be greater when the game player closely identifies with an aggressive game character.

3. What features, if any, could be added to violent video games to decrease the impact on subsequent aggression by the game player? For instance, does the addition of pain responses by the game victims make players less reluctant to reenact the aggression in later real-world situations, or do such pain responses in the game further desensitize the player to others' pain?

4. Can exciting video games be created that teach and reinforce nonviolent solutions to social conflicts?

5. What are the long-term effects of exposure to violent video games?

6. What types of people are most susceptible to violent video game effects, and who is relatively immune?

Answers to these questions are vital, but will require considerable effort by the research community and considerable funding by federal and other research agencies and foundations. Violence in contemporary American culture is a major social concern, and media violence plays an important role. Ideally, social policy decisions are grounded in solid empirical research. However, policy decisions are made regardless of whether there are good and relevant data. To date, researchers have studied violence and video game questions with virtually no governmental support. As video games continue to evolve in the digital age, becoming ever more realistic and violent, a commitment by the federal government is needed to fund basic research that will more adequately inform policy about the role that these games play in the development of childhood aggression. Both the relatively small research base (relative to the TV/movie literature) and the paucity of funding for video game research are at least partly the result of the fact that such electronic gaming is a fairly new phenomenon. It is clear from the present chapter that there are legitimate concerns about the effects of playing violent video games. It is clear from other chapters in this volume that video gaming already consumes many hours of children's leisure time, and that the amount consumed is rapidly growing. What we've learned so far has taken almost 20 years, in part because of the lack of research funding. It is timely for researchers and governmental agencies to work together to complete the next round of studies on this vital topic.

NOTES

1. A list of the studies included in the meta-analysis can be obtained from the following web site: http://psych-server.iastate.edu/faculty/caa/abstracts/2000-2004/01ABtable.html.

2. For studies that reported effects separately for players and observers, we used the player results. One might expect video game effects to be greater on players than observers (on average), and that studies that report only the combined player/observer results might, therefore, underestimate the true obtained effect on players. For this reason, such studies were dropped in meta-analyses reported in a later section in this chapter.

3. Averaging entails computing separate effect sizes for the male and female participants, and then averaging the two effect sizes using appropriate sample size weightings. Because the meta-analysis did not yield reliable sex effects, the present re-analyses collapsed across sex when possible, that is, used effect size estimates generated by analyses in which sex was not in the statistical model.

4. Frustration and boredom can themselves cause increases in aggression, so "control" conditions which are experienced by participants as highly boring or frustrating do not provide appropriate comparisons for the violent video game conditions, unless, of course, the comparison video game condition also induces boredom and/or frustration.

REFERENCES

Abelson, R. P. (1985). A variance explanation paradox: When a little is a lot. *Psychological Bulletin, 97,* 129–133.

Anderson, C. A. (1983). Imagination and expectation: The effect of imagining behavioral scripts on personal intentions. *Journal of Personality and Social Psychology, 45,* 293–305.

Anderson, C. A., & Bushman, B. J. (2001). Effects of violent video games on aggressive behavior, aggressive cognition, aggressive affect, physiological arousal, and prosocial behavior: A meta-analytic review of the scientific literature. *Psychological Science, 12,* 353–359.

———. (2002). Human aggression. *Annual Review of Psychology, 53,* 27–51.

Anderson, C. A., & Dill, K. E. (2000). Video games and aggressive thoughts, feelings, and behavior in the laboratory and in life. *Journal of Personality and Social Psychology, 78,* 772–790.

Anderson, C. A., & Godfrey, S. (1987). Thoughts about actions: The effects of specificity and availability of imagined behavioral scripts on expectations about oneself and others. *Social Cognition, 5,* 238–258.

Bandura, A. (1971). Social learning theory of aggression. In J. G. Knutson (Ed.), *Control of aggression: Implications from basic research* (pp. 201–250). Chicago: Aldine-Atherton.

———. (1973). *Aggression: A social learning analysis.* Englewood Cliffs, NJ: Prentice-Hall.

Berkowitz, L. (1993). *Aggression: Its causes, consequences, and control.* New York: McGraw-Hill.

Buchman, D. D., & Funk, J. B. (1996). Video and computer games in the '90s: Children's time commitment and game preference. *Children Today, 24,* 12–16.

Bushman, B. J., & Anderson, C. A. (2001). Media violence and the American public: Scientific facts versus media misinformation. *American Psychologist, 56,* 477–489.

CIRP (1998, 1999). *Cooperative Institutional Research Program survey results.* Ames, IA: Office of Institutional Research.

Cohen, J. (1988). *Statistical power analysis for the behavioral sciences* (2nd ed.). Hillsdale, NJ: Lawrence Erlbaum.

Crick, N. R., & Dodge, K. A. (1994). A review and reformulation of social information-processing mechanisms in children's social adjustment. *Psychological Bulletin, 115,* 74–101.

Dietz, T. L. (1998). An examination of violence and gender role portrayals in video games: Implications for gender socialization and aggressive behavior. *Sex-Roles, 38,* 425–442.

Fighting violence. (1968). *Time, 92,* December 27, 58–59.

Fiore, M. C., Smith, S. S., Jorenby, D. E., & Baker, T. B. (1994). The effectiveness of the nicotine patch for smoking cessation. *Journal of the American Medical Association, 271,* 1940–1947.

FTC. (2000). *Marketing violent entertainment to children: A review of self-regulation and industry practices in the motion picture, music recording, & electronic game industries.* Report of the Federal Trade Commission. Federal Trade Commission. Available online: www.ftc.gov/reports/violence/.

Funk, J. B., Flores, G., Buchman, D. D., & Germann, J. N. (1999). Rating electronic games: Violence is in the eye of the beholder. *Youth & Society, 30,* 283–312.

Geen, R. G. (1990). *Human aggression.* Pacific Grove, CA: McGraw-Hill.

Gentile, D. A., & Walsh, D. A. (2001). *A normative study of family media habits.* Minneapolis, MN: National Institute on Media and the Family.

Glick, D., & Keene-Osborn, S. (1999). Anatomy of a massacre (Columbine High School shootings). *Newsweek, 133,* May 3, 24–30.

Hagell, A., & Newburn, T. (1994). *Young offenders and the media: Viewing habits and preferences.* London: Policy Studies Institute.

Hedges, L. V., & Olkin, I. (1985). *Statistical methods for meta-analysis.* New York: Academic Press, 1985.

Huesmann, L. R. (1986). Psychological processes promoting the relation between exposure to media violence and aggressive behavior by the viewer. *Journal of Social Issues, 42,* 125–139.

Lindsay, J. J., & Anderson, C. A. (2000). From antecedent conditions to violent actions: A general affective aggression model. *Personality and Social Psychology Bulletin, 26,* 533–547.

Marsh, R. L., Hicks, J. L., & Bink, M. L. (1998). Activation of completed, uncompleted, and partially completed intentions. *Journal of Experimental Psychology: Learning, Memory, and Cognition, 24,* 350–361.

Needleman, H. L., & Gatsonis, C. A. (1990). Low-level lead exposure and the IQ of children. *Journal of the American Medical Association, 263,* 673–678.

Panee, C. D., & Ballard, M. E. (in press). High versus low aggressive priming during video game training: Effects on game violence, state affect, heart rate, and blood pressure. *Journal of Applied Social Psychology.*

Provenzo, E. F. (1991). *Video kids: Making sense of Nintendo.* Cambridge, MA: Harvard University Press.

Rideout, V. G., Foehr, U. G., Roberts, D. F., & Brodie, M. (1999). *Kids and media*

Violent Video Games 119

at the new millennium: Executive summary. Menlo Park, CA: Kaiser Family
Foundation.
Rosenthal, R. (1990). How are we doing in soft psychology? American-Psychologist, 45, 775–777.
See no evil? (1954). Scholastic, November 10, 7–8.
Smith, A. H., Handley, M. A., & Wood, R. (1990). Epidemiological evidence indicates asbestos causes laryngeal cancer. Journal of Occupational Medicine, 32, 499–507.
The World Today. (2000). Atlanta, GA: Cable News Network, May 12.
Video Game Sales. (2001). Video game sales slide 5 percent in 2000. January 19, Reuters.
Violence bill debated in Washington: Most panelists argued against legislation. (1990). Broadcasting, 118 (6), 77.
Walsh, D. (2000). Interactive violence and children: Testimony submitted to the Committee on Commerce, Science, and Transportation, March 21. Downloaded from http://www.mediaandthefamily.org/senateviolence-full.html on March 24, 2000.
———. (2001). 5th annual video and computer game report card. Minneapolis, MN: National Institute on Media and the Family.
Wells, A. J. (1998). Lung cancer from passive smoking at work. American Journal of Public Health, 88, 1025–1029.
Welten, D. C., Kemper, H.C.G., Post, G. B., & van Staveren, W. A. (1995). A meta-analysis of the effect of calcium intake on bone mass in young and middle aged females and males. Journal of Nutrition, 125, 2802–2813.
Zillmann, D. (1983). Cognition-excitation interdependencies in aggressive behavior. Aggressive Behavior, 14, 51–64.

Part III

Cognitive Effects of Media

Chapter 7

"We Have These Rules Inside": The Effects of Exercising Voice in a Children's Online Forum

Justine Cassell

I was earlier like an unlit lamp. Jrsummit has lit a spark in me. So, now I spread the light around. I talk to my friends, read newspapers, do not take any injustice lying down.

—Pooja, India

Some kids do really bad things and get a lot of publicity. Some kids do great things but get very little publicity. This will be a story about kids all across the US and the world who are working together to do something globally great!

—Jason, United States

The discussion of the role of computational technology in children's development has become increasingly polarized over the last year or so. On the one hand we find a frantic push to place computers and Internet access into all U.S. schools, based on a belief that computer literacy will increasingly be required for success in the job market (Committee on Information Technology Literacy, 1999), and on the other hand, a frantic push *back* to place a "moratorium" (Cordes & Miller, 2000) on children's access to computers, based in part on a belief that the negative effects of computers on children have not been sufficiently studied. Clearly the answer lies at neither end of this long spectrum, and a careful review of existent studies shows a number of benefits, a palmful of harmful effects, and a plethora of unknowns (Wartella, O'Keefe, & Scantlin, 2000). History teaches us that whereas initial fears about movies or radio or television concern the very presence of the medium, it is the content of the medium—the message—that must be evaluated and improved. However, one difference between the computer and earlier media is that never before has a technology so effectively allowed people from around the world to congregate. Never before has a technology been so fundamentally *bi-directional*: allowed those who consume to also create. That is, with this particular technology, the medium is available for anybody to create the message. Although it would seem as if such a technology would be lauded for its ability to allow community, quite the contrary has been the case. Many believe, as forcefully expressed by Hern and Chauk (1997), that:

The Internet, after the automobile and television, is the third technological innovation this century powerful enough to challenge and mutate our disintegrating collective vision of community. Although useful for exchanging e-mail and performing fact-based research, the Internet inherently denies and denigrates the crux of direct democratic theory, the possibility of face-to-face relationships.

In this chapter I discuss an Internet-based democratic global learning community. The Junior Summit program was a $2.1 million international project that brought together 3,000 children, aged 10 to 16, from 139 different countries, in an online forum that allowed the children to communicate with each other across languages on topics of international concern. This forum culminated in a six-day program at MIT (November 1998) where 100 of the children (from 54 countries) met with world leaders, heads of industry, and international press to describe, get feedback, and garner support for their ideas about how to use technology to improve children's lives. The children then returned to the online forum to implement the projects that they had designed, and to amplify the voices of the Junior Summit by bringing in more children from their respective communities. The community was democratic in the sense that children decided on the topics of interest, organized themselves into workgroups, elected delegates, and determined outcomes. In the remainder of this chapter, I first describe the philosophical and design underpinnings of the Junior Summit—the notions of voice, underdetermined design, designing to the lowest common denominator—then turn to the organization of the program, some outcomes to date, and the lessons we can learn in order to use the Internet and other communication technologies in the service of children's well-being.

VOICE

One of the principal concerns that emerges in contemplation of technological "progress" is that those whose stories have not been heard (girls and women, ethnolinguistic minorities, developing nations, children) may be even more silenced as technology advances. As a designer of new technology for children, and as a developmental psychologist, I wished to ensure that the bi-directional promise of computers be upheld and that technology not become increasingly more America-centric, more English-centric, more geared to selling stuff to children, rather than eliciting words from children.

My earlier work investigated computer games for girls, and I designed and implemented several new technologies in this arena, as well as writing on the topic. I argued that girls were not being taken into account in the design of computer games, however designing games "specially for girls" risks ghettoizing girls as a population that needs "special help" in their relation to technology. In contrast to this stance, my own design work contributed games for both boys and girls that encouraged them to express aspects of self-identity that transcend stereotyped gender categories. In a volume coedited with Henry Jenkins (Cassell & Jenkins, 1998), researchers in education, psychology, cultural theory and technology, along with the foremost players in the industry of computer games for girls, contributed chapters on the topic of implications of the "girls' market" in computer games. My own contribution to the volume (Cassell, 1998) focused on what I termed "feminist software design" (FSD) and how to apply it to the design of storytelling software for children. Modeled after feminist pedagogy (Lewis, 1993), my design philosophy of FSD rested on five principles:

- Transfer design authority to the user
- Value subjective and experiential knowledge in the context of computer use
- Allow use by many different kinds of users in different contexts
- Give the user a tool to express her voice and the truth of her existence
- Encourage collaboration among users

I argued that storytelling systems were the ideal genre for experimentation with this design philosophy, and that, additionally, the ideal way for girls to learn about themselves, and to construct their selves, is through first-person storytelling and other kinds of participatory narratives. What is meant by "storytelling" here is not professional storytelling: fairytales, retellings of Goldilocks, Disney's version of "Winnie the Pooh." Instead, an approach consonant with construction of social identity gives girls the role of narrator and also allows them to choose whether to be the subject of the narration—that is, to give them voice. This enables them to tell whatever story they like, while the computer constructs a willing listener. It is a way for a child to represent his or her unique perspective on the world—the first-person perspective—to the world. As Ochs and Taylor write (1995), "[G]ender identities are constituted through actions and demeanors . . . among other routes, children come to understand family and gender roles through differential modes of acting and expressing feelings in narrative activity" (p. 98).

Some of the issues that face girls in the United States and elsewhere are similar to the issues faced by other children outside the mainstream—racial minorities, children from developing nations, children with disabilities. These children are at risk of not being taken into account in the design of technology, but yet there is likewise a danger of marginalizing their participation if we design technology only for them. It is for children who fit into these categories that empowerment, self-efficacy, and the notion of *voice* take on importance. The term "voice" in narrative theory has referred to whether an author speaks through a narrator or a character, or speaks as herself—it is the taking of different perspectives on a story. But, popular books on adolescence, and much feminist theory, use the terms "voice," "words," and "language" metaphorically, "to denote the public expression of a particular perspective on self and social life, the effort to represent one's own experience, rather than accepting the representations of more powerful others" (Gal, 1991, p. 176).

The Junior Summit was designed to allow children to deploy their voices—to be heard in a very essential way. That is, the Junior Summit was designed to allow children of all sorts, from everywhere, to come to know their own experience as primary, to try out versions of themselves, to tell their stories, to describe their version of the world, and learn to trust the value of their perceptions. These opportunities, we believed, would allow the growth of self-efficacy—the belief that they can have an effect on the world around them.

UNDERDETERMINED DESIGN AND DESIGNING TO THE LOWEST COMMON DENOMINATOR

The technology and design of the Junior Summit focused on bringing voices to the table that are not often recognized, and giving them the means to be heard. This included (a) setting up computers and Internet connections for needy participants so that not just the "digerati" (i.e., those wealthy enough to afford digital technologies were involved, (b) training to ensure that moderators were prepared to help children reach beyond clichés (the "children say the darnedest things" statements that so often define children's contribution) to the areas in which they could make truly valuable contributions, and (c) designing the interaction among the children, and the shape of the online space in such a way that children were helped to respect one another's views during the summit, and to increase their role on the world stage afterwards.

In my work on girls and computer games, I had developed an interface design philosophy called "underdetermined design"—designing just enough to make the system engaging, easy to learn, and intuitive, but not so much as to determine how to use it. Users themselves determined how the system was to be used. That philosophy was essential to the implementation of the Junior Summit online forum, but I found that I needed to extend it with a set of principles that I call "Designing to the Lowest Common Denominator." Whereas most web sites for children did and do feature as many bells and whistles as possible, appeal as much as possible to children's love for the new, the novel, the technological, the Junior Summit was designed to the lowest common denominator: no feature of the forum was available to some children and not to others. All children were equal participants whether they used an Apple IIC, or a Pentium 4, whether they could support Flash plug-ins, or just e-mail, whether they logged in from a dedicated T1, or used a 1,200-baud modem in the local Internet café, whether they were "clickerati" (i.e., had grown up clicking a computer mouse) or had never before seen a screen. Underdetermined design put all participants on an equal footing.

Technologically, and ethically, the challenges of underdetermined design were immense. We implemented a way to relay all messages typed into real-time online chat automatically to e-mail for those children without Web access. And, we turned down a big donation from a major software company, when the "gift" was accompanied by a request to have Junior Summit kids test drive a computation-heavy 3D graphical online world that would only work on Pentium 4 machines. With a simple environment, it was the children's words that became salient, as opposed to the animations that adorned their personal Web pages.

IMPLEMENTATION OF UNDERDETERMINED DESIGN AND DESIGNING TO THE LOWEST COMMON DENOMINATOR

Many organizations have used communication technologies as diverse as the telegraph and television to bring children together. In autumn 1997, there were a handful of programs already in place that either gathered children on the Internet, or gathered children at an in-person summit to discuss the Internet. Though some of these programs were extremely impressive, there were a number of features common to most of them that diminished the impact of children's own voices. In the following sections, I describe how the Junior Summit differed from previous programs in terms of (1) the children who participated, (2) the format of the online forum, (3) the role of adults, (4) how the issue of language was dealt with, (5) the children's representation on the world stage, and (6) how talk might lead to action.

DESIGN AND METHOD

Participants

The vast majority of previous programs targeted children who were already online. The goal of the Junior Summit was to accept 1,000 participants who represented every country in the world, those who used a

Figure 7.1
Excerpt from Junior Summit Entry Form

If you will be between 10 and 16 years old in November 1998 and would like to participate in the Junior Summit, you must submit an entry by March 31, 1998. We want to know how you see the state of children in your community and in the world, what changes you think can and should be brought about, and how these changes could be affected by the growth of the Internet and other new communication technologies.

In your application you should do one or more of the following:

- suggest an important problem (either local or global) that you think children should take action on.
- describe the work that you have already done to change the world, and how you would like to expand that work.
- discuss how the Internet and other new communication technologies can change the roles that children play in the world.

You can express your ideas in words, pictures, video, music, or any other medium (a web site, a story). You can submit an entry as an individual or as a group.

Participation in the Junior Summit is for you if you have an opinion about whether people your age should have a greater say and a more active role in changing the world locally and globally.

We are aiming for the greatest diversity of participants. We will include those who use a computer on a daily basis and those who have never had the chance to touch one.

Representatives will be chosen from each region of the world, both boys and girls, and older and younger children.

---

computer on a daily basis and those who didn't know what a computer was, those who struggled to exist on the margins of their society and those who received every benefit their society has to give. In order to achieve this goal Junior Summit distributed entry forms (see Figure 7.1) in every way possible, so as to try to reach every child in every country. Following UNESCO, who carry out 90% of their outreach in English, French, and Spanish, we sent out 80,000 copies of the entry form in those three languages, around the world. Entry forms were sent to every ministry of education in the world, all UNESCO offices, offices of Education International in 300 countries, the 2,500 schools of the worldwide Associated Schools Project, the 850 members of the Association of Secondary School Principals, 300 offices of the Junior Achievement program, headquarters of Education International, and many NGOs and international conferences. Over 100 educational web sites around the world linked to the Junior Summit '98 web site. In addition, requests for entry forms received by fax and by mail were responded to, as well as a large number of requests by e-mail.

Entries were received from more than 8,000 children in 139 countries, in 30 different languages, and every medium imaginable. Because of a zealous local NGO, nearly 400 entries were received from China. More surprisingly, more than 30 entries (from every child of appropriate age, as it turned out) were received from Nieue, a country of 1,800 people—so small that the mailing address reads "Nieue, near New Zealand." With the help of international graduate students and faculty from across MIT, 1,000 entries were chosen, representing 3,062 children between the ages of 10 and 16, from 139 countries. Entry criteria included:

- *Quality of entry.* Do they have creative ideas and visions about changing the world, particularly through technology? Are they able to articulate those ideas well, through some medium? Have they answered the questions?
- *Effort.* Seems to have invested time, care, and passion into the entry.
- *Commitment.* Seems to take the project seriously, understand it as a valuable opportunity and responsibility, and indicate a commitment to participate regularly (i.e., don't just want to win a free computer).
- *Past experience.* Have they demonstrated their capacity to change the world, or a serious attempt to do so?
- *Fit the following description.* Children with the gift of expression through such media as language, music, and images. Children who can document the digital [or nondigital] state of children in their country or community. Children with a vision of how to harness the digital revolution in the service of kids. Children who can convince adults of this vision.

Examples of successful entries included a moving essay about female circumcision in Benin with documenting photos *taken by the 13-year-old applicant herself* that described how access to information about girls around the world could help local girls resist, and how technology could help in other ways.

Other successful entries included a video documenting the technological collaboration between an international school and a rural school for local children, both located in Tamil Nadu, in Southern India, and a sketch demonstrating how the energy gleaned from walking could be used to power technology located in shoes. Despite worries about fair, equitable, nonethnocentric criteria for judging, it turned out that *passion* was the key criterion, and that it was quite simple to distinguish passionate essays from children who hoped to improve the world, from essays or drawings from children (or from adults behind the scenes) who simply hoped to acquire a free computer. And, in only one case did we later become convinced that a parent had written the entry and was continuing to write the child's contributions online.

Although neither gender nor age were taken into account in the judging, successful entrants were roughly 55% girls and 45% boys, and represented a bell-shape curve of ages. The gender mix was particularly interesting given that other online fora for children reported greater numbers of boys than girls, and that computers and new technology were still in 1997 perceived as primarily masculine activities. We guessed that the even gender mix was due to explicit wording in the entry form about a mix of boys and girls, and to the relative salience in the entry form of the notion of changing the world, with respect to the notion of new technology. Forty percent of the participants chosen did not have computer fluency. The minority of accepted entries came from children working alone—many entries represented the work of school classes or self-constituted groups. Thus, the 1,000 accepted entries comprised over 3,000 children.

Format

In previous online fora for children, topics of discussion, rules and interaction format were chosen by adults and policed by adults. Adult moderators on the Junior Summit forum were carefully trained to keep the discussion on track without directing the outcome, to make no decisions for the children, and not to influence the direction of the discussion. A striking example comes from the group that decided to work on the topic of "bringing about peace." Early in the discussion, when the participants were introducing themselves, a worrisome debate developed between an Israeli and a Palestinian child. In this debate the conversation soon turned personal, and even threatening, with one of the children talking about revenging the death of his uncle. The moderator was at first frightened and then managed to hold fast to the desire to let the children find their voices. Within a day or so, the other children in the topic group chimed in; one of the children in the debate stepped back and suggested that their conversations concern only the present and future, and not the past of their countries.

This topic group was subsequently more productive than many of the other topic groups, in terms of the numbers of concrete action projects suggested, more tightly knit, in terms of communication among the members, and more long-lasting, in terms of how long after the in-person summit this group continued to work together. This early chance to resolve conflict autonomously, without adult intervention, to learn listening skills, to use their voices to prevent harm to one another, seems to have allowed this group to feel more capable and more in control of their environment—more self-efficacious, leading to more action (Bandura, 1997). As one child from Norway remarked, "We all are sharing one world and today's children are tomorrow's leaders. We have to start learning empathy and sympathy, not only in thinking, but also in handling."

Excerpts from the beginning of the conversation, the point at which other children intervened, and the response by one of the fighting children, are reproduced below (spelling and grammar have not been corrected):

Palestinian Child: Axxxx, i am delighted to find a person from israel with me on the same topic, as i mentioned later i am palestinian, and i carry a Israeli ID (ta3odat zehout) and i beleive in peace, but not according to Madrid, Oslo treaties etc. . . . i beleive in eternal peace, solutions that will get peace into the soceity not peace that we show the americans that we are living happily while the truth is that we are stabbing each other from the back.

Axxxx and the rest in topic 11, before i start talking about peace let me go back in history at tell you this story:

Once upon a time in a land called Palestine (originally the land of Canaan), the Palestinian people (Christians, Muslims, and a few Jews) dwelled happily. One day, out of nowhere, outside intruders started to flock down claiming their right to the land. Soon, these ravenous intruders started appropriating the land by force, until the aboriginal people of Palestine found themselves denied the right to live on their own soil.

Israeli Child: Dear Ahxxx and Topic 11 group, Ahxxxx didn't tell the full story of history. but that argue with the palastiens is not new, and i'm not going to open it again because it will not end.

i will just say that that before all the jewes that come from all over the world to israel they suffered the holocaust. and the only right think to do is to build a jew country. the UN devided ISRAEL to two parts, ARAB part and JEW part, they was almost equil in their size, but the day of the declaration about the new jewish country all the arabs aroud attacked the jewes and left theme no chanse but to fight. in the fight the jews won after more the 2,000 victoms and conquer the Land of Israel.

Ahxxxx, please don't react to wat i wrote, the argue will not end. so please from u, let's live it like that.

i disagree with your opinion, that ISRAEL will become Palastine, because that is unposibble and it will never be.

American Child: I'm probably butting in where I'm not wanted here, but I truly want the discussion between Axxx and Ahxxx to stop. Why? Because it's counterproductive and will lead us nowhere.

Yes, I will probably receive word that you guys are not fighting, but talking. Well, I say, B*ll Sh*t! You guys are definitely not talking, for you don't have an open mind. Answer me this, after all that "talking," has your point of view changed? Would you go around saying: "Yes, we should not have founded Israel, we were wrong," or "Israel is our friends, let us share." NO!

After all this bickering (because frankly that is what it is) you guys will only have even more resentment. You guys may argue all you want, but you won't change the other's point of view. The arguing must stop sooner or later. So, I ask: "Please do it NOW!" You guys want peace? Then set the example! Forget about this matter, don't talk about it ever again and let us talk about something that will help for peace. Alternatives that I thought of: Start from the home and community. Start by talking to your friends and providing cool and simple facts that it no longer is the time to shove the blame but to put that all aside and look for solutions. Forget the grudges and to think of those in the future . . . the children that you will have . . . do you want them to live in the conditions that you do? In fear of war? To hate others?

New Zealand Child: Ahxxx, did you see the importance of preconception in your life? You have to take your bad experience and not to take a revange, but to take it to help other people. You have to fight because you don't want this to happen to other people. In summary, I want to say that you have to take it as an example to not do again. We don't wish your experience to anyone and this is why we have to work on peace. Bye.

Israeli Child: Dear Ahxxx, I guess we didn't understand each other. i want to you very much! Please understand it, i want us to build our future together. what i meant in the previus letters is that i won't answer letters about issues that belong to the past, that's it. So please understand me and tell me what you think of my project, because it will work if you just understand that it's up to us, if we (the three of us) won't talk than how is the project will work? Please write soon.

Spanish Child: Hello! I felt a real emotion to see your effort to make peace. If this topic room ends with a friendship between its members everything will be worthy!

In general terms, the format of the online forum progressed from a structured exercise to total freedom. The 1,000 participating children and teams spent their first week online in "homerooms" participating in a guided exercise of initiation to the technology and the principles of the summit. After that, the children themselves brainstormed 20 topics on which they wished to work, and they could suggest and implement new ways of forming groups. We designed the online forum interface so that it supported— encouraged even—these *spontaneous forms of community*. In order to respond to this demand, rather than maintaining the role as the "keepers of the forum" we implemented technology whereby the children themselves could build new spaces on the forum.

The children then divided into topic groups to work on developing the 20 proposals to an actionable stage. The children were responsible for working on the proposals, and for posting weekly updates to the public externally viewable Junior Summit web site so that outsiders could view the progress of the forum. Next, each topic group voted for six children to serve as delegates to the in-person Cambridge Summit. The organizers chose five out of those six children, based on an overall fair representation of region, age, gender, and language, and then made sure that all underrepresented countries also sent representatives. During the Cambridge Summit week, the delegates were responsible for keeping in touch with their constituencies at home. After the summit, the final phase consisted of the children reuniting online (see Figure 7.2) to carry forward their projects with the support of the influential people they met at the summit, and taking advantage of the press that the summit garnered.

Two examples of topics that the children chose to work on included:

• The use of computers to link disabled children to their peers, and to educate children about the disabled. One 14-year-old girl in South Africa with cerebral

Figure 7.2
Technologies of the Online Forum

The online forum was a showcase for technologies that encourage and support a multilingual digital community. In particular, it allowed:

- Synchronous communication (real time chat)
- Asynchronous communication (such as e-mail, mailing lists, threaded chat)
- Different discussions for different topics
- Intelligent and child-friendly archiving
- Multilingual communication (through automatic and human translation)
- Children's own web site construction (for novice users)
- Sharing of photographs and other images
- Collaborative storytelling
- Voting (to allow children to elect the 100 delegates who came to Cambridge)
- A graphical timeline to illustrate what stage of the online forum is currently going on
- A map to show who was logged in from each country at any one time.

As we designed, we kept in mind that the forum was meant to support "deep chat" (sustained, contentful discussion) and thinking before speaking rather than the shallow talk found in most chat groups.

---

palsy wrote, "The computer is in some ways my hands and feet and it even gives me wings to fly to other countries and far away places."
- Bridging the double gap between speakers of different languages, and between the literate and illiterate in the world. One child from the United States wrote that the computer could provide a natural link between pictures and words and sounds that would allow children both to learn to read, and to learn other languages.

Role of Adults

Most previous Internet communities for children were classroom-based: Teachers initiated participation, and chose participants and involvement was organized through the schools. In the Junior Summit, children could apply individually or in teams or as school classes. But no adult participation was required or allowed. The decision to forbid adult participation (except for 20 moderators) was controversial. Our stance came from the belief that, in many cases, for those whose voices are not generally encouraged (such as children, especially from developing nations), having powerful adults present may prevent them from finding their own voice and speaking out (Cassell & Ryokai, 2001). In addition, research shows that children's moral reasoning and linguistic skills demonstrate more complexity when they talk with peers than when they talk with adults (Kruger, 1988). And parents differ greatly in their ability to help children disclose, or use their voices (Fagot, Luks, & Poe, 1995). We decided that the children should have the chance to reason and to talk on their own, before presenting their thoughts to the adult world. With adults playing such a minimal role, we found that children became their own moderator, as in the following interaction between two children who had just arrived in their topic groups:

HELP ME!!!!!
WHAT'S THIS TOPIC 11 EVERYONE IS REPLYING TO?!! AM I ALSO SUPPOSED TO HAVE A TOPIC 11 TO REPLY TO?????? WELL, I DON'T!!!!!!!!!
PLEASE CAN SOMEONE TELL ME WHAT'S GOING ON!
THANKS
M
Hi M, It's Mo here, don't panic, we're just talking about war, and the causes of it, and ideas for preventions and solutions, good to here from you, I hope to get some of your ideas!!!!!!!!!!

The online forum was not linked to the public Junior Summit web site, so only children and moderators had access. However, children regularly posted updates about their work to the public Junior Summit site (http: www.jrsummit.net), where adults were welcome. Our decision to not allow teachers and parents to contribute to the forum was often challenged by those adults, but often supported by the children. One child, from the United Arab Emirates, wrote to complain about an overzealous moderator:

She almost replies to every single message. Don't you think she should leave the kids there to give their opinions freely without stressing every single word they say? She's a grown-up after all, and with someone studying their every move believe me, kids won't be at their ease. I'm not saying she should stop giving comments she's doing a great job, but I personally believe she should ease off a bit.

Of course, not allowing adults on the online forum did not prevent parents and teachers from becoming involved. Because of a number of e-mails that we received from parents, we ended up deciding that it was important to run a parallel but strictly separate in-person summit for those parents who accompanied their children to Cambridge (roughly 30 parents). This program was run across campus from the children's program, and lasted from 8:00 A.M. until 9:00 P.M., leaving no time for the parents to participate in the children's work.

Language

All of the previous Internet programs for children were either conducted in English or, when there were several languages, children could only participate with other children who spoke the same language. We implemented automatic translation of all messages between five languages (Chinese, English, French, Portuguese, Spanish) and, more importantly, we set up a system whereby the participants could send out a message requesting clean up of the admittedly poor automatic translation, and receive a reply from a board of bilingual children in the forum who acted as translators for one another. We even built a multilingual simultaneous chat system (now being used by other online programs for children).

Our primary goal in implementing language policies was, as Bandura says in describing how to build community-wide efficacy for social change, to "never do anything for someone that they can do for themselves" (Bandura, 1997, p. 500). Thus, technical approaches were simply supports to the children's own translation work. With respect to the goal of providing equal access to speakers of all languages, however, we were not entirely successful. The automatic translation setup was imperfect, even for *gisting* (giving the basic meaning of a text), and children were often too busy replying to messages to translate messages for other participants. The sad result was that English speakers were more likely to contribute than speakers of other languages, and that a Spanish-speaking group coalesced in a separate room. In the future, establishing a rotating board of translators might be a more successful approach.

Representation

Previous Internet programs for children were either Internet-only or, if they did bring the children together in the physical world, simply directed to adult organizers. In order to give the children a representation on the world stage for their ideas, and support for bringing the ideas to fruition, we decided that the online forum would culminate in a week-long, in-person summit where representatives of each topic group in the forum could hone their ideas through intense interaction with each other and with experts in new technology, and could then present those ideas to the press and to governmental and industry officials. This goal led us to structure the in-person Cambridge summit to comprise:

• One general session each morning, with a press briefing attended by child reporters from around the world
• Many group meetings so that the delegates could refine their proposals

- Meetings not just of the participants topic groups, but also of their super-topics, and their task forces (for example the task force on technological infrastructure)
- Immersion workshops, during which participants had the opportunity to design, explore, and create with the new technologies for children that the MIT Media Lab is famous for (music, filmmaking, storytelling, manipulatives, etc.)

In addition we planned that:

- On Friday the participants would deliver their final proposals to one another, and decide which proposals should be delivered to the general assembly on the last day. They would also hold a video conference with the UN general assembly in New York.
- On Saturday a half-day assembly would be convened at MIT where children presented their impassioned proposals to attendees that included press from around the world, ministers of technology, industry executives, digital notables.

The 900 online forum participants who did not come to Cambridge could participate in many events through online activities linking them to their representatives, and through special two-way pager systems at the conference that allowed the representatives to check in with their work-groups at home.

These were *our* plans. The children themselves had other ideas. In fact, on the evening the children arrived, at their welcome reception, I showed up to find that the children had kicked out our staff members and were staffing the check-in desk themselves: handing out name badges and welcome packets. After dinner, I led a discussion about rules that we would adhere to—respect for one another, no wandering off to explore Boston, cooperation and not competition. I had hardly jotted down the first point on a huge whiteboard when a 14-year-old Indian girl stood up to say, "We have these rules inside. We don't need this written down." The others clamored their agreement, and I sat down.

A little after the end of the activities on the evening of the first day of the summit, I received similar e-mails from two participants. One is included below:

I need to let you know about the task group I'm in—the "Kid's Bank" which went, to be honest, terribly today. I feel awful about it and I need to tell you before I can sleep. Basically what we did: Had lectures—a student/teacher relationship, everyone falling asleep, no interaction between us kids in the least. [. . .] There was some lady who had her laptop computer and was making "mission statements" and almost telling us how we should do our project. None of us kids were able to connect to each other or even discuss—everyone was half asleep and most were disinterested in the topic. The adults were taking complete control over it and didn't just leave it up to us to work on like it would have worked just fine as—if not much better. The list goes on . . . I feel like screaming. I think we have to change this whole organization.

As with the fight online, my first reaction was *panic*. Our carefully crafted summit going down the tubes before the end of the first day. But I managed to remind myself once again that I had promised these children that their voices would be heard—that included concerning issues of process as well as of content. We turned over the second day's plenary meeting to the delegates and they began to change things around. In fact, after a half-day of meetings with one another and with us, the summit returned to the activities that we had planned. However, important changes were made: the quietest children and the children who spoke languages that only they and their interpreters understood, sat at the front of the room where they were more likely to make a contribution. The children began to design an overarching organization to coordinate all of their action plans, and met to work on that idea. And, as they requested, adults no longer stood at the front of the room, if they were in the room at all.

On the last day of the in-person summit, the children stood up in front of an audience of 2,000—ministers of technology, members of the press, CEOs of *Fortune* 500 companies—and gave presentations that blew the socks off the adults. Two presentations in particular left not a dry eye in the house: on child labor, and on disability. One of the children participating described the disability presentation as follows: "What we tried to do is to tell people stories and through these stories make them listen."

Action

In previous fora, for the most part discussions among children, no matter how exciting, remained at the level of "just talk." The Junior Summit intended to bring children together and give them the means to come up with—and to bring to fruition—radical ideas to change the world for children. Already during the online forum, we had examples of children bringing ideas home and implementing them. One child in India began a "fistful of grain" program where she collected "only a single fistful of grain" from each of the families in her neighborhood and then, with the help of the other children in her school, set up a storehouse in a local vacant building so that poor families could come get grains for food. Another team of two children in Malta sent the following message to their topic group:

For those of you who have seen our reply to Kxx's message, we said that we have already contacted and interviewed personally the President of Malta, Madame Speaker and the former Minister of Education. Now, we are awaiting an appointment from the present Minister of Education, since last month we had the elections and the party was changed.

Today, we have another POSITIVE result. We came across the lyrics of a Maltese song, which was placed second for the concert known as the "Maltese Song for Europe." The text is really excellent for our topic. It is called "Listen to our Voices," so ... we called the singer to ask for her permission to publish the words. She was so glad to hear of our effort, that she also offered to support us. In fact, she has invited us on a TV show that she herself presents, which is open for all citizens to see our point of view. Isn't that great??!

Also, we have contacted a radio station that holds a programme called "DOT.NET," which is all about modern technology. After telling him how we're participating by means of the Internet, he was also interested and invited us to go "on-air," live-in-show.

Wow!! Our voices are beginning to be heard locally. Why don't you guys out there try it too?! See what's the response?

During the week in Cambridge, a number of additional projects got off the ground. For example, the child laborers were very concerned about getting their stories out, and publishing photo essays to illustrate their lives. From this idea was born the "Junior Journal," an online newspaper written and edited by Junior Summit participants. The first issue was published during the week of the online summit; a visiting Reuters news crew wasn't allowed to take pictures or interview the children until they agreed to donate an unlimited Reuters news feed. At the end of the week, software was put in place to allow the children to continue from home: to submit, revise, and edit without any of the authors being in the same room. They also requested a mechanism to allow a rotating edition editorship, so that participants got the chance to be journalist and editor. Remarkably, the "Junior Journal" continues today. Currently in its thirtieth edition (an edition which sports 50 stories and photos from 32 different countries), the journal recently won the prestigious international Global Junior Challenge award in Rome.

Nation1 was also born during the in-person summit, as a way of realizing the wish for an overarching organization to allow participants to pursue their different action projects. On the fifth day of the in-person summit, the children passed out a press release, entitled "A Nation1 Declaration":

Young people of the world, entering the age of communication without barriers, you are already part of an emerging nation, Nation1. Join us there.

Nation1 is a global nation made of young minds. It is created, governed, and sustained by the young. It is a place where adults may not enter unless invited, and may not stay if asked to leave.

We believe that Nation1 has always existed. There has always been a universal culture of young humanity, but only now are the means arising for us to make common cause, using technology to bring all of us closer. Together we can harness the natural virtues of youth: tolerance, energy, playfulness, hope, and a willingness to share.

Kids from all over the world have much in common, despite cultural and national differences. Nation1 is a place to combine the strength of our similarities with the genius of our differences and create a strong bond between people physically separated by distance and national borders. Through integration, we can gain knowledge, support, and friends, and authority in the "real" world.

Because of press coverage of the last day of the summit, the children who were spearheading the Nation1 effort received more than 500 requests for information in the week after the in-person summit had ended. Nation1 has continued to grow since the summit by opening its web site to non–Junior Summit children.

At the time of writing, two Junior Summit participants are employed full-time in a Nation1 office in New York. They have set up a foundation, been successful at raising funds, and are forming alliances with other non-profit organizations for children, in the hope that together they can maintain an umbrella organization to support children in doing more for the world than they are expected to be capable of. Despite these quite extraordinary accomplishments, the children have, since the summit, reported feeling frustrated by how little action has been accomplished. It is possible that without the support of and interchanges among a vast and varied collective, some other kind of outcome is required to maintain collective efficacy. That is, during the online forum, the children were receiving constant feedback from others, allowing them to know that their voices counted. Without that demonstration of *voice*, more action is required. As one of the children wrote, six months after the in-person summit ended,

When you're one person working on a dream, you can get hung up, wondering if there are people who care if you succeed, if you will ever make it happen, and sometimes you lose motivation along the way. Besides that, one person has a difficult time making a huge impact on their own. Through Junior Summit, we were 3,000 children working together. Even when we split off into our separate interests there could be 20 of us working together, and we knew that in the long run all of us, despite our different focuses, were working on the same project—making the world a better place.

EVALUATION

The evaluation of a program with such large scope represents a formidable challenge. My own interests concerned the evaluation of the technology and interface design principles, and the evaluation of the effects of the Junior Summit on children's lives. Some of the effects of the Junior Summit interface and format decisions have been documented above, for example, the positive effect of allowing the children to solve their own battles, and come up with their own solutions, and the not completely successful attempt to deal with a multiplicity of languages. Like speakers of languages other than English, those children who had no prior experience whatsoever with computers and the Internet found themselves hand-icapped, and were less likely to continue on the online forum, and less likely to be chosen as delegates (roughly 30% of delegates had no prior computer or Internet experience). Children who were not computer literate before-hand were more likely to persevere if they were members of a team, and not solo participants. Thus, for example, a small school in rural India had three teams accepted to the Junior Summit, and two children from the school were actually elected delegates of two separate topic groups. These children, both the delegates and the others, despite their lack of computer literacy, did stick with the forum, and in fact a number of them are still active today, three years later.

The notion of underdetermined design appears to have been very suc-cessful in this diverse context. At first children wanted to create hundreds of rooms for special interest groups, but after they had created rooms and found that nobody congregated in them, this desire quickly subsided, and gave way to some powerful cross-cutting organizing principles. As de-scribed above, participants organized themselves into topics (20 groups dis-cussing different ways for children to use technology to make the world better for children), supra-topics, task forces, and electives.

Roughly 140 children from 32 countries filled out a presummit ques-tionnaire. An additional 25 children filled out the questionnaire one month after the forum had begun. For the following countries (in order of largest number of questionnaire takers), more than 5 children filled out the ques-tionnaire: India, Finland, Senegal, Sweden, Uruguay, Bangladesh, Japan, Jamaica, and Estonia. This noisy data set is still being analyzed, but some quantitative results are interesting and worth reporting in this overview chapter. Correlations revealed a significant trend in the data where better global self-worth, meaning an overall sense of satisfaction and regard for oneself (Harter, 1987) corresponded to more computer experience, and more belief in the educational value of computers. As found by others (Oettingen, 1995), we found no differences in global self-worth or in self-efficacy due to country of origin.

A t-test for independent samples revealed that ($t = -7.43, p < .000$) the children who filled out the questionnaire after one month online demon-strated more global self-worth (M= 3.24, S.D.= .41) than those children who filled out the questionnaire before the forum started (M= 2.54, S.D.= .55). Global self-worth was assessed by asking the children which descrip-tion fit them better, and how well it fit them, in pairs such as the following: "Some kids don't like the way they are leading their lives BUT other kids do like the way they are leading their lives." Likewise, an effect was found for more "meaningful instrumental activity" (MIA) (Maton, 1990), that is, those activities that require children to use their skills, and lead them to desired ends ($t = -2.81, p < .005$). Children tested after the beginning of the forum reported engaging in more MIA (M = 3.62, S.D. = .792) than those tested before the summit (M = 3.14, S.D. = .903). MIA is measured through questions such as "How often during the last week did you perform a challenging or difficult task well?" Scores on this instrument are important since Maton's research with at-risk urban teenagers found that engagement in "meaningful instrumental activity" was significantly related to their life satisfaction, well-being, and overall self-esteem—and was as powerful a factor as that of social support (Maton, 1990). Of course, these results must be interpreted with caution, since the sample size is small and since most of the participants were downright exuberant after one month online, and these effects might well have diminished over the course of the online forum. However, further analysis of these data, and of continuing follow-up data may allow us to look at some of the effects of the Junior Summit on self-worth, self-esteem, and self-efficacy.

Although preliminary studies by Kraut, Lundmark, Patterson, Kresler, Mukopadhyay, & Scherlis, (1998) found that the Internet was associated with increased loneliness and depression, reports from Junior Summit children, three years after the summit ended, are anything but depressed. A teacher from Spain wrote several months after the in-person summit that the way that the summit was conducted led her students to "feel empowered to act as leaders, as world-wide ambassadors of digital culture. They regard school with new eyes, as a GLOBAL place where people may meet people easily, where they can learn and voice their opinions about the world that surrounds them. A place where they may feel loved, heard, taken into consideration, where technology is (for the first time in history) a powerful tool that they employ better than adults."

Outcomes and Lasting Contribution of the Junior Summit

Three years after the summit's supposed conclusion, the children have refused to consider the project over. They continue to use the online forum, continue their communication with one another, and continue their Junior Summit work. One Junior Summit participant gave a speech at the White House on New Year's Eve 2000 as a part of a roundtable about voices of the new millennium. Several others traveled to the Hague Appeal for Peace (from their respective countries of India, Jamaica, Australia, France, and the United States) to meet with Kofi Annan. Still others gave workshops about the Junior Summit to the nongovernmental organization I*EARN's conference in Beijing, China. In October 2000, one of the summit participants won the $5,000 Global Youth Peace & Tolerance Award, presented at the United Nations. Another child won the ACS International Peace Prize. In January 2001, the children obtained grant money to continue their work on the Nation1 online country for kids.

CONCLUSION

The scope of the Junior Summit program meant that my role came to include everything from coming up with the initial design, the philosophy, the developmental underpinnings, and the technical specifications of the entire program, to making relationships with nongovernmental organizations around the world to ensure that the application form was actually distributed to *all* children in a given country, to assembling an international group of professors and graduate students from around MIT and the Boston area to wade through 5,000 applications from kids from 139 countries. It also included traveling around the world, with computers hidden from customs in big suitcases, to deliver and install computers and Internet connections, and sleeping in my office for several nights at a stretch in order to be able to send and receive faxes and phone calls with rather uncooperative American embassies in Eastern Europe and Africa in order to allow children to get the visas to permit them to attend the Cambridge Summit.

Organizing such a global community for children, therefore, encompasses not only educationally relevant and empowering technical and design work, but also *fundraising* for computers, Internet connections, and in some cases electricity and phone lines, so that children in all parts of the world could have access to the forum, *footwork* to deliver the computers, *policy and political work* to deal with the intricacies of relationships within and among nations, *education* to help the adults in the program do their best . . . and the occasional late-night pizza run when the participants of one's summit don't like the food planned for them. In my case, I have continued as advisor, cheerleader (I never suspected that one outcome of the summit would be that I would find myself writing 3,062 letters of recommendation for colleges, summer programs, etc.), agent, fundraiser, and technical staff. Most importantly, I continue to try to ensure that the children's voices are heard and that in using their voices they can develop the belief that they can control the world around them and their own destinies. We know that those reporting low levels of voice in a given context also report low self-esteem (Harter, 1997). The question is whether high levels of voice in a given context can have transfer effects to other contexts. One child from Brazil wrote, "We think we have matured in this project; it has made us feel more secure about ourselves. It hasn't changed us!"

Although the Junior Summit officially ended in 1998, its purview is spreading today—the ideas that the children came up with are coming to be more widely known: the "Junior Journal" online newspaper, the Nation1 online country, delegations to the Hague Peace Appeal, and the Olympics. Houghton Mifflin will even be running some images of the Junior Summit in a forthcoming new edition of a high school history textbook, to illustrate "the large scale meeting of young minds, and the global dimension of technological developments!" Finally, an understanding of the harm wrought by a thoughtless digital divide is better understood today than it was when plans for the Junior Summit began in 1997–1998.

Recently Amy Aidman, former researcher at the Washington-based Center for Media Education, gave a public testimony to the Democracy Online National Task Force that included reference to the Junior Summit's democratic basis. She wrote to me:

I was looking for sites that are emblematic of involving young people in the public sphere and in social change as part of CME's public testimony for the Democracy Online National Task Force: In Search of Democracy's Domain in a Dot-Com World. Part of what impressed me was the level of discourse that is going on through the site and the kinds of issues that are being addressed, also the fact that kids can participate in 5 languages. I found an exchange between a 14-year old boy from Greece and Noam Chomsky about the future of the Internet that I ended up quoting in my testimony. It showed the potential of the Internet for the future of democracy in the finest light—crossing cultural, geographical, generational, and status boundaries. When a teen from Greece can get a response to a question from one of the great thinkers of the world—and the great thinkers can have access to the questions of promising young people in other parts of the world, I think we are seeing the Internet's potential as a tool for the future of democracy expanded in the best sense.

ACKNOWLEDGMENT

Thanks to David Berg, Isolde Birdthistle, Steve Buka, and Mary Beth O'Hagan for assisting with the design of an evaluation of the Junior Summit, to Mia Keinanen, Anindita Basu, Lira Nikolovska, and Jennifer Smith for assisting with gathering and coding data. I am indebted to Pam Smith of Merrill Lynch for a research grant to study the Junior Summit, as well as to the other generous sponsors of the MIT Media Lab. Most of all, thanks to the 3,062 Junior Summit participants who have illuminated my vision of what it means to be a child, and a citizen of the world, and have made my life immeasurably better.

REFERENCES

Bandura, A. (1997). *Self-efficacy: The exercise of control.* New York: W. H. Freeman and Company.

Cassell, J. (1998). Storytelling as a nexus of change in the relationship between gender and technology: A feminist approach to software design. In J. Cassell & H. Jenkins (Eds.), *From Barbie to Mortal Kombat: Gender and computer games* (pp. 298–326). Cambridge, MA: The MIT Press.

Cassell, J., & Jenkins, H. (Eds.). (1998). *From Barbie to Mortal Kombat: Gender and computer games.* Cambridge, MA: The MIT Press.

Cassell, J., & Ryokai, K. (2001). Making space for voice: Technologies to support children's fantasy and storytelling. *Personal Technologies, 5* (3), 203–224.

Committee on Information Technology Literacy. (1999). *Being fluent with information technology.* Washington, DC: National Research Council.

Cordes, C. M., & Miller, E. (2000). *Fool's gold: A critical look at computers in childhood.* Washington, DC: Alliance for Childhood.

Fagot, B., Luks, K., & Poe, J. (1995). Parental influences on children's willingness to disclose. In K. J. Rotenberg (Ed.), *Disclosure processes in children and adolescents* (pp. 148–165). Cambridge: Cambridge University Press.

Gal, S. (1991). Between speech and silence. In M. di Leonardo (Ed.), *Gender at the crossroads of knowledge: Feminist anthropology in the postmodern era* (pp. 175–203). Berkeley: University of California Press.

Harter, S. (1987). The determinants and mediational role of global self-worth in children. In N. Eisenberg (Ed.), *Contemporary topics in developmental psychology* (pp. 219–242). New York: Wiley.

Harter, S. (1997). The personal self in social context: Barriers to authenticity. In R. Ashmore & L. Jussim (Eds.), *Self and identity: Fundamental issues.* New York: Oxford University Press.

Hern, M., & Chauk, S. (1997). The Internet, democracy and community: Another big lie. *Journal of Family Life, 3* (4), 36–39.

Kraut, R., Lundmark, V., Patterson, M., Kiesler, S., Mukopadhyay, T., & Scherlis, W. (1998). Internet paradox: A social technology that reduces social involvement and psychological well-being? *American Psychologist, 53* (9), 1017–1031.

Kruger, A. C. (1988). *The effect of peer and adult-child transactive discussions on moral reasoning.* Paper presented at the Conference on Human Development, Charleston, SC.

Lewis, M. (1993). *Without a word: Teaching beyond women's silence.* New York: Routledge & Kegan Paul.

Maton, K. (1990). Meaningful involvement in instrumental activity and well-being: Studies of older adolescents and at risk urban teenagers. *American Journal of Community Psychology, 18* (2), 297–320.

Ochs, E., & Taylor, C. (1995). The "Father Knows Best" dynamic in dinnertime narratives. In K. Hall & M. Bucholtz (Eds.), *Gender articulated: Language and the socially constructed self.* New York: Routledge & Kegan Paul.

Oettingen, G. (1995). Cross-cultural perspectives on self-efficacy. In A. Bandura (Ed.), *Self-efficacy in changing societies* (pp. 149–176). Cambridge: Cambridge University Press.

Wartella, E., O'Keefe, B., & Scantlin, R. (2000). *Growing up with interactive media.* New York: Markle Foundation.

Chapter 8

Developmental Implications of Commercial Broadcasters' Educational Offerings

Amy B. Jordan, Kelly L. Schmitt, and Emory H. Woodard IV

Through the years, television has offered children both the good and the bad. Programs such as *Sesame Street, Mister Rogers' Neighborhood,* and *Blue's Clues* have been found to provide children with skills and confidence to make them more ready to learn (Anderson, 1998). Nevertheless, the economic structure of the medium has worked against the provision of a wide array of beneficial programs, as advertisers seek to mass market their products and programs aim to sell toys. The result has been a proliferation of violence-laden, educationally devoid, toy-driven cartoons (Jordan, 1996), leading to periodic efforts by regulators to improve the quality of children's television programs (Sullivan & Jordan, 1999).

This chapter explores the ways in which the Children's Television Act of 1990 (CTA) and a subsequent processing guideline have affected the amount and the availability of television that might aid in children's social and intellectual development. It considers the types of programs broadcasters now offer children to satisfy their public-interest obligations, the educational strength of programs labeled as educational and informational (E/I), and whether the current educational offerings reflect the interests and needs of children from different developmental stages and ethnic backgrounds.

REGULATING CHILDREN'S TELEVISION

The CTA of 1990 mandates that all commercial broadcasters provide educational programming for children in order to qualify for license renewal. The law is based in the Communications Act of 1934, which states that, in return for receiving a portion of the public broadcast spectrum for free, broadcasters must "serve the public interest, convenience and necessity" (Communications Act of 1934, Section 307a). Under the CTA, the child audience was considered part of that public-interest obligation.

Research on the impact of the CTA by advocacy groups and scholars revealed that broadcasters claimed that programs of dubious educational value satisfied their public-interest obligations. The vagueness of the legislation allowed for questionable assertions, since broadcasters could fulfill their responsibilities to the child audience by offering content that "furthers the positive development of the child in any respect, including the child's cognitive/intellectual or emotional/social needs" (Federal Communications Commission, 1991). Left undefined, however, were issues such as how much programming was adequate, when the programs should air, and whether the programs should be designed with children as a primary audience (Jordan, 1996). Evaluations of license renewal applications uncovered wide variation in the amount of educational programming provided (8% of the stations did not claim any educational programming and over half aired two hours or less per week) (Kunkel & Canepa, 1994). In addition, the types of programs offered were of questionable pedagogical value, such as *The Jetsons*, *Mighty Morphin Power Rangers*, and *Yogi Bear* (Center for Media Education, 1992; Kunkel & Canepa, 1994).

Thus in 1996, under pressure from the White House, Congress, and advocacy groups, the Federal Communication Commission (FCC) developed a set of guidelines that would further specify the children's educational programming requirements. This processing guideline, known as the Three-Hour Rule, mandates that commercial broadcasters air a minimum of three hours per week of educational programming for children in order to receive an expedited license renewal. Programming may still address either children's social/emotional needs (prosocial programming) or their cognitive/intellectual needs (traditional academic programming), but the parameters around the audience and the scheduling have been clarified. Under the guidelines of the Three-Hour Rule, core programming (that which counts toward the three hours) must be specifically designed for children, have education as a significant purpose, air between the hours of 7:00 A.M. and 10:00 P.M., and be labeled as educational on the air. Finally, the educational objective and target age of the child audience addressed by the program must be specified in the children's programming report filed quarterly with the FCC and kept on file at the local stations.

An assumption inherent in the Three-Hour Rule is that educational television is beneficial to children, presumably because they learn from it. Therefore, a brief overview of research on what children learn from television follows. In addition, a review of research on content that may be harmful for children—namely violence and stereotypy—is also included (as implicit in much of the legislation is the expectation that such content may be reduced by an increase in educational content).

LEARNING FROM TELEVISION

The crafters of the legislation argued that television "can assist children to learn important information, skills, values, and behavior while entertaining them and exciting their curiosity to learn about the world around them" (CTA of 1990, p. 303a). This assertion has a basis in decades of research that finds that children benefit from watching programming designed to teach or strengthen academic skills (for reviews, see Anderson, 1998; Huston & Wright, 1998). Research conducted during the last decade, for example, indicates that watching educational programs such as *Sesame Street* helps prepare preschoolers for kindergarten (Zill, Davies, & Daly, 1994).

A recent longitudinal study found that watching educational television during early childhood appears to have a long-term impact on scholastic achievement, possibly by providing children with a positive attitude toward learning and offering information that helps them to do well in school. In this study, researchers found that exposure to children's educational programming at age 5, in particular *Sesame Street*, was associated with better grades in school and decreased aggression 10 years later, even after controlling for parents' educational levels, child's initial ability levels, birth order, and gender (Anderson, Huston, Schmitt, Linebarger, & Wright, 2001).

Television programs designed to strengthen school skills have also shown benefits for school age viewers. For example, one study found that almost all of the viewers of *Ghostwriter* read along with the print on the screen (e.g., messages to *Ghostwriter*), and many children kept casebooks along with the characters recording clues from the program (KRC Research and Consulting, 1993). Results of two studies on the efficacy of *Cro*, a Saturday-morning cartoon about science and technology aimed at 6- to 11-year-olds, indicated that watching *Cro* increased children's understanding of technology, especially for girls (see Fisch, 1998 for a review).

Television has been found to contribute to the development of children's prosocial skills—such as honesty, perseverance, and cooperation—as well (e.g., Collins & Getz, 1976). A recent meta-analysis of the research on the prosocial effects of watching educational television found a positive relationship between viewing prosocial programs and prosocial behaviors (Mares & Woodard, in press). The meta-analysis of 34 studies (with a total sample of 5,473 children) indicates that prosocial content has a weak to moderate effect on children's prosocial behaviors (roughly equivalent to a Pearson correlation of .27). The effects of prosocial television content were significantly strengthened by the addition of support materials, such as guided lessons, games, and general discussion to enhance program content.

THE DETRIMENTAL EFFECTS OF VIOLENCE AND STEREOTYPING ON TELEVISION

Though the debate over the impact of televised violence on children is far from over, there is a significant amount of evidence that indicates there is likely a relationship between violence viewing and aggressive impulses and behaviors. A meta-analysis of the studies examining this relationship conducted by Paik and Comstock (1994) reported clear, positive relations between exposure to TV violence and antisocial behavior. This relationship was most significant for field studies and for time-series studies. An earlier meta-analysis by Wood, Wong, and Chacere (1991) found less consistency across studies but found a stronger relationship with exposure to violence in laboratory settings. They argue that "exposure to media violence may have a small to moderate impact on a single behavior, but cumulated across multiple exposures and multiple social interactions, the impact may be substantial" (p. 378).

Importantly, studies have shown that the inclusion of violence in an educational program may have detrimental effects on learning the intended lesson. Research by Rule and Ferguson (1986) illustrates that children are less likely to remember prosocial or academic lessons when viewed alongside the more perceptually salient scenes incorporating aggressive behaviors.

In addition to violence, the lack of diversity on the small screen and the preponderance of stereotyped characters may be problematic for children developing a sense of their role in the world (Graves, 1996). Television often presents a world that contains a homogeneous population. In fact, studies reveal that gender images in children's television are often *more* stereotyped than programs directed at adults (Feldstein & Feldstein, 1982). Saturday morning cartoons are dominated by Caucasian males, with minority characters inhabiting, at best, minor roles (Calvert, Stolkin, & Lee, 1997). Nevertheless, research indicates that children learn best when they have a character with whom they can relate (Van Evra, 1998), and benefit from seeing themselves reflected in a positive light (Greenberg & Brand, 1994).

METHOD

A content analysis was conducted to examine the educational goals and educational strength of the commercial broadcasters' E/I offerings. The children's educational programs examined in this study were those which were identified as core programs in a December 1998 FCC report.[1] Phone calls were also made to local station representatives in charge of children's programming (called a children's television liaison) to verify series currently airing as core programming under the Three-Hour Rule.

Sample

The sample of programs consisted of the "core educational and informational (E/I) programs" from the 10 commercial broadcast stations that serve the Philadelphia market. These stations included all the major broadcast networks (ABC, CBS, NBC, FOX), the weblets (UPN, WB, PAX, and the Home Shopping Network), and two unaffiliated "independent" stations. Because previous research indicates that network-affiliated broadcasters air primarily network-provided children's educational programs, this sample can be considered representative of large media markets (Sullivan & Jordan, 1999).

Forty-four individual titles of children's educational programs were identified as core E/I shows. Networks and syndicators were contacted and asked to submit three episodes of each program title for inclusion in the evaluation. Programs that were not submitted by the program producer (a total of 10 individual titles) were taped off the air during the spring of 1999. Comparison of submitted tapes with those taped randomly off the air indicates that they received similar evaluations of educational strength in a different content analysis (Woodard, 1999).

This data-collection procedure resulted in a census of 132 programs (44 individual titles). Only one episode of *Awesome Adventures, Wild about Animals,* and *Vegetable Soup* was evaluated, however, due to the submission of less than three episodes and taping difficulties. In order for these programs to be appropriately represented in the sample, the data from the episodes coded were duplicated to create three episodes.[2]

Coding Procedure

The unit of analysis for the study was the program, including opening sequences and closing credits and excluding advertisements, or other program segments unrelated to the program's content (e.g., "We'll be right back after this message"). Each program was coded for the following variables: target age, primary lesson, episode lesson, educational strength, violence, and gender/ethnic diversity.

Target Age

Commercial broadcast stations are required to indicate the target age for their educational programs. The information provided by the broadcasters and/or producers was used to classify the age range at which the programs are targeted. The groupings were preschool (0 to 4), elementary school age

(5 to 11), and preteen/teen (12 to 16). Programs spanning two or more age groupings were reclassified into one of the three age groupings based on the coders' judgment of the age appropriateness of the content and/or the air times.

Primary Lesson

Programs were also classified according to the primary educational lesson of the program. Lessons centering on knowledge (e.g., facts, ideas, or cultures) or cognitive skills (e.g., problem-solving approaches, classification skills) were classified as *traditionally academic*. Lessons focusing on interpersonal skill development (e.g., cooperation, accepting diversity) or intrapersonal skills development (e.g., recognizing emotions, self-esteem) were classified as *prosocial*. Lessons conveying information about physical well-being/health and development (e.g., exercise, safety, nutrition) were classifed as *physical well-being*. Some program episodes emphasized more than one lesson type equally, and were classified as *mixed*. Other episodes did not convey any discernible lesson and were coded as *unclassifiable*.

Educational Strength

An educational strength scale with five items was developed to evaluate the primary lesson in each episode. These items were developed based on the FCC's requirements for core E/I programming (e.g., must be specifically designed for children, must have education as a significant purpose) as well as through consultation with experts in child development, education, and children's TV production. The objective portion of the scale consisted of four items: lesson clarity, lesson integration, lesson involvement, and lesson applicability (see Table 8.1). Each item was scored as present (1) or absent (0), with the exception of Lesson Involvement, which was given a score of 0, .33, .67, or 1, depending on the extent to which the three criteria were met. The combined objective scores therefore ranged from 0 to 4.

The Subjective Assessment reflected the coders' overall judgment of the program's educational quality. Using the subjective assessment, episodes were judged as highly educational (engaging, challenging, and relevant to the target age group with no significant problems in the conveyance of the lesson); moderately educational (containing educational content but suffering from problems that might interfere with children's learning of the lessons); or minimally educational (does not contain a discernible lesson or have education as a significant purpose). The Subjective Assessment score ranged from 0 to 2. Objective and subjective measures were highly correlated $r = .74$, $p < .01$.

The Subjective Assessment score (0 to 2) was doubled in order to give equal weight when summed with the Objective Measure. This provided an overall numeric score for *educational strength*. Programs were then recoded

Table 8.1
Objective Items in the Educational Strength Scale

Item	Definition
Lesson Clarity	The presence of a message that is clearly and explicitly laid out so that it can be easily comprehended by the target audience.
Lesson Integration	The consistent conveyance of the lesson or the culmination of the program in a lesson so that it is integral to the program as a whole.
Lesson Involvement	Presentation of the lesson in a way that is engaging and appropriately challenging for the child audience, including the incorporation of (a) children or childlike characters in significant roles, (b) age-appropriate production techniques, and (c) age-appropriate lessons.
Lesson Applicability	The inclusion of carefully conveyed, realistic situations and solutions that the target audience can translate to their own lives and experiences.

as *highly educational* (score of 6.67–8.0), *moderately educational* (score of 3.34–6.66), and *minimally educational* (score of 0–3.33).

Violence

Programs were coded for the extent to which violence is included in the scenes. "Violence" was defined using a modified version of both Kunkel's (1997) and Gerbner and Gross's (1976) measures. Our definition for violence involves the overt depiction of an intentional and/or malicious threat of physical force or the actual use of such force intended to physically harm an animate being or group of beings. A scene was defined as a sequence of related shots in which there was no change in location or time. Programs with three or more scenes containing violence were coded as "violent" and programs containing violence in zero to two scenes were coded as "nonviolent."

Diversity

Programs were evaluated for the extent to which they included characters representing members of diverse ethnic and racial groups and characters of both genders. Ethnic diversity was assessed by evaluating whether programs included characters of different races and ethnicity (at least one major and minor character of different ethnic groups). Gender diversity was evaluated by assessing whether programs contained both males and females in major and minor speaking roles.

Interobserver reliability was obtained by having the seven coders double-code 15% of the sample ($n = 20$), with an overall reliability score of .90 (range = .70 to 1.0).

RESULTS

In the 1998–1999 season, all of the commercial broadcast stations in the Philadelphia area offered a minimum of three hours a week of educational and informational programming for children during the required hours of 7:00 A.M.–10:00 P.M. (Range = 3–6.5 hours, Median = 3.5 hours). During a typical week in May 1999, 42.5 hours of E/I programming were offered to children. Although the major networks tended to concentrate their programming on Saturday and Sunday mornings, over half (58.8%) of the E/I programming was found on weekdays.

Sixty-one percent of the commercial broadcasters' E/I programs were targeted to elementary school-age children. Preteens and teens were the intended audience for another 32% of the programs. Only 7% of the shows were primarily intended for preschoolers.

Teaching Goals

Approximately one-half (51%) of the programs focused their lessons around social/emotional issues (prosocial programming). Traditional academic or knowledge lessons were the focus of another one-third (37%) of the programs. Physical well-being lessons were the primary theme of 5.3% of the programs. Only 2.3% of the episodes equally emphasized two or more lesson types. Major networks (ABC, CBS, NBC, and FOX), and weblets (WB, UPN, PAX) were significantly more likely to provide programming with social lessons, whereas independent stations were more likely to provide programming in the other categories, $\chi^2(2) = 10.88$, $p < .01$.

Table 8.2 indicates that the educational focus of the series that are directed to elementary school-age children is fairly diverse, though programs for this age group that are provided by the networks are more likely to focus on prosocial lessons than any other type. Of the 61.4% of shows primarily targeting this age group, a little more than half (53.8%) are prosocial. Programs designed for the preteen/teen audience are no more likely to be prosocial than traditionally academic, although there appears to be a trend in this direction (e.g., four out of the five programs NBC offers in its exclusively teen line-up are prosocial).

Table 8.2 also illustrates the types of lessons emphasized in each E/I series (traditionally academic, prosocial, physical well-being, or mixed), as well as the lesson included in each of the three submitted episodes. In order to assess episode lessons, three judges (the authors of this article) summarized the coders' written descriptions of the lessons. The table reveals that prosocial lessons in the individual episodes range from lessons that teach children intrapersonal skills (self-esteem, self-acceptance, adjusting to life change) to lessons about interpersonal skills (cooperation, friendship, and competition). Though less common than these prosocial lessons, several of the series centered on providing children with knowledge and information of a more traditionally academic nature. These lessons included topics that ranged from dinosaurs to world history to music. Five series for elementary school-age children center on the physical sciences (*Popular Mechanics for Kids, Bill Nye the Science Guy, Squigglevision, Algo's FACTory,* and *Inquiring Minds*).

Episodes directed at preteens and teens include more mature social themes, as illustrated by Table 8.2. These include programs that address gun control, alcoholism, and sleep deprivation. Programs for teens also tap into adolescent interest in sports and physical well-being (e.g., basketball). In contrast to programming for elementary school-age children, academic/ knowledge programs targeting teens were unrelated to school topics. Instead, academic/knowledge programs included lesson topics such as outdoor exploration or conveyed general trivia on a vast array of subjects, such as the type found on game shows.

The three programs in the Philadelphia sample that targeted preschoolers were mainly prosocial in nature and included lessons on appreciating others, being true to oneself, and overcoming anxiety. The one program that centered on developing preschoolers' appreciation of physical well-being also included the prosocial theme of cooperation.

Table 8.2 also illustrates that there was a small percentage of episodes with no discernable lesson (3.8%). In these instances, coders were unable to detect any lesson or judged a lesson to be so confusing and/or contradictory as to render it unclear.

Educational Strength

The overall measure of educational strength for the 132 programs produced the following distribution: 33.3% of the programs were considered *highly educational,* 45.5% were considered *moderately educational,* and 21.2% were considered *minimally educational.* Thus, the majority of the E/I episodes in this evaluation (79%) can be considered as meeting the FCC's requirements for the provision of educational and informational programming for children. Some programs air only once per week, whereas others air multiple times. Thus, after weighting the sample according to the frequency of airing in a typical week, the data reveal that 4.5 hours of the 42.5 hours of programming cannot be considered educational by the benchmarks used in this study (i.e., the programs do not have clear and salient lessons that are involving and relevant to children).

There were no significant differences in the educational strength of pro-

Table 8.2
Commercial Broadcasters' 1998–1999 E/I Programming in the Philadelphia Broadcast Area

Program Name	Program Source	Target Age	Series Emphasis	Episode Lessons	APPC Evaluation
Bill Nye the Science Guy	SYNDICATED	Elementary	Academic	deserts; pollution; weather	High
Disney's Pepper Ann	ABC	Elementary	Prosocial	parental dating; age discrimination; trust and empathy	High
Inquiring Minds	PAX	Elementary	Academic	each episode deals with popular science	High
Magic School Bus	FOX	Elementary	Academic	immune system; water; digestive system	High
New Zoo Revue	SYNDICATED	Elementary	Prosocial	keeping promises; perseverance; telling the truth	High
Popular Mechanics for Kids	SYNDICATED	Elementary	Academic	special effects; zoos; aquariums	High
Awesome Adventures*	SYNDICATED	Preteen/teen	Academic	Hawaii	High
Hang Time	NBC	Preteen/teen	Mixed Emphasis	personal safety; HIV/ discrimination; how to treat people with disabilities	High

Show	Network	Age Group	Type	Lessons	Level
Saved by the Bell: The New Class	NBC	Preteen/teen	Prosocial	dangers of addictions; sexual harassment; sleep deprivation	High
Imagineland	SYNDICATED	Preschool	Prosocial	dealing with anxiety; respect for others; privacy	Moderate
New Adventures of Winnie the Pooh	ABC	Preschool	Prosocial	appreciation of others; be yourself; no clear lesson in third episode	Moderate
Bloopy's Buddies	SYNDICATED	Preschool	Physical well-being	cooperation and exercise; exercise; exercise and sharing	Moderate
Life with Louie	FOX	Preschool/Elementary	Prosocial	death; cooperation; responsibility	Moderate
Algo's FACTory	SYNDICATED	Elementary	Academic	aerodynamics; robotics; astronomy	Moderate
Birdz[v]	CBS	Elementary	Prosocial	sensitivity; materialism; self-esteem	Moderate
Disney's 101 Dalmatians[v]	ABC	Elementary	Prosocial	respect; cooperation; no clear lesson	Moderate
Disney's Doug	ABC	Elementary	Prosocial	Be yourself; first kiss anxiety; friendship	Moderate
Disney's Recess	ABC	Elementary	Prosocial	be yourself; over-competitiveness; friendship	Moderate

Table 8.2 (continued)

Program Name	Program Source	Target Age	Series Emphasis	Episode Lessons	APPC Evaluation
Dumb Bunnies[v]	CBS	Elementary	Prosocial	no one's perfect; honesty; evaporation	Moderate
Field Trip	SYNDICATED	Elementary	Academic	movie studio; bakery; police officers	Moderate
Flying Rhino Jr. High[v]	CBS	Elementary	Prosocial	humility and confidence; dinosaurs; Egyptian myths and symbols	Moderate
Get Along Gang	SYNDICATED	Elementary	Prosocial	cooperation; overcompetitiveness and greed; no clear lesson in third episode	Moderate
Histeria![v]	WB	Elementary	Academic	Renaissance; American Revolution; Civil War	Moderate
Musical Encounter	SYNDICATED	Elementary	Academic	string instruments; Native American music and dance; musical composition	Moderate
Mythic Warriors[v]	CBS	Elementary	Prosocial	girls' self-esteem; overcoming prejudice; resisting temptation	Moderate

Title	Network	Audience	Category	Themes	Violence
Rupert	CBS	Elementary	Prosocial	humor; one good turn deserves another; sharing	Moderate
Squigglevision	ABC	Elementary	Academic	work and levers; Newton's third law of motion; perseverence and pendulums	Moderate
Sylvanian Families	SYNDICATED	Elementary	Prosocial	feeling comfortable with life changes; acceptance of family quirks; gender roles and life changes	Moderate
The Lionhearts	SYNDICATED	Elementary	Prosocial	self-acceptance; peer pressure; accepting diversity	Moderate
*Vegetable Soup***	SYNDICATED	Elementary	Prosocial	accepting diversity	Moderate
Critter Gitters^v	SYNDICATED	Elementary/ Teen	Academic	termites; veterinary forensics; Costa Rica	Moderate
Homer's Workshop	SYNDICATED	Elementary/ Teen	Academic	building a terrarium; creating a gumball machine; making toys and boxes	Moderate
*Wild About Animals**	SYNDICATED	Elementary/ Teen	Academic	animal stories	Moderate

157

Table 8.2 (continued)

Program Name	Program Source	Target Age	Series Emphasis	Episode Lessons	APPC Evaluation
Animal Adventures	SYNDICATED	Preteen/teen	Academic	animal lessons	Moderate
California Dreams	SYNDICATED	Preteen/teen	Prosocial	dating; honesty; transitions	Moderate
City Guys[v]	NBC	Preteen/teen	Prosocial	conflict resolution; don't do drugs; gun control	Moderate
More than a Game	SYNDICATED	Preteen/teen	Prosocial	overcoming obstacles; altruism; third episode has no clear lesson	Moderate
One World	NBC	Preteen/teen	Prosocial	adoption issues; alcoholism; Affirmative Action	Moderate
Saved by the Bell	SYNDICATED	Preteen/teen	Mixed	two episodes about friendship; third episode has no clear lesson	Moderate

158

Young Americans Outdoors	SYNDICATED	Preteen/teen	Academic	each episode deals with various topics related to the outdoors	Moderate
Adventures of Swiss Family Robinson[v]	PAX	Elementary	Prosocial	no clear lesson in any episode coded	Minimal
Anatole[v]	CBS	Elementary	Prosocial	self-reliance; no clear lesson in remaining two episodes	Minimal
Click	SYNDICATED	Preteen/teen	Academic	each episode presents general trivia for teens	Minimal
NBA Inside Stuff	NBC	Preteen/teen	Physical well-being	none of the episodes has a clear lesson	Minimal
Peer Pressure	SYNDICATED	Preteen/teen	Prosocial	episodes present various topics related to teen life; including peer pressure; the ethics of friendship	Minimal

*Only one episode was submitted.

**Only one episode was obtained due to taping difficulties.

[v] Violence found in at least one episode examined.

grams targeted to children of different ages, χ^2 (4) = 6.42, p > .10. There were also no differences in the educational strength of narrative or expository lessons, χ^2 (2) = 1.02, p > .10. However, programs having traditionally academic topics as their main lesson were significantly more likely to receive *highly educational* scores than programs emphasizing prosocial/emotional skills χ^2 (2) = 5.80, p < .05. Almost half of the programs with traditionally academic/knowledge lessons (44.1%) were considered *highly educational* whereas one quarter (26.5%) of the programs with prosocial lessons were rated as *highly educational*.

We were interested in whether the programs deemed highly educational were presenting children with socially diverse characters. We examined the extent to which these programs contained characters of different ethnicity and gender. The majority of highly educational programs contained ethnic diversity (65%) and gender diversity (84.1%). These highly educational programs were generally more successful at conveying social diversity but not gender diversity (because almost all of the programs contained gender diversity).

We also examined the prevalence of violence in educational programming. Of the programs that were highly educational, 10.3% contained a lot of violence. This did not differ from the overall sample—overall, only a small amount of the E/I programs airing in Philadelphia contained violence (12.1%). All of the programs containing violence were provided to the commercial broadcaster by the networks or weblets. All but one episode containing violence was aimed at school-age children.

DISCUSSION

The content analysis of the 1998–1999 E/I programs offered by commercial broadcasters to satisfy their public interest obligations under the Three-Hour Rule reveals that programming provided by the major networks is significantly more likely to be prosocial—that is, programs that address children's social/emotional needs. Programming acquired through syndication and airing on weblets and independent channels, however, was more diverse, perhaps because weblets and independents are more likely to see their audiences as *niche* than *mass*. These providers offered programs that addressed not only prosocial issues (such as dating or friendship lessons) but also traditionally academic topics (such as science lessons) and physical well-being lessons (such as exercise instruction). The child audience for E/I programs are more likely to be exposed to prosocial lessons from networks rather than school-related topics reaching it through syndication, since audiences for the Big Four networks (which provide mainly prosocial programs to their affiliates) are much larger than those for weblets and independents (A. C. Nielsen, 1996). Though both types of programs are acceptable under the FCC's definition of "educational and informational programming," this study finds that traditionally academic types of programs were more often highly educational while prosocial programs were mostly moderately educational.

Broadcasters direct their programs to children of all ages, although it is the elementary school-age child that receives the lion's share of E/I offerings (61% directed at elementary children versus 32% directed at preteens/teen and 7% directed at preschoolers). Perhaps as a result, 6- to 11-year-olds have the most diverse menu of E/I programs available. Programs for this age group are more likely to be prosocial in nature, but they are also the only age group that has a significant amount of programming that is relevant to a school curriculum such as science (*Algo's FACTory, Squigglevision*), history (*Histeria!*), or music (*Musical Encounters*).

Though the majority of E/I programs do meet the letter if not always the spirit of the children's television regulations, our analyses reveal that one-fifth of the programs cannot be considered as "contributing to the positive development of the child" (FCC, 1996). These programs lacked any clear lesson and/or failed to provide educational content that would be discernible to the target audience.

The introduction of E/I programs may also have had the consequence of encouraging producers and programmers to think more carefully about the content they offer children. This analysis reveals that there is very little violence in E/I programs, particularly when one compares it to the larger slate of children's programming on commercial and cable television (Woodard, 1999). In addition, programs with the most educational strength were also more likely to include strong representations of children from a variety of racial and ethnic backgrounds. The absence of violence and the inclusion of socially diverse child characters may make it more likely for children from a variety of backgrounds to attend to and learn from these educational programs.

The networks that provide the majority of programs to their local affiliates have responded to the new regulations by providing primarily prosocial programming (75% of their offerings are prosocial). While there is evidence that such programming can be beneficial to the developing child (see Chapter 9, this volume), there is also evidence that programming that is of a more academic nature may be equally, if not more, valuable. The relatively small number of traditionally academic programs in this sample tended to overwhelmingly focus on science. There is clearly room for programming based on other topics such as literature, language, culture, mathematics, and geography.

Though a great deal of research has been done with public television's preschool programs (such as *Sesame Street* or *Mister Rogers' Neighborhood*), there is very little understanding of how the school-age child responds to educational programming or how parents use such programming. In addition, more research is needed on the overall media environment of the American home. Children's television programs now also have a symbiotic relationship with other media and children increasingly have access to these new media (Rideout, Foehr, Roberts, & Brodie, 1999). Many programs have web sites (Center for Media Education, 1999; Schmitt, 1999), books, music, games, CD-ROMs, and toys that go along with the program. Therefore, television may stimulate children's interest in other activities that could also be potentially valuable as well.

Television viewing still dominates children's leisure-time use and broadcast television is universally available to all children—even those who might otherwise have few educational resources at hand (Rideout et al., 1999; Stanger & Gridina, 1999). There is evidence that children from low-income families watch more television than children from higher income families (St. Peters, Fitch, Huston, Wright, & Eakins, 1991; Woodard, 2000) and that children from disadvantaged families may benefit more from it (Huston, Donnerstein, Fairchild, Feschbach, Katz, Murray, Rubenstein, Wilcox, & Zuckerman, 1992). Television may, therefore, be a centralized and universal educational resource for this nation's children.

ACKNOWLEDGMENTS

Portions of this research were presented at the Annenberg Public Policy Center's Fourth Annual Conference on Children and Television in Washington, D.C. in June 1999.

We wish to thank Mark Brewin, Lubianska Espinosa, John Sindoni, Carolyn Strom, and Rebecca Zeit for assisting with coding of the video tapes and Jenn Goldstein and Mark Brewin for cataloging the video tapes and assisting with data collection. Thanks are also due to our Advisory Panel on Educational Television, who worked with us to define "educational" programming and test our measures of educational strength. Its members are Daniel Anderson, Sandra Calvert, Eliot Larson, Valeria Lovelace, Ann McGillicudy-DeLisi, and John Zimmerman.

Reprinted from *Applied Developmental Psychology*, Vol. 22 (1), A. Jordan, K. Schmitt, & E. Woodard. Developmental implications of commercial broadcasters' educational offerings, pp. 87–101, © 2001, with permission from Elsevier Science.

NOTES

1. Stations must file their report by the tenth day of each quarter. Online reporting is required the final quarter.
2. Two of these duplicate programs were rated as "highly educational"; one was rated "moderately educational."

REFERENCES

A. C. Nielsen. (1996). *Top 100 network children's programs*. Special report to the Annenberg Public Policy Center of the University of Pennsylvania, March.

Anderson, D. (1998). Educational television is not an oxymoron. *Annals of the American Academy of Political and Social Science, 557,* 24–38.

Anderson, D. R., Huston, A. C., Schmitt, K. L., Linebarger, D., & Wright, J. C. (2001). Early childhood television viewing and adolescent behavior. *Monographs of the Society for Research in Child Development, 66* (1, Serial No. 264).

Calvert, S., Stolkin, A., & Lee, J. (1997). Gender and ethnic portrayals in Saturday morning television programs. Poster presented at the biennial meeting of the Society for Research in Child Development, Washington, DC, April.

Center for Media Education. (1992). *A report on station compliance with the children's television act.* Washington, DC.

————. (1999). The E/I programs online. *Infoactive Kids,* Spring.

Children's Television Act of 1990 (CTA). (1990). Publ. L. No. 101–437, 104 Stat. 996–1000, codified at 47 USC Sections 303a, 303b, 394.

Collins, W. A., & Getz, S. (1976). Children's social responses following modeled reactions to provocation: Prosocial effects of a television drama. *Journal of Personality, 44,* 488–500.

Communications Act of 1934, 47, U.S.C. Section 307a. Washington, DC: Federal Communications Commission.

Federal Communications Commission (FCC). (1991). Policies and rules concerning children's television programming. *Federal Communications Commission Record, 6,* 2111–2127.

————. (1996). Policies and rules concerning children's television programming: Revision of programming policies for television broadcast stations. MMDocket No. 93–48.

Feldstein, J. H., & Feldstein, S. (1982). Sex differences on televised toy commercials. *Sex Roles, 8,* 581–87.

Fisch, S. (1998). The children's television workshop: The experiment continues. In R. G. Noll & M. E. Price (Eds.), *A communications cornucopia: The Markle Foundation essays on information policy.* Washington, DC: Brookings Institute Press.

Gerbner, G., & Gross, L. (1976). Living with television: The violence profile. *Journal of Communication, 26* (2), 172–199.

Graves, S. B. (1996). Diversity on television. In T. M. MacBeth (Ed.), *Tuning in to young viewers* (pp. 61–86). Thousand Oaks, CA: Sage.

Greenberg, B., & Brand, J. (1994). The question of media violence. In J. Bryant & D. Zillman (Eds.), *Media effects: Advances in theory and research* (pp. 163–212). Hillsdale, NJ: LEA.

Huston, A., Donnerstein, E., Fairchild, H., Feschbach, N., Katz, P., Murray, J., Rubenstein, E., Wilcox, B., & Zuckerman, D. (1992). *Big world, small screen.* Lincoln: University of Nebraska Press.

Huston, A. C., & Wright, J. C. (1998). Television and the informational and educational needs of children. *The Annals of the American Academy of Political and Social Science, 557,* 9–33.

Jordan, A. (1996). *The state of children's television: An examination of quality, quantity and industry beliefs.* Report No. 2. Philadelphia, PA: The Annenberg Public Policy Center of the University of Pennsylvania.

KRC Research and Consulting. (1993). *An evaluative assessment of the Ghostwriter Project*. New York: Author.

Kunkel, D. (1997). *National television violence study* (Vol. 2). Thousand Oaks, CA: Sage.

Kunkel, D., & Canepa, J. (1994). Broadcasters' license renewal claims regarding children's educational programming. *Journal of Broadcasting and Electronic Media*, Fall, 397–416.

Mares, L., & Woodard, E. (in press). The positive effects of television on children's social interactions. In R. Carveth and J. Bryant (Eds.), *Meta-analyses of media effects*. Hillsdale, NJ: LEA.

Paik, H., & Comstock, G. (1994). The effects of television violence on antisocial behavior: Meta-analysis. *Communication Research, 21* (4), 516–546.

Rideout, V., Foehr, U., Roberts, D., & Brodie, M. (1999). *Kids and media at the new millennium: Executive summary*. Menlo Park, CA: Kaiser Family Foundation.

Rule, B. G., & Ferguson, T. J. (1986). The effects of media violence on attitudes, emotions, and cognitions. *Journal of Social Issues, 42* (3), 29–50.

Schmitt, K. (1999). *The Three-Hour Rule: Is it living up to expectations?* Report No. 30. Philadelphia, PA: The Annenberg Public Policy Center of the University of Pennsylvania.

St. Peters, M., Fitch, M., Huston, A. C., Wright, J. C., & Eakins, D. J. (1991). Television and families: What do young children watch with their parents? *Child Development, 62* (6), 1409–1423.

Stanger, J., & Gridina, N. (1999). *Media in the home 1999: The fourth annual survey of parents and children*. Survey No. 5. Philadelphia, PA: The Annenberg Public Policy Center of the University of Pennsylvania.

Sullivan, J., & Jordan, A. (1999) Playing by the rules: Impact and implementation of children's educational television regulations among local broadcasters. *Communication Law and Policy, 4*, 483–511.

Van Evra, J. (1998). *Television and child development*. Mahwah, NJ: LEA.

Wood, W., Wong, F., & Chacere, J. (1991). Effects of media violence on viewers' aggression in unconstrained social interaction. *Psychology Bulletin, 109* (3), 371–383.

Woodard, E. (1999). *The 1999 state of children's television report: Programming for children over broadcast and cable television*. Report No. 28. Philadelphia, PA: The Annenberg Public Policy Center of the University of Pennsylvania.

———. (2000). *Media in the home 2000*. Survey No. 6. Philadelphia, PA: The Annenberg Public Policy Center of the University of Pennsylvania.

Zill, N., Davies, E., & Daly, M. (1994). *Viewing of Sesame Street by preschool children in the United States and its relation to school readiness*. Rockville, MD: Westat.

Chapter 9

Children's Online Reports about Educational and Informational Television Programs

*Sandra L. Calvert, Jennifer A. Kotler, William F. Murray,
Edward Gonzales, Kristin Savoye, Phillip Hammack,
Susan Weigert, Erin Shockey, Christine Paces,
Melissa Friedman, and Matthew Hammar*

With television sets in 99% of homes (Roberts, Foehr, Rideout, & Brodie, 1999), television content is readily accessible to almost all American children. Indeed, American children spend more time watching television programming than in any other activity but sleeping (Roberts et al., 1999). Moreover, longitudinal follow-ups reveal that children who grow up watching educational television programs such as *Sesame Street* later have better grades in high school (Huston, Anderson, Wright, Linebarger, & Schmitt, 2001). Realizing the unique potential of television as a medium that can educate as it entertains, Congress passed the Children's Television Act of 1990. The law required broadcasters to air educational and informational programs for young viewers as a condition for license renewal (Children's Television Act, 1990).

Although a decade has passed since the Children's Television Act (CTA) became a law, we still know virtually nothing about what, if anything, children learn from these programs. The purpose of this study was to analyze second- through sixth-grade children's learning from television programs that broadcasters label as educational and informational. To do so, children accessed our Internet site, located at *http://data.georgetown.edu/kidtv*, and reported their viewing patterns and their learning from educational and informational television programs.

WHAT IS AN EDUCATIONAL TELEVISION PROGRAM?

When the Federal Communications Commission (FCC) implemented the Children's Television Act, they defined educational and informational programming as "any content that serves to further the positive development of the child in any respect, including the child's cognitive/intellectual or emotional/social needs" (FCC, 1991, p. 21). This definition set the stage for prosocial as well as academically oriented programs to qualify as educational and informational.

Controversy quickly arose over what an educational program is when some of the initial television programs broadcast to meet the requirements of the Children's Television Act were of marginal educational value (Kunkel & Canepa, 1994). For instance, academic and advocacy groups monitored the kinds of programs that broadcasters listed as educational and informational on their license renewal forms (e.g., Center for Media Education & Institute for Public Representation, Georgetown University, 1992; Kunkel & Canepa, 1994). One broadcaster claimed that *GI Joe* taught children patriotism. The findings from these kinds of analyses led the FCC to implement more stringent standards, including the Three-Hour Rule that required each broadcaster to provide a minimum of three hours of educational and informational television programming each week (FCC, 1996).

Content analyses of educational and informational television programs became another focal point of the effort to monitor the quality of children's programs (e.g., Jordan & Woodard, 1997; Chapter 8, this volume). These content analyses reveal that the major networks provide their affiliate stations primarily with programs that contain social and emotional lessons rather than cognitive skills, knowledge information, or physical skills lessons. The educational strength of these programs, measured by the clarity, salience, involvement, and applicability of program lessons, has varied over time, but about one-fifth of E/I programs are consistently low in educational strength.

Although the body of knowledge about educational and informational programs has flourished in the children's television area, children's learning from these programs has not been examined. Therefore, feedback from children has not influenced the national debate about the kinds of programs that are and should be available for them.

CHILDREN'S LEARNING FROM EDUCATIONAL TELEVISION PROGRAMS

The literature about children's learning from television programs has almost always been derived from laboratory investigations. In such studies, children view specific television programs and are later asked questions which assess their memory of the content (Calvert, 1999b). Some of these television programs are narrative stories whereas others, like *Sesame Street*, are comprised of discrete vignettes that are put together in an expository, magazine format. Narrative stories tend to teach social and emotional lessons whereas expository magazines tend to teach traditional academic lessons. Studies have documented a developmental increase in children's memory for important over irrelevant program content, particularly for narrative stories (Collins, 1970). Although young children are often deficient in television story comprehension, televised stories are the main type of program being created by broadcasters to meet the requirements of the Children's Television Act (Calvert, 1999a).

Laboratory studies have contributed significantly to our knowledge about what children take away from television viewing experiences, but they are limited in several respects. First, laboratory studies offer the benefit of controlled conditions, thereby increasing the internal validity of the research, but they lack ecological validity, thereby limiting the generalizability of the findings and the external validity of the research. In the laboratory, for example, the researcher selects the program that children view. In real life, children may rarely, if ever, choose to view that program. We need to know more about what children are learning from the programs that they view in their homes, an external validity issue. Second, while delays in testing children's memories are sometimes built into experimental designs (Watkins, Calvert, Huston, & Wright, 1980), most studies collect data only immediately after exposure to a television program (Collins, 1970). Therefore, we know little about the durability of the messages that children take away from television viewing. Third, researchers typically construct measures to assess their own views, rather than children's views, of what should be important and memorable. We need to know more about what children think is important in the television programs they view.

One important exception to this pattern was a longitudinal study that examined the impact of educational television. In this study (Huston et al., 2001), two research teams collected initial data on the naturalistic viewing patterns of children during early childhood and examined these subjects a decade later, when these children had become adolescents. The researchers found that adolescents who had been frequent viewers of children's informative programs, such as *Sesame Street* and *Mister Rogers' Neighborhood*, had better grades in high school than those who had been infrequent viewers of this kind of educational fare. These differences held up even when other important family characteristics—such as family income and parental education—were taken into consideration. *Sesame Street* focuses on traditional academic lessons, such as number and letter identification, decoding, subtraction, counting strategies, and addition whereas *Mister Rogers' Neighborhood* focuses on prosocial themes (Calvert, 1999a). The long-term naturalistic findings document the enduring impact of high quality children's television programming on the academic achievement of our youth.

Our project was especially interested in what children were learning during middle childhood, an age group for whom relatively few quality educational programs have traditionally been created. Younger children, particularly boys, watch more Saturday morning cartoons than older children do (Huston & Wright, 1998). Educational and informational programs created by three of the four major commercial networks are broadcast by their affiliates on Saturday morning (though NBC chose to create a live action rather than an animated program line up). Therefore, we expected that younger children would view more of the presented educational programs than would older children. However, developmental differences in children's comprehension of essential plot-relevant television content and in verbal skills, which have long been documented in the literature, led us to predict advantages favoring older children in the number of lessons learned and in the educational strength of their reports.

GENDER DIFFERENCES

Gender differences in computer usage patterns document that boys are more likely to use computers than girls are (Calvert, 1999a). However, this pattern often emerges because computer software is generally directed at male interest patterns (Calvert, 1999a). Girls become interested in computers if they perceive the activity as relevant for them.

One computer activity that both boys and girls do is word processing (Calvert, 1999a). Therefore, the Internet computer game that we created for data collection involved writing stories. As both boys and girls use computers for writing activities, we expected similar involvement for both genders. Because girls often have better verbal and expressive skills than boys do early in development (Ruble & Martin, 1998), we also expected girls' reports to have greater clarity, integration, and applicability than boys' reports.

HYPOTHESES

Our main hypotheses were (1) younger children would view more educational and informational programs than older children, primarily because younger children are more likely to view cartoons which are typically broadcast on Saturday morning television programs (though the NBC line-up was in a live-action format); (2) older children would learn more academic and social lessons than younger children, primarily because older children can understand and convey lessons better; (3) older children would generalize program themes better than younger children, again because of their superior skills at understanding, integrating, and conveying lessons; (4) children who viewed more PBS and Nickelodeon than network programs would learn more academic (PBS) and social lessons (Nickelodeon) and generalize program themes better than would frequent viewers of commercial programs, primarily because PBS and Nickelodeon broadcast more educational and informational programs on a daily basis; and (5) girls would write reports with greater clarity, integration, and generalizability than boys because of girls' greater verbal and expressive skills.

METHOD

Participants

Children accessed our web site primarily from their schools, thereby allowing us to gather information about boys and girls representing various socioeconomic groups. Because developmental changes take place in children's comprehension of television programs (Calvert, 1999a), we compared two age groups: second/third/fourth (13 boys, 19 girls) versus fifth/sixth graders (30 girls, 35 boys). For year 1, the 97 children visited our site primarily from public schools in Shaker Heights, Ohio; West Chester, Pennsylvania; Silver Springs, Maryland; Norwalk, Connecticut; and private schools in Tampa, Florida and Salt Lake City, Utah.

Procedure and Internet Web Site for "The Georgetown Hoya TV Reporters"

Our web site, located at http://data.georgetown.edu/kidtv, is part of the Georgetown University site. Georgetown athletic teams are called "Hoya Bulldogs." Hence, the Internet site is called "The Georgetown Hoya TV Reporters."

The child-friendly web site, used to evaluate children's learning from educational and informational television programming, is designed as a game in which children become Hoya Reporters. Children reported from their schools or homes to tell us about: (1) what they viewed, (2) what their favorite program was, and (3) what they learned from their favorite program.

Using the Internet has distinct methodological advantages over other techniques. The Internet promotes: (1) ecological validity based on assessments of naturalistic viewing patterns, (2) immediate data transmission, (3) ease of reporting for children, and (4) interest value for children.

The first time that children entered the Hoya Reporter web site, new reporters went to a page that described what we were doing, and then went to a page where they provided descriptive information about themselves. After identifying information was provided, children moved to the *TV Guide* page. Here children selected the names of the weekly educational and informational programs that they had viewed the preceding week.

Because most network affiliates are broadcasting network feed for their educational and informational programs (Schmitt, 1999), a finite set of television programs was studied. For comparison purposes, educational and informational programs targeted at grade-school children from PBS and Nickelodeon were included in the sample. There were 30 programs on the site during year one. Network programs were selected based on educational and informational labels that were provided at the beginning of programs, as mandated by FCC requirements. The PBS and Nickelodeon programs were selected by our research team. Initially, our research team used descriptions and ratings from the October 1998 *Kidsnet Media Guide,* a computerized clearinghouse for children's television programs, to select potential programs for our sample. Then a panel of six judges from our project selected the actual programs for our study by viewing and classifying sample episodes of these programs for educational and informational content.

For the 1998–1999 season, our 30 target programs for second- through sixth-grade children were as follows:

ABC: *Disney's Doug; Disney's Pepper Ann; Disney's Recess; Squigglevision; Disney's 101 Dalmatians.*

CBS: *Anatole; Flying Rhino Junior High; Birdz; Mythic Warriors.*

FOX: *Magic School Bus; Life with Louie.*

NBC: *City Guys; Hang Time; Saved by the Bell; NBA Inside Stuff; One World.*

PBS: *Bill Nye, the Science Guy; Where in Time Is Carmen Sandiego?; Wishbone; Kratt's Creatures; Zoom.*

Nickelodeon: *Hey Arnold!; The Mystery Files of Shelby Woo; The Secret World of Alex Mack; Nick News; Clarissa Explains It All; Cousin Skeeter; Adventures of Pete and Pete; My Brother and Me; The Wild Thornberrys; Doug.*

Overall, there were 14 PBS/Nickelodeon programs and 15 network programs. *Doug* was a network, a Nickelodeon, and a syndicated program, and *Bill Nye, the Science Guy* also appeared in syndication.

The Annenberg Public Policy Center (APPC) coding system, a reliable system that has face validity, was selected for coding the programs and adapted for coding children's reports (see Chapter 8, this volume). Using the APPC content coding system, two independent raters classified all programs for: (1) *genre,* the kind of program, and (2) *program structure,* expository (lessons shape content) or narrative (lesson woven into a story). For genre, 13 programs (45%) were animated comedies, 11 (38%) were live action comedies or dramas, 2 (7%) were news, 1 (3%) was a quiz game show, 1 (3%) was a magazine, and 1 (3%) was a mixture of 2 or more genres. For program structure, 24 programs (83%) were narratives and 5 (17%) were expository. Interobserver reliability was 93% for genre and 97% for program structure.

After television viewing patterns were reported, children selected their Favorite Program for the past week. Then children went to the Reporting page where they described the lessons that they learned from their favorite program. Finally, children posted their reports to an animated boy or girl reporter on the site.

Reward structures were embedded within the game to sustain children's interest. Children who wrote the best reports at their grade levels became one of The Top Dogs, and their reports were published in our Internet "newspaper." These weekly winners received Blue Ribbon and Gray Ribbon Awards, the colors of Georgetown University. Children also could view their own reports in an individual, cumulative file.

Scoring System: Dependent Variables

The dependent variables were: (1) the number of educational and informational programs viewed by each child; (2) the favorite educational and informational programs viewed by each child; (3) the kind of lessons learned by children, a measure adapted from the *APPC television content analyses*, consisting of (a) cognitive skills, (b) knowledge/information skills, (c) social emotional skills, and (d) physical well-being/motor development skills; and (4) the educational strength of children's reports, another measure adapted from the *APPC television content analyses*, consisting of: (a) lesson clarity: Does the child present a clear lesson in his or her report?; (b) lesson integration: Does the child discuss the lesson consistently throughout his or her report?; (c) lesson involvement: Does the child report the lesson in an engaging manner (e.g., excitement); and (d) lesson applicability/generalizability: Does the child describe the lesson in relation to his or her own life, drawing links between the television content with events that have or could happen to them? The definitions of integration and involvement varied from the APPC definition because we were studying children's reports and they were studying the actual programs (see Chapter 8, this volume). We also examined the kinds of programs that children were viewing (i.e., narrative versus expository and the program genre).

Interobserver reliability, calculated as $2 \times$ the number of agreements divided by the total number of scores for Observer 1 and Observer 2, was computed on 20% of the data. Interobserver reliability for the kinds of lessons learned was 93% for cognitive skills, 95% for knowledge/information skills, 100% for social and emotional skills, and 100% for physical well-being skills. Interobserver reliability for the components of educational strength was 93% for the educational goal, 84% for lesson clarity, 84% for lesson integration, 80% for lesson involvement, and 84% for lesson generalization.

RESULTS

This study examined age and gender differences in: (1) the educational and informational programs children view; (2) their favorite educational programs; (3) the kinds of lessons they learn from favorite programs; and (4) the strength of the lessons. Only first reports are analyzed.[1]

Number and Types of Educational Programs Viewed

Children viewed an average of 3.81 (SD = 3.01) educational programs per week. Eight children reported that they did not view any of the educational and informational programs.[2] A 2 (sex) × 2 (age: second to fourth versus fifth to sixth graders) analysis of variance (ANOVA) was conducted to examine whether there were sex and age differences in the number of educational programs viewed. There was a marginal main effect for age $F(1, 93) = 2.972$, $p < .10$. Younger children viewed slightly more educational and informational programs than the older children did (M = 4.59, SD = 3.75 vs. 3.43, SD = 2.52, respectively).

To examine sex and age differences in whether children watched educational and informational programs on commercial broadcast stations versus Nickelodeon/PBS, a 2 (sex) × 2 (age) × 2 (station: commercial broadcast versus Nickelodeon/PBS) mixed ANOVA was conducted with sex and age as the between-subjects factors and station as the within-subjects factor. The dependent variable was the number of programs children viewed on the two types of stations. There was a significant main effect for station, $F(1, 85) = 27.04$, $p < .001$. As predicted, children watched more programs from PBS and Nickelodeon than from broadcast stations (M = 2.75, SD = 2.21 vs. 1.39, SD = 1.44, respectively).

A 2 (sex) × 2 (age) × 2 (genre: animated vs. live-action vs. magazine vs. mixed vs. news) mixed ANOVA was conducted with the number of programs viewed as the dependent variable. Sex and age were between-subjects factors and genre was a within-subjects factor. The analysis yielded a main effect for genre $F(4, 82) = 31.52$, $p < .001$. Simple contrasts indicated that children watched significantly more animated comedies and dramas (M = 1.98, SD = 1.61) than any other type of program. Children also viewed more live-action comedies and dramas (M = 1.31, SD = 1.38) than magazine (M = .33, SD = .52), mixed (M = .37, SD = .51), or news (M = .11, SD = .32) genres.

A 2 (grade) × 2 (sex) × 2 (structure: narrative vs. expository) mixed ANOVA was computed with the number of programs viewed as the dependent variable. Structure was the within-subjects factor and sex and age were between-subjects factors. The analysis yielded a significant main effect for structure $F(1, 85) = 93.51$, $p < .001$. Children viewed more narrative programs than expository programs (M = 3.55, SD = 2.67 vs. M = .60, SD = .82, respectively).

In summary, children viewed more Nickelodeon and PBS programs than broadcast programs; they viewed more narrative than expository programs; and they viewed more animated and live-action programs than other types of programs.

Most Frequently Viewed Programs

For each program, we computed the percentage of child viewers. As seen in Table 9.1, the most frequently viewed programs were *Doug, Hey Arnold!, Saved by the Bell, Recess, Cousin Skeeter,* and *Wishbone.* Other popular programs for subgroups of children included *Bill Nye, the Science Guy* for boys, *The Wild Thornberrys, Zoom,* and *Magic School Bus* for younger girls, and *Clarissa Explains It All* for older girls.

Least Frequently Viewed Programs

Some programs were rarely viewed by children. These programs were *Squigglevision, Birdz, Flying Rhino Junior High, One World, Where in Time Is Carmen Sandiego?,* and *Mythic Warriors.* In addition, younger boys never watched *City Guys, Hangtime,* or *Life with Louie;* younger girls never watched *NBA Inside Stuff* or *Bobby's World;* and older girls never watched *City Guys.* See Table 9.1.

Favorite Programs

The top five favorite programs chosen by children were: (1) *Doug,* (2) *Hey Arnold!,* (3) *Saved by the Bell,* (4) *Bill Nye, the Science Guy,* and (5) *Cousin Skeeter. Doug* was the favorite program of all age groups except for older girls who liked *Saved by the Bell.* Other favorite programs included *Zoom* and *The Wild Thornberrys* for younger girls and *Recess* for older girls. See Table 9.1.

Lessons Learned from Favorite Programs

To examine the types of lessons children learned from their favorite program, a 2 (sex) × 2 (age) × 4 (lessons: cognitive, knowledge/information, social and emotional, and physical well-being) mixed ANOVA was conducted with sex and age as between-subjects factors and lessons as the within-subjects factor. The dependent variable was the presence or absence of each lesson type (scored 0 vs. 1) in the children's reports. It was expected that children would report more social and emotional lessons than any other type of lessons, that older children would learn more lessons than younger children, and that girls' reports would have the most educational strength.

The means for lessons learned by sex and grade are presented in Table 9.2. As expected, there was a significant main effect for sex, $F(1, 85) = 6.377, p < .05$. Girls reported learning more lessons than boys (M = .86, SD = .71 vs. .53, SD = .55, respectively). There was also a significant main effect for lesson, $F(3, 83) = 13.270, p < .001$. Simple contrasts indicated that social and emotional lessons were reported more often than cognitive

Table 9.1
Frequencies of Programs Viewed and Favorites by Age and Sex[a]

	Total Children (N = 97)	Younger Boys (N = 13)	Younger Girls (N = 19)	Older Boys (N = 35)	Older Girls (N = 30)
Most Frequently Viewed Programs	Doug (49.5%)	Doug (46.2%)	Doug (62.5%)	Doug (44.4%)	Doug (55.2%)
	Hey Arnold! (39.2%)	Bill Nye (38.5%)	Hey Arnold! (50%)	Hey Arnold! (41.7%)	Hey Arnold! (34.5%)
	Saved by the Bell (24.7%)	Saved by the Bell (38.5%)	Wild Thornberrys (37.5%)	Cousin Skeeter (30.6%)	Saved by the Bell (34.5%)
	Recess (23.7%)	Hey Arnold! (38.5%)	Zoom (37.5%)	Bill Nye (19.4%)	Recess (31%)
	Cousin Skeeter (22.7%)	Recess (25%)	Wishbone (37.5%)	Saved by the Bell (19.4%)	Clarissa (24.1%)
	Wishbone (20.6%)		Magic School Bus (37.5%)		Wishbone (20.7%)
Least Viewed Programs[b]	Squigglevision (1%)	City Guys	Carmen Sandiego	Birdz	Birdz
	Birdz (2.1%)	Flying Rhino	Flying Rhino	Carmen Sandiego	City Guys
	Flying Rhino (2.1%)	Hangtime	NBA Inside Stuff	Flying Rhino	One World
	One World (2.1%)	Life with Louie	Squigglevision	One World	Mythic Warriors
	Carmen Sandiego (3.1%)			Squigglevision	Squigglevision
	Mythic Warrior (3.1%)				

174

Favorite Programs[c]	(N = 89)	(N = 12)	(N = 18)	(N = 31)	(N = 28)
	Doug (15.7%)	Doug (16.7%)	Doug (16.7%)	Doug (16.1%)	Saved by the Bell (21.4%)
	Hey Arnold! (12.4%)	Hey Arnold! (16.7%)	Zoom (16.7%)	Hey Arnold! (16.1%)	Doug (14.8%)
	Saved by the Bell (10.1%)		Wild Thornberrys (16.7%)	Bill Nye (12.9%)	Recess (11.1%)
	Bill Nye (9%)			Cousin Skeeter (9.7%)	
	Cousin Skeeter (6.7%)				

Notes:

[a] The percentages represent the proportion of children who indicated that they viewed each program.

[b] The total column indicates the least viewed programs for all children. The breakdowns by age and sex indicate which shows were not viewed at all.

[c] Favorite programs were only computed for children who watched at least one program.

Table 9.2
Means and Standard Deviations for Lessons Learned and Educational Strength of Report

	All Children (n = 89)	Younger Boys (n = 12)	Younger Girls (n = 18)	Older Boys (n = 31)	Older Girls (n = 28)
Lessons Learned					
Cognitive skills	0.06 (0.23)	0.08 (0.29)	0 (0)	0 (0)	0.14 (0.36)
Knowledge/ information skills	0.19 (0.40)	0.25 (0.45)	0.33 (0.49)	0.16 (0.37)	0.11 (0.32)
Social and emotional skills	0.38 (0.49)	0 (0)	0.33 (0.49)	0.39 (0.50)	0.58 (0.50)
Physical well-being skills	0.06 (0.23)	0 (0)	0.11 (0.32)	0.06 (0.25)	0.04 (0.19)
Educational Strength					
Clarity	0.91 (.89)	0.50 (0.80)	1.28 (0.89)	0.77 (0.85)	1.00 (0.90)
Integration	0.79 (.80)	0.50 (0.80)	1.00 (0.84)	0.68 (0.79)	0.89 (0.79)
Involvement	0.88 (.77)	0.67 (0.78)	0.94 (0.73)	0.71 (0.69)	1.11 (0.83)
Applicability	0.84 (.92)	0.08 (0.29)	1.22 (0.88)	0.68 (0.87)	1.11 (0.96)

Notes: Only children who chose a favorite program were included in the means. For lessons learned, scores were 0 (not present) or 1 (present). For educational strength, scores were 0 (not at all), 1 (somewhat), or 2 (very well). Means are presented without parentheses and standard deviations are presented within parentheses.

skills lessons $F(1, 85) = 24.395$, $p < .001$, and physical lessons $F(1, 85) = 20.995$, $p < .001$, but not significantly more often than informative lessons $F(1, 85) = 1.959$, $p = $ n.s. Additional simple contrasts indicated that informative lessons were reported more often than cognitive lessons $F(1, 85) = 8.542$, $p < .01$ and physical lessons $F(1, 85) = 4.457$, $p < .01$. Lessons involving physical well-being and cognitive skills were rarely reported. In short, a diversity of lessons was found in children's reports. Most lessons probably reflect social and emotional lessons because the majority of educational programs (67%) posted on this site are designed to teach social and emotional lessons.

Although there was no main effect for age, there was an age-by-sex-by-

lesson interaction $F(3, 83) = 2.916$, $p < .05$ and an age-by-lesson interaction $F(3, 83) = 3.315$, $p < .05$. To examine the direction of these
interactions, each lesson type was examined separately in a 2 (sex) $\times$ 2
(age) ANOVA. For social and emotional lessons, there were significant sex
$F(1, 85) = 6.046$, $p < .01$ and age $F(1, 85) = 8.819$, $p < .01$ main effects.
Girls reported more social and emotional lessons than boys (M = .48, SD
= .51 vs. .28, SD = .45, respectively). Older children reported more social
and emotional lessons than younger children (M = .48, SD = .50 vs. M=
.20, SD = .41, respectively). For knowledge/information lessons, there was
a marginal age main effect $F(1, 85) = 3.105$, $p = .10$. In contrast to the
results for social and emotional lessons, younger children tended to learn
more informative lessons than older children did (M = .30, SD = .47 vs.
.14, SD = .35, respectively). For cognitive lessons, there was a significant
sex-by-age interaction $F(1, 85) = 4.838$, $p < .05$. Older girls reported more
cognitive lessons than any other group followed by younger boys (M =
.14, SD = .36 vs. M = .08, SD = .29, respectively); older boys and younger
girls did not report any cognitive skills lessons. There were no significant
effects for physical well-being lessons.

Educational Strength

Differences in educational strength were examined by a 2(sex) $\times$ 2(age)
multivariate analysis of variance (MANOVA) with the four measures of
educational strength (i.e., clarity, integration, involvement, and applicability) as dependent variables. Each measure of educational strength had
scores that could range from 0 (not at all) to 1 (somewhat) to 2 (very well).
As seen in Table 9.2, older children's reports were not of significantly
greater quality than the younger children's reports. As predicted, there was
a main effect for sex, $F(4, 82) = 5.020$, $p < .01$. Univariate tests indicated
that girls' reports scored higher than boys' reports on clarity $F(1, 85) =
6.463$, $p < .05$, and applicability $F(1, 85) = 16.445$, $p < .001$. There was
a marginal sex effect for integration $F(1, 85) = 3.862$, $p < .06$, and involvement F (1, 85) = 3.849, p < .06, both in favor of the girls' reports.

A one-way MANOVA analysis, controlling for sex, examined the difference between PBS/Nickelodeon programs versus the four major commercial
broadcasters on the four measures of educational strength. Contrary to
prediction, reports about PBS/Nickelodeon programs were no stronger than
reports about ABC, CBS, NBC, or FOX offerings. Moreover, reports about
PBS programs were no stronger than reports about Nickelodeon programming.

The Relation between Lessons Learned and Educational
Strength

Partial correlations controlling for sex and grade examined the relation
between lessons learned and educational strength. Reports citing social and

emotional lessons learned were related to all measures of educational strength. Such reports of social/emotional lessons tended to be clear ($r = .590, p < .001$), integrated ($r = .498, p < .001$), demonstrated involvement ($r = .268, p < .05$) and demonstrated that children generalized the messages ($r = .701, p < .001$). Reports citing informative lessons learned were positively related to how clear ($r = .317, p < .01$) and how integrated ($r = .320, p < .01$) children's reports were but were not related to involvement or generalization. Children's reports citing cognitive or physical well-being lessons were unrelated to any measure of educational strength. In summary, children were most involved with and learned most from programs with social and emotional themes but also clearly understood knowledge/information lessons presented in the programs they viewed.

DISCUSSION

The Children's Television Act of 1990 encourages greater availability of educational and informational television offerings for children over the nation's free airwaves, but independent evaluations are needed to ensure that broadcasters' claims that their programs are educational and informational, are in fact, valid. By providing a web site where children can report their viewing behavior, we can determine if educational television programs are attracting an audience and providing any lessons of value for the viewing audience.

Our findings generally support broadcast industry claims of educational value for their "educational and informational" offerings with children primarily learning social and emotional lessons. PBS and Nickelodeon programs, particularly Nickelodeon programs, are viewed more than those broadcast by the affiliates of the four major networks, perhaps because ABC, CBS, and NBC run their programs against each other on Saturday mornings. By contrast, programs on Nickelodeon, PBS, and FOX are broadcast throughout the week, allowing children greater access to these educational offerings. Even so, there were no differences in the educational strength of reports written about Nickelodeon/PBS programs versus the four major networks.

The kinds of reports that children wrote dovetail with the kinds of programs being made for them by most broadcasters. Specifically, most reports are story narratives focusing on social and emotional themes. Consider the following social and emotional theme reported by a fifth-grade boy about *Hey Arnold!*, a Nickelodeon program:

I watched *Hey Arnold!* It was about Arnold and his class going to an aquarium. There was a big turtle that was at the aquarium and they kept it in horrible condition. There was gerfidy on his shell and a kid threw an ice cream cone at the turtle. Arnold felt sorry for the turtle. When he got home he told his grandmother about what happened and they went to the aquarium to rescue the turtle. They got the turtle out and put it in the ocean. I learned that you need to take good care of animals in this episode.

By contrast, cognitive skills or physical skills are rarely learned from educational and informational television programming, a finding that supports the APPC report that prosocial rather than traditionally academic programs are the focus of broadcaster offerings (Chapter 8, this volume). Even so, some of the favorite educational programs of boys, such as *Bill Nye, the Science Guy* (a PBS and syndicated offering), are academic in nature, and young girls like *Magic School Bus*, a science program that is currently broadcast on FOX. Commercial broadcasters might find an audience for well-made academic programs as well as for the prosocial stories.

The developmental prediction that younger children would view more educational programs than older children was partially supported, but the hypothesis that older children would generalize program messages better than younger children was not supported. Older children did learn more social and emotional lessons than the younger children, but the younger children learned more knowledge/information lessons than did older children. These findings probably reflect the kinds of programs children chose as favorites at varying ages. More specifically, older children chose more favorite programs with social and emotional themes, such as *Saved by the Bell*, whereas younger children selected more academically oriented programs such as *Wishbone*, a program focusing on the language arts integrated with social and emotional themes. The broadcasters' belief that younger children like academically oriented programs more than older children do (Jordan & Sullivan, 1997) is partially supported by our research.

Gender differences were prevalent throughout our findings. Although both boys and girls viewed an equal amount of educational programming, girls' reports demonstrated more educational strength. Specifically, girls' reports were clearer, more integrated, and had more applicability to their real-life activities than the reports of boys. These findings are consistent with literature that documents the advanced verbal and expressive skills of girls over boys during middle childhood (Ruble & Martin, 1998). Moreover, viewing patterns suggest that unlike strictly commercial entertainment cartoons, which draw a boy audience (Huston & Wright, 1998), girls and boys are equivalent viewers of educational and informational programs. These findings suggest that educational television has a male and a female audience, making its benefits equally available for all children.

The kind of lesson emphasized and the gender of key characters in programs seemed to influence the kinds of programs children viewed and selected as their favorites. The finding that girls like more socially oriented areas of achievement and enjoy arts and crafts areas are supported by the kinds of programs that they selected as favorites. Older girls liked *Saved by the Bell* the most while younger girls liked *Zoom* and *The Wild Thorn-berrys*, programs which feature female interest patterns and female characters. Only boys frequently viewed *Bill Nye, the Science Guy*, and only young girls frequently viewed *Magic School Bus*. Both programs are about science, but boys chose the program with the male host whereas young girls chose the program featuring a female lead and a multiracial cast of boys and girls. In 1999, both of these programs received awards from the Annenberg Public Policy Center as excellent educational and informational programs. Perhaps the appeal of each is more determined by the gender of the host and cast than by the content area of science, an area that has traditionally been stereotyped as a male domain. The implication is that girls may become more interested in science programs if they see other girls and women involved in enjoyable science lessons. Both age groups did like *Doug* and *Hey Arnold!*, perhaps because the stories conveyed social and emotional themes that involve both boys and girls, and even though male leads are featured, central female characters are included in both casts.

Using the Internet as a research tool has distinct advantages over traditional data collection techniques. Children from across the United States could transmit their viewing preferences and knowledge about programs by having a computer interface with our site. This type of methodology provides a future way to sample children from a wide range of locations, but is limited in that adults have to coordinate children's participation, at least initially.

Another methodological issue was that at the time of data collection, many schools were not yet wired to the Internet, and teachers did not always have the computer skills to bring their children online. Many of the wiring and training problems are being resolved in the twenty-first century, making the Internet a viable research tool for collecting data throughout this country and the world.

In conclusion, this study demonstrates that children benefit from viewing the educational and informational television programs that are the result of the Children's Television Act of 1990. Broadcasters have found an effective way to meet their obligation to the child audience while entertaining them with engaging prosocial content. Whether broadcasters will make the investment to create comparable academically oriented fare remains a question, particularly if there are no additional requirements from the Federal Communications Commission to do so.

ACKNOWLEDGMENTS

This research was supported by a grant from the Smith Richardson Foundation and by a Teaching Research Nexus Award from Georgetown University. We thank the students, parents, teachers, and principals from schools in Shaker Heights,

Ohio; West Chester, Pennsylvania; Norwalk, Connecticut; Silver Spring, Maryland; Salt Lake City, Utah; and Tampa, Florida, who participated in this research.

Reprinted from *Applied Developmental Psychology*, Vol. 22 (1), S. L. Calvert, J. A. Kotler, W. F. Murray, E. Gonzales, K. Savoye, P. Hammack, S. Weigert, E. Shockey, C. Paces, M. Friedman, M. Hammar, Children's online reports about educational and informational television programs, pp. 103–117, © 2001, with permission from Elsevier Science.

NOTES

1. Because *Doug* was broadcast almost daily on Nickelodeon and once a week on ABC, we estimated that children viewed *Doug* on Nickelodeon 7 times for every 1 time they viewed *Disney's Doug* on ABC. This formula was supported when compared to year two of our data collection when there were separate icons for *Doug* and *Disney's Doug*. When programs were syndicated, we defaulted to the primary major networks where the programs were broadcast for analyses.

2. For all other ANOVA's, only children who watched at least one program were included because those who did not watch any of these television programs could not be classified as viewing a particular category of programming, and they did not submit a report that could be analyzed for the lesson type or for its educational strength.

REFERENCES

Calvert, S. L. (1999a). *Children's journeys through the information age*. Boston: McGraw-Hill.

———. (1999b). The form of thought. In I. Sigel (Ed.), *Theoretical perspectives in the concept of representation*. Hillsdale, NJ: Erlbaum.

Center for Media Education & Institute for Public Representation, Georgetown University. (1992). *A report on station compliance with the Children's Television Act*. Washington, DC: Center for Media Education, September 29.

Children's Television Act of 1990 (CTA). (1990). Publ. L. No. 101–437, 104 Stat. 996–1000, codified at 47 USC Sections 303a, 303b, 394.

Collins, W. A. (1970). Learning of media content: A developmental study. *Child Development, 41,* 1133–1142.

Federal Communications Commission (FCC). (1991). Policies and rules concerning children's television programming. *Federal Communications Commission Record, 6,* 2111–2127.

———. (1996). Policies and rules concerning children's television programming: Revision of programming policies for television broadcast stations. MMDocket No. 93–48.

Huston, A. C., Anderson, D. R., Wright, J. C., Linebarger, D. L., & Schmitt, K. L. (2001). Sesame Street viewers as adolescents: The recontact study. In S. Fisch & R. Truglio (Eds.), *G is for growing: Thirty years of Sesame Street*. Mahwah, NJ: Erlbaum.

Huston, A. C., & Wright, J. C. (1998). Mass media and children's development. In

W. Damon, I. Sigel, & K. A. Renninger (Eds.), *Handbook of child psychology, Vol. 4: Child psychology in practice* (5th ed). New York: John Wiley.

Jordan, A., Schmitt, K., & Woodard, E. (2001). Developmental implications of commercial broadcasters' educational offerings. *Applied Developmental Psychology, 22* (1), 87–101.

Jordan, A., & Woodward, E. (1997). *The 1997 state of children's television report: Programming for children over broadcast and cable television.* Report No. 14. Philadelphia, PA: The Annenberg Public Policy Center of the University of Pennsylvania, June.

Jordan, A. B., & Sullivan, J. L. (1997). *Children's educational television regulations and the local broadcaster: Impact and implementation.* Report No. 13. Philadelphia, PA: The Annenberg Public Policy Center of the University of Pennsylvania, June.

Kunkel, D., & Canepa, J. (1994). Broadcasters' license renewal claims regarding children's educational programming. *Journal of Broadcasting and Electronic Media, 38,* 397–416.

Roberts, D. F., Foehr, U. G., Rideout, V. J., & Brodie, M. (1999). *Kids and media at the new millennium: A comprehensive national analysis of children's media use.* Menlo Park, CA: Kaiser Family Foundation.

Ruble, D., & Martin, C. (1998). Gender development. In W. Damon (Ed.) & N. Eisenberg (Vol. Ed.), *Handbook of Child Psychology, Vol. 3: Social, emotional and personality development* (5th ed.). New York: John Wiley.

Schmitt, K. L. (1999). *The Three-Hour Rule: Is it living up to expectation?* Report No. 30. Philadelphia, PA: The Annenberg Public Policy Center of the University of Pennsylvania.

Watkins, B. A., Calvert, S. L., Huston-Stein, A., & Wright, J. C. (1980). Children's recall of television material: Effects of presentation mode and adult labeling. *Developmental Psychology, 16,* 672–674.

Chapter 10

The AnimalWatch Project: Creating an Intelligent Computer Mathematics Tutor

Carole R. Beal and Ivon Arroyo

Just as computers and Internet access are becoming ubiquitous in the home (Chapter 1, this volume), so too are they becoming ubiquitous at school. Yet the mere presence of computers in schools does not always mean that their promise is fulfilled. In fact, many teachers have reported to us that their computers are often underutilized. It can be difficult to find software that is easy to use, effective, that will engage students' interest, and that meshes well with the existing curriculum. All too often, the powerful computers end up being used for game playing or Internet surfing as a reward to students when their academic assignments are completed (Jennings, 2001). We have even seen computers being used as expensive plant holders and doorstops.

At the same time that powerful computer technology is becoming more readily available to schools, there is an urgent need for new approaches to instruction that will help schools meet growing challenges. These challenges include the need to serve an increasingly diverse student population, including accommodations for students with special learning characteristics and disabilities. Educators must also cope with rising expectations on the part of parents, politicians, and others about educational standards. There is growing pressure for accountability in the form of frequent high stakes achievement tests even for elementary school students.

One possibility for improving the educational system is to use computer-based teaching systems to help educators address the needs of all their students through "adaptive instruction." Adaptive instruction refers to the ability of the computer to tailor teaching to individual students as a function of their problem-solving progress (Andriessen & Sandberg, 1999; Beck & Stern, 1999; Bruer, 1997; Fletcher-Flynn & Gravatt, 1995).

Computer-based tutoring systems have been around for decades, yet their use in K–12 classrooms was rare until quite recently (Burton, 1982; Koedinger, Anderson, Hadley, & Mark, 1997; Schofield, Eurich-Fulcer, & Britt, 1994). Computer-based tutors were traditionally very expensive to develop, and they tended to be brittle, meaning that a computer tutor that had been developed for one particular domain could not be easily updated or modified by the teacher for another purpose. However, recent developments in the area of artificial intelligence and machine learning now support the design of systems that can be used more flexibly in the classroom (Gertner, Conati, & Van Lehn, 1998; Major, Ainsworth, & Wood, 1997; Paliouras, Karkaletsis, Papatheodorou, & Spyropoulos, 1999; Shute, 1995; Sigalit & Van Lehn, 1995). For example, the intelligent teaching component of the tutor can now be more clearly distinguished from the domain content, allowing teachers to add their own material (Ainsworth, Underwood, & Grimshaw, 2000). Also, increased access to the Internet has made it possible for tutoring systems to be updated frequently, and for teachers to use design and authoring tools to customize the tutoring system for their own needs (Ritter, Anderson, Cytrynowicz, & Medvedeva, 1998).

THE ANIMALWATCH PROJECT

The goal of the AnimalWatch project has been to develop a computer-based mathematics tutoring program for 10- to 12-year-olds that can be integrated into the classroom curriculum and customized by teachers through an accompanying web site. AnimalWatch provides instruction in the mathematics topics most often taught in American fifth and sixth grades: whole number operations (addition, subtraction, multiplication, and division), introduction to fractions, and addition and subtraction of like and unlike fractions and mixed numbers. The project's focus on mathematics as the target domain for adaptive instruction came about for several reasons. First, mathematics is an area of the curriculum in which American schools tend to falter. International comparisons consistently indicate that students from the United States perform at best only on an average level in math and, often, far below students in other countries (Beller & Gafni, 1996; Stevenson & Lee, 1990). At the same time, there is a growing need for a technically skilled workforce, a need that has been met in part by the importation of mathematically proficient workers from other countries (Raloff, 1991).

A second reason for the focus on mathematics is that teachers frequently reported to us that they would appreciate support in this area of the curriculum. Many teachers at the elementary level, most of whom are female, feel underprepared to teach math (Delamont, 1990; Spender, 1984). The response in teacher education programs has not always led to an improvement in math skills. For example, one of our project members gave a guest lecture at an institution in which student teachers were prepared for math lesson planning primarily through writing poetry about their feelings about math.

The third reason for our focus on mathematics is that there are important issues of equity in this domain (Beal, 1994; Eccles & Jacobs, 1986). Specifically, although female students now enroll in almost as many math courses as males, the long-standing gender gap in math achievement tests persists. There is also reason to be concerned about female students' level of competence in math, particularly when they must work under time pressure or transfer skills to problems not previously seen (Willingham & Cole, 1997). A related concern is that enrollment by female students in careers that require mathematical proficiency remains discouragingly low. Educators, researchers, and funding agencies have called for new approaches to mathematics learning that can engage more students, particularly girls and women (Alper, 1993; Camp, 1997; Campbell, 1992).

THEORETICAL FRAMEWORK

The overall design of the AnimalWatch tutor reflects the theoretical framework of Eccles, Wigfield, Harold, and Blumenfeld (1993). Specifically, students' motivation and, in turn, their achievement in a particular academic subject such as math is thought to reflect their attitudes about the domain. These attitudes include students' liking of the subject, their belief that it is important and valuable to learn, and their concept of their own ability to master the subject. These constructs may vary independently. For example, a male student might dislike math but feel that it is important to learn and believe that he can succeed with effort, whereas a female classmate might dislike math and feel that it is not important for her to learn, but believe that she could master the material if she really tried. Extensive work by Eccles et al. has shown that students in elementary school and beyond can accurately report their attitudes, and that their attitudes are related to motivation and achievement in math as well as other academic domains (Beal, Beck, & Woolf, 1998).

One implication of the Eccles et al. theoretical framework is that computer-based teaching should help students see the value of learning mathematics. To accomplish this, math-problem solving in the Animal-Watch tutor is linked with real-world information and problems are embedded in real-world contexts (Cordova & Lepper, 1996). One of our partner teachers, a master teacher of fifth graders known for her work on environmental science, had found that both her male and female students were very interested and engaged in class projects about endangered species. She suggested the idea of creating computer-based math problems about endangered species (hence the name, "AnimalWatch"). We began by creating mathematics word problems about the Atlantic Right Whale, then added problems about the Giant Panda, and the Takhi Wild Horse (also known as the Przewalksi Wild Horse).

THE DEVELOPMENT OF ANIMALWATCH

Many teachers had told us that they felt most commercially available software for mathematics was focused more on entertainment than education. To address teachers' concerns, the AnimalWatch project involved an interdisciplinary team of computer scientists, developmental psychologists, and classroom educators. The computer scientists also had graduate degrees in education and were able to consider curriculum and pedagogy while solving the technical challenges involved in designing the intelligent mathematics tutor.

When students log on to AnimalWatch, they choose a species and are greeted with a personalized letter inviting them to serve as wildlife biology consultants who will help to assess the status of the species. Students then are presented with a series of math word problems about the species. For example, a student working on the Right Whale adventure might view a problem about the average distance traveled per day on the whales' annual migration down the Atlantic coast. Each problem is accompanied by an image that serves as an illustration, or that presents information needed for the problem such as a graph, chart, or other data sources that the student must examine to find relevant information. The content information represented in the word problems is as accurate as possible. For instance, the distances are factually accurate; sizes and weights of the animals are within known ranges; and related historical and geographical information is correct.

Adaptive Teaching in Narratives

In early field trials, students reported that they enjoyed working on math about the endangered species and that they felt that it was a good way to learn mathematics. However, we found that simply working on an indefinite series of math word problems about endangered animals was not sufficiently engaging for students; they needed to have some sense that they were making progress as they worked. We did not want to make the program into a competitive game, because this tends to appeal much more to boys than girls (Frenkel, 1990; Lawry, Upitis, Klawe, Anderson, Inkpen, Ndunda, Hsu, Leroux, & Sedighian, 1994). Rather, we decided to merge the word problems into a narrative through which students would progress as they worked on math.

Each narrative currently has four sections or "contexts." For example, the Takhi Wild Horse story begins with word problems concerning background information about the species, its history, and its distinctive characteristics. Then the student moves to a section on Mongolia, the original home of the Takhi, learning about its history, geography, and culture. The third context focuses on how the Takhi horse was saved from complete extinction through the efforts of zoos around the world. In the final segment, the student takes a virtual trip to accompany a group of wild horses that are being returned to a nature reserve in Mongolia. Each context has a distinctive background color, and the transitions from one context to another are explicitly marked by text screens congratulating the student on his or her work and introducing the next section of the adventure.

Although we found that the addition of narrative to the tutor was very effective, one challenge presented by this strategy is how to move all student users through the story even though they may be working on different areas of mathematics. That is, a student who is still struggling with multiplication should ideally reach the final segment of a story in roughly the same amount of class time as a classmate who has moved on to fractions. Or, as we say in our project, "everyone has to get on the boat," referring to the Right Whale narrative which culminates in the student going on a virtual whale watching trip. Our reasoning was that it would not be helpful to students' confidence and motivation to be stuck in the first context while a student in the adjacent seat had completed the narrative. This was of particular concern because we had observed that students did frequently lean over to the next computer to see what classmates were working on.

In order to adapt the narrative to students working on different math topics, we made the problem set space deep as well as wide. That is, word problems were required not only for all the math topics in our target domain (addition through mixed numbers), but each topic had to have four to six word problems for every section of the story. The goal was to ensure that a student with low skills who had reached the end of the story could still be solving addition problems if necessary, even if other students have progressed to fractions in the same amount of time. Sometimes, it was a challenge to find real-world content that would support this problem set depth; to put it bluntly, there are only so many interesting math problems about whales. One strategy was to include problems about related topics such as history (e.g., some Takhi Wild Horses were captured by the Nazis at the start of the Second World War), geography and culture (e.g., nomads of Mongolia), and other species (e.g., how the loss of the Mongolian steppes has also affected the Snow Leopard) in order to broaden the scope of our problem set.

A second strategy was to use problem templates that could be filled in "on the fly" with specific numbers, rather than relying on a fixed set of canned problems. AnimalWatch uses hundreds of problem templates, each with a range of possible numerical values that are realistic given the problem content. When a problem of a specific level of difficulty is needed for a particular student, the system searches a candidate space of problem templates (e.g., the set of two-digit multiplication problems available for that particular part of the story), selects one, and fills it with specific numerical values that are appropriate for the student's current level of mastery. Creating novel problems as needed increases the flexibility of the system and helps to ensure that there are enough problems available at different levels of difficulty.

Adaptive Teaching Strategies and Mechanisms

The theoretical framework guiding the AnimalWatch project implies that teaching methods should encourage students to believe that they can learn difficult academic subjects, given sufficient effort (Eccles et al., 1993). AnimalWatch addresses this issue by presenting mathematics problems that are targeted to the edge of each student's expertise, while also providing substantial help and problem-solving support as needed to ensure success. The ability of the computer to assess and adapt its instruction on a minute by minute basis is a major advantage compared to traditional classroom instruction with one teacher working with groups of students. Studies in other domains suggest that the personalized instruction provided by an intelligent tutor can dramatically accelerate adult student learning, because the student works on areas at the edge of his or her understanding, whereas traditional instruction moves either too quickly or too slowly (Anderson, 1990; Lesgold, Lajoie, Bunzo, & Eggan, 1990; Shute & Regian, 1990; Woolf, Hart, Day, Botch, & Vining, 2000).

The selection of appropriate math problems in AnimalWatch is determined by its student model function: an artificial intelligence module that "knows" the mathematics domain and creates an estimate of what the student understands of the domain (Beck, Stern, & Woolf, 1997). This estimate is continually updated as the student works, relying on errors made during problem solving and latency to enter a response via the keyboard. If a student makes many errors on a particular problem, AnimalWatch will prompt the student to try harder. It will also present another problem of about the same or less difficulty, both to check that the student actually has the prerequisite knowledge and to boost confidence. If a student solves a couple of similar problems quickly and without errors, AnimalWatch estimates that the student is ready to move on to problems involving a new mathematics operation or a new level of difficulty.

The ability to adapt instruction depends heavily on a good estimate of the student's comprehension. Yet determining what a student actually understands is technically quite difficult. Whereas a human teacher would be able to consider behavioral observations such as expressions of puzzlement and direct questions from the student, the computer tutor only has access to fairly crude indirect measures such as the latency of response, and the number and type of errors. These data are noisy because there are considerable individual differences in how quickly and accurately students work. For example, some students navigate the keyboard more expertly than others. Also, a small computational mistake at the beginning of the problem-solving process can drastically impact the time required to solve a problem, but this does not necessarily imply that the student is seriously confused about the mathematical concept. Thus, AnimalWatch must continually evaluate its predictions about the student's behavior on a particular problem against what the student actually does and adjust its estimates accordingly.

Adaptive Help

AnimalWatch provides help when students make errors, selecting from a battery of hint types. Hints include simple text messages, dynamic graphic demonstrations of procedures such as digit carrying, and highly structured and interactive hints that walk the student through a complex procedure such as finding the least common multiple for unlike fractions. The choice of which hint to present for a particular student on a particular problem is guided by the student modeling function. When a student makes a problem-solving error, AnimalWatch will usually respond first with a simple text hint, such as "Try again!" or "Are you sure you are adding problem quantity 1 and problem quantity 2?" This encourages the student to try to figure out what went wrong in the problem-solving process. In fact, about half the time, students can identify and correct their own errors after one message hint, encouraging them to believe that they can achieve the answer through their own efforts.

When the student makes a second error, increasingly specific help is offered until the student gets the answer, even to the point of presenting the answer in the hint area of the screen and requiring the student to reenter it in the problem-solution area. The more extensive hints used in AnimalWatch range from fairly concrete, highly structured, and interactive (meaning that the student is required to make many small steps) to more abstract, procedural hints. For example, a student who has made errors on an addition problem might see a concrete hint screen in which the two quantities are displayed in the form of screen objects (e.g., blocks that can be dragged and dropped together into groups of 10 that in turn become rod units). Dragging and dropping the screen objects parallels the grouping of concrete manipulatives in the classroom, and helps the student to observe directly the physical regrouping that is represented by numerical digit trading (carrying and borrowing).

In another case, the student who is struggling with a multidigit subtraction problem may receive a procedural hint in which the trading algorithm is displayed step by step. Generally speaking, AnimalWatch has a bias to first draw on concrete hints to help the student, and gradually shift to more abstract, procedural help as a topic (e.g., multidigit addition) is mastered. However, this is somewhat constrained by the particular topic and the level of problem difficulty. For example, if the student is working on a four-digit addition problem, requiring the student to drag and group, thousands of blocks would be impractical given limits on time and screen size, and so the abstract-procedural hints must be used instead.

FORMATIVE RESEARCH WITH ANIMALWATCH

Much of our research with AnimalWatch has focused on how the tutor can adapt its instruction to students on the basis of gender and cognitive developmental stage (Arroyo, Beck, Schultz, & Woolf, 1999; Arroyo, Beck, Woolf, Beal, & Schultz, 2000). With regard to gender, other researchers have reported that female students tend to rely on more concrete and complete strategies, such as counting on fingers, or setting up equations and working out full solutions step by step (Carr & Davis, 2001; Fennema, Carpenter, Jacobs, Franke, & Levi, 1998; Zambo & Follman, 1994). These approaches tend to be accurate but are often slower than guessing and estimating, retrieving answers from memory, or reasoning on the basis of past examples of similar problems, all strategies that are more commonly observed among male students (Mills, Ablard, & Stumpf, 1993; Royer, Tronsky, Chan, Jackson, & Merchant, 1999). Therefore, what constitutes effective instruction in math may be somewhat different for girls and boys. For example, hints requiring the student to perform multiple problem-solving steps without guidance may be less effective for girls than the more concrete, structured hints that involve manipulating screen objects.

Another potential predictor of response to hints of different types is the student's level of cognitive development (Arroyo et al., 1999). This is particularly important at the transition to adolescence. In a class of 11- to 12-year-olds, some students may still be at the concrete operational stage, reasoning about problems on the basis of direct observation, whereas others may have moved into early formal operations and be capable of more abstract, hypothetical reasoning. The variation in the cognitive developmental level can present a challenge to teachers in terms of selecting the right form of instruction in math. Students who are still reasoning with concrete examples may benefit more from screen manipulatives, whereas their formal operational classmates may find dragging and grouping virtual blocks to be tedious and less helpful than a dynamic screen demonstration of a trading procedure.

Matching AnimalWatch Help Features to Student Characteristics

To investigate the impact of different hints as a function of gender and cognitive developmental level, we analyzed detailed student problem-solving data that are automatically collected by the computer as students work. The primary data include time required to solve problems, the number of errors made, and the student's response to hints, meaning the probability that a hint on one problem was followed by problem-solving success on a subsequent problem of similar difficulty. In one study, 64 fifth-grade students worked with AnimalWatch for three sessions over the course of one week (Arroyo et al., 2000). AnimalWatch was configured with a strong hint-selection bias either toward hints that were highly structured and concrete, or hints that were more abstract and procedural in nature. Hints also varied in the degree of interactivity required from the student. Hints that are highly interactive are also highly structured and walk the student through the solution process in incremental steps. We hypothesized that highly structured hints would be more helpful to girls than to boys.

Hint effectiveness was assessed by comparing the number of errors made on subsequent problems of the same type, the idea being that if a particular hint is helpful then the student should be able to move on to solve a similar problem with significantly fewer errors. Students' cognitive developmental stage was assessed via a computer-presented battery of Piagetian reasoning problems. At the end of the activity, students completed a survey about their AnimalWatch experience, including questions in which they were asked to rate the helpfulness of the different types of hints that they saw.

As expected, the results indicated that male and female students did have different responses to the hint conditions. Specifically, girls made better progress with hints that were highly structured and interactive, in terms of a lower error rate on subsequent problems. In contrast, boys tended to prefer and make more progress when the hints were less structured. The students' cognitive developmental stage was also important in determining response to hints. Not surprisingly, both boys and girls in concrete operational thought needed more hints to solve the problems than students who had advanced to the stage of formal operations. The concrete operational students also benefited more from more concrete and structured hints, whereas formal operational students performed better with more abstract, procedural hints.

We also investigated students' preferences for different types of help. Students were shown screen shots of the various hints and were asked if they had seen such hints and, if so, to rate how helpful they had been. There was a strong relation for girls between their cognitive developmental stage and their ratings of how helpful the different hints were. Girls who were still at the concrete operational stage rated the more concrete, highly structured hints as being much more helpful than the more abstract feedback, and as noted above, the structured hints did in fact work better for these students. In contrast, girls who were at the formal cognitive stage were more likely to think that the more abstract hints were most helpful. This was particularly true for hints that focused on multiplication and division.

Overall, the results indicated that not only is adaptive feedback especially important for girls, certain specific types of feedback are preferred by girls. This pattern paralleled an earlier study in which the fully adaptive version of AnimalWatch was compared to a no-help version in which all problem-solving errors were greeted with the response, "Try again." In this case, girls' performance faltered considerably in the no-help version, whereas the impact on boys was much less dramatic (Beck, Arroyo, Woolf, & Beal, 1999). In current studies, we are investigating whether information about the student's gender and assessments of his or her cognitive developmental level can be directly integrated into AnimalWatch in order to guide its hint selection.

Using Past Performance as a Guide to Adaptive Teaching

Another way to improve the adaptivity of intelligent tutors such as AnimalWatch is to use data from past users as an additional guide to optimize teaching decisions. That is, the problem-solving performance of hundreds of students who have used AnimalWatch in the past can serve as a database resource for the student model function. When an estimate is made of a student's knowledge and a problem is selected, AnimalWatch can use its "knowledge" of past students with similar estimated knowledge to gauge the likely outcome of the problem-solving process and make adjustments as needed. Thus, as more students use the system, its teaching performance can be continually refined and improved. It, therefore, becomes increasingly likely that the system will be able to find a past user who has a problem-solving profile similar to the current user and to evaluate the probable impact of a teaching decision based on past outcomes.

One constraint on this approach is that, as the number of stored problem-solving records increases, the time and resources required to search the space of problems expands dramatically. Given that Animal-Watch is being used on fairly low-end classroom computers and must reason in real time while the student user is waiting for the next problem, the search must be pruned. Techniques such as rollouts, which involve randomly choosing a path through the search space and then performing an immediate evaluation of its utility, can be used to limit the search space while maintaining the predictive power of the past-performance database (Beck, Woolf, & Beal, 2000).

ADAPTIVE SUPPORT FOR TEACHERS

Computer-based teaching systems will only have wide impact in the classroom if they can be used flexibly and can help teachers achieve their own goals. To support flexible use, AnimalWatch can be configured to adapt the story line to the amount of time available for the student to work.

In our field trials, students have typically worked with AnimalWatch for several sessions, but the length of each session and the number of sessions available have varied considerably for different grades and schools.

To increase flexibility, the duration of each context can be adjusted by specifying the number of minutes or number of problems in each, so that the narrative can adapt to fit the anticipated time available. Also, when students have completed one narrative, they can choose another species and begin another narrative. The system will keep them at their current level of mathematics problem solving. That is, they do not "start over" with simple addition in the new story but rather are presented with problems similar in difficulty to those that they worked on at the end of the previous story.

One long-term goal of the project is to increase teachers' ability to adjust AnimalWatch's teaching without having to become computer programmers. Ideally, teachers could specify a goal and allow the tutor to figure out how to accomplish the goal on its own. As an initial step toward this goal, Beck designed a machine-learning agent that would accept a specific teaching goal and then use stored performance data from hundreds of past users to run simulations that allowed the tutor to train itself to make appropriate teaching decisions. Beck found that the machine-learning version of AnimalWatch could significantly reduce the time needed for students to progress through the mathematics curriculum (Beck et al., 2000). Although not currently practical for a classroom-based tutor due to the intense processing demands, this approach should eventually permit teachers to enter a teaching goal and allow AnimalWatch to evaluate and modify its own performance accordingly.

Another strategy to promote adaptive use by teachers is the availability of authoring tools and support through the AnimalWatch web site. Here, teachers are provided with options and strategies for customizing the program and extending it to meet their specific needs. The web site provides information about the curriculum and options for downloading the program (although the very large number of images currently makes distribution via CD-ROM more practical for most users). A bulletin board allows teachers to share ideas about ways to use the tutor and to discuss what needs to be fixed or improved, and what new features would be worth adding.

Most importantly, teachers can propose new word problems and select images or upload their own graphics to accompany the problems. The web site is designed to make the word-problem authoring tool easy to use, and the overall philosophy is open source, meaning that although researchers provided the initial content, it will be expanded by the community of users (Murray, 1998). An important part of the open source philosophy is that users should evaluate the utility and evolution of AnimalWatch, judging what problems are the best to download, what people are the most reliable creators of word problems, and which adventures are most effective for use with students. To accomplish this goal, rating mechanisms are provided, along with a discussion forum in which teachers can comment on the features of the system and contribute ideas about how to use it effectively in their classrooms.

Because the student modeling component of the tutor is separated from the story content, teachers can create their own endangered species adventure and customize AnimalWatch to fit their curriculum. For example, if a teacher is developing a unit on Borneo, he or she might download the student modeling component to integrate with a new adventure that he or she created about the orangutan, including maps and background information about the country and its people. Although the original focus of AnimalWatch was on mathematics tutoring, the inclusion of real-world content would support interdisciplinary projects in the classroom, including e-mail contact with experts, environmentalists, and students in countries that are home to the endangered species under study.

SUMMARY

Cognitive strengths, motivation, and interests vary dramatically from one student to another, even if they are the same age, and these characteristics affect the success of classroom instruction. The philosophy that instruction should be adapted to individuals, or at least to groups of students with similar characteristics, has long been valued in education (Bloom, 1984; Snow, 1977). Increasingly, computer-based tutoring systems offer a way to accomplish this goal. Computer-based teaching systems have long been able to adjust instruction on the basis of student performance, by adjusting the difficulty of problems, by trying a different type of hint, or returning to an earlier topic to review a critical concept. New approaches in intelligent teaching systems are leading to the development of tutors like Animal-Watch that can consider the learning style and cognitive stage of the student as a guide to teaching decisions, and that can be customized and extended by teachers.

Formative research that is based on a theoretical model of children's learning will play a vital role in the development of software for effective classroom instruction. Research to document clear outcomes will also become increasingly important as computer tutors are integrated into classroom settings. Although it is unlikely that computer-based systems will ever entirely replace human teachers, it does seem probable that such systems will become increasingly important as tools for teachers to use to enhance children's education.

ACKNOWLEDGMENTS

The AnimalWatch project was supported by the National Science Foundation Program in Gender Equity (HRD-9714757). The views, opinions, and recommendations expressed here are those of the authors and do not necessarily reflect the views of the granting agency.

We would like to acknowledge our project colleagues Beverly Woolf, David Hart, Joseph Beck, and Rachel Wing. We would also like to express our deep appreciation to Charlene Galenski, Diana Campbell, and Amy Ryan for their enthusiastic support of our field work, as well as to Douglas Tierney, principal of the Deerfield Elementary School in South Deerfield, Massachusetts, and Dr. Mario Cirillo, principal of the Chestnut Accelerated Middle School in Springfield, Massachusetts.

REFERENCES

Ainsworth, S., Underwood, J., & Grimshaw, S. (2000). Using an ITS authoring tool to explore educators' use of instructional strategies. *Proceedings of the 5th International Conference on Intelligent Tutoring Systems*, Montreal, Canada, June.

Alper, J. (1993). The pipeline is leaking women all the way along. *Science, 260*, 409–441.

Anderson, J. R. (1990). Analysis of student performance with the LISP tutor. In N. Frederiksen, R. Glaser, A. M. Lesgold, & M. Shafto (Eds.), *Diagnostic monitoring of skill and knowledge acquisition*. Hillsdale, NJ: Erlbaum.

Andriessen, J., & Sandberg, J. (1999). Where is education heading and how about AI? *International Journal of Artificial Intelligence in Education, 10*, 130–150.

Arroyo, I., Beck, J. E., Schultz, K., & Woolf, B. P. (1999). Piagetian psychology in intelligent tutoring systems. *Proceedings of the 9th International Conference on Artificial Intelligence in Education* (600–602), Le Mans, France, June.

Arroyo, I., Beck, J. E., Woolf, B. P., Beal, C. R., & Schultz, K. (2000). Micro-adapting AnimalWatch to gender and cognitive differences with respect to hint interactivity and symbolism. *Proceedings of the 5th International Conference on Intelligent Tutoring Systems* (574–583), Montreal, Canada, June.

Arroyo, I., Schapira, A., & Woolf, B. P. (2001). Authoring and sharing word problems with AWE. *Proceedings of the 10th International Conference on Artificial Intelligence in Education* (527–529), San Antonio, TX, May.

Beal, C. R. (1994). *Boys and girls: The development of gender roles*. New York: McGraw-Hill.

Beal, C. R., Beck, J. E., & Woolf, B. P. (1998). *Impact of intelligent computer instruction on girls' math self concept and beliefs in the value of math*. Poster presented at the annual meeting of the American Educational Research Association, San Diego, April.

Beck, J. E., Arroyo, I., Woolf, B. P., & Beal, C. R. (1999). An ablative evaluation. *Proceedings of the 9th International Conference on Artificial Intelligence in Education* (611–613), Le Mans, France, June.

Beck, J. E., & Stern, M. (1999). Bringing back the AI to AI & Ed. *Proceedings of the 9th International Conference on Artificial Intelligence in Education* (233–240), Le Mans, France, June.

Beck, J. E., Stern, M., & Woolf, B. P. (1997). Using the student model to control problem difficulty. *Proceedings of the 6th International Conference on User Modeling* (277–288), Chiahaguna, Italy, June.

Beck, J. E., Woolf, B. P., & Beal, C. R. (2000). ADVISOR: A machine learning architecture for intelligent tutor construction. *Proceedings of the 17th National Conference on Artificial Intelligence*, Austin, TX, July.

Beller, M., & Gafni, N. (1996). The 1991 International Assessment of Educational Progress in mathematics and sciences. *Journal of Educational Psychology, 88* (2), 365–376.

Bloom, B. (1984). The 2 sigma problem: The search for methods of group instruction as effective as one-on-one tutoring. *Educational Researcher, 13*, 3–16.

Bruer, J. T. (1997). *Schools for thought.* Cambridge, MA: MIT Press.

Burton, R. (1982). Diagnosing bugs in a simple procedural skill. In D. Sleeman & J. S. Brown (Eds.), *Intelligent tutoring systems* (pp. 157–182). New York: Academic Press.

Camp, T. (1997). The incredible shrinking pipeline. *Communications of the ACM, 40*, 103–110.

Campbell, P. B. (1992). *Encouraging girls in math and science: Working together, making changes.* Report from the Office of Educational Research and Improvement, U.S. Department of Education.

Carr, M., & Davis, H. (2001). Gender differences in strategy use: A function of skill and preference. *Contemporary Educational Psychology, 26*, 330–347.

Cordova, D. I., & Lepper, M. R. (1996). Intrinsic motivation and the process of learning: Beneficial effects of contextualization, personalization, and choice. *Journal of Educational Psychology, 88*, 715–730.

Delamont, S. (1990). *Sex roles and the school* (2nd ed.). London: Routledge.

Eccles, J. S., & Jacobs, J. E. (1986). Social forces shape math attitudes and performance. *Signs, 11*, 367–380.

Eccles, J. S., Wigfield, A., Harold, R. D., & Blumenfeld, P. (1993). Age and gender differences in children's self and task perceptions during elementary school. *Child Development, 64*, 830–847.

Fennema, E., Carpenter, T. P., Jacobs, V. R., Franke, M. L., & Levi, L. W. (1998). A longitudinal study of gender differences in young children's mathematical thinking. *Educational Researcher, 27* (June–July), 6–11.

Fletcher-Flynn, C. M., & Gravatt, B. (1995). The efficiency of computer assisted instruction (CAI): A meta analysis. *Journal of Educational Computing Research, 12*, 219–241.

Frenkel, K. A. (1990). Women and computing. *Communications of the ACM* (November), 34–46.

Gertner, A. S., Conati, C., & Van Lehn, K. (1998). Procedural help in ANDES: Generating hints using a Baysian network student model. *Proceedings of the 15th National Conference on Artificial Intelligence* (106–111), Madison, WI, July.

Jennings, N. (2001). *Children's use of technology in multiple settings.* Paper presented at the biennial meeting of the Society for Research in Child Development, Minneapolis, April.

Koedinger, K. R., Anderson, J. R., Hadley, W. H., & Mark, M. A. (1997). Intelligent tutoring goes to school in the big city. *International Journal of Artificial Intelligence in Education, 8*, 30–43.

Lawry, J., Upitis, R., Klawe, M., Anderson, A., Inkpen, K., Ndunda, M., Hsu, D., Leroux, S., & Sedighian, K. (1994). *Exploring common conceptions about boys and electronic games.* Unpublished report; Departments of Computer Science & Education, University of British Columbia, April.

Lesgold, A., Lajoie, S., Bunzo, M., & Eggan, G. (1990). A coached practice environment for an electronics troubleshooting job. In J. Larkin, R. Chabay, & C. Sheftic (Eds.), *Computer assisted instruction and intelligent tutoring systems: Establishing communication and collaboration.* Hillsdale, NJ: Erlbaum.

Major, N., Ainsworth, S., & Wood, D. (1997). Exploring symbiosis between psychology and authoring environments. *International Journal of Artificial Intelligence in Education, 8,* 317–340.

Mills, C. J., Ablard, K. E., & Stumpf, H. (1993). Gender differences in academically talented young students' mathematical reasoning: Patterns across age and subskills. *Journal of Educational Psychology, 85,* 340–346.

Murray, T. (1998). Authoring knowledge based tutors: Tools for content, instructional strategy, student model, and interface design. *Journal of the Learning Sciences, 7,* 5–64.

Paliouras, G., Karkaletsis, V., Papatheodorou, C., & Spyropoulous, C. (1999). Exploiting learning techniques for the acquisition of user stereotypes and communities. *Proceedings of the 7th International Conference on User Modeling* (169–178), Banff, Canada, June.

Raloff, J. (1991). Science: Recruiting nontraditional players. *Science News, 140,* 396–397.

Ritter, S., Anderson, J., Cytrynowicz, M., & Medvedeva, O. (1998). Authoring content in the PAL algebra tutor. *Journal of Interactive Media in Education, 98,* 3.

Royer, J. M., Tronsky, L. N., Chan, Y., Jackson, S. J., & Merchant, H. (1999). Math fact retrieval as the cognitive mechanism underlying gender differences in math test performance. *Contemporary Educational Psychology, 24,* 181–266.

Schofield, J. W., Eurich-Fulcer, R., & Britt, C. L. (1994). Teachers, computer tutors, and teaching: The artificially intelligent tutor as an agent for classroom change. *American Educational Research Journal, 31,* 579–607.

Shute, V. (1995). Smart evaluation: Cognitive diagnosis, mastery learning, and remediation. *Proceedings of Artificial Intelligence in Education, 5,* 123–130.

Shute, V., & Regian, J. W. (1990). *Rose garden promises of intelligent tutoring systems: Blossoms or thorns?* Paper presented at the Space Operations, Automation and Robotics Conference, Albuquerque, NM, June.

Sigalit, U., & Van Lehn, K. (1995). Steps: A simulated, tutorable physics student. *Artificial Intelligence in Education, 6,* 405–437.

Snow, R. E. (1977). Individual differences and instructional theory. *Educational Researcher, 6,* 11–15.

Spender, D. (1984). Sexism in teacher education. In S. Acker & D. W. Piper (Eds.), *Is higher education unfair to women?* (pp. 132–143). Surrey, UK: University of Guildford Press.

Stevenson, H. W., & Lee, S. (1990). Contexts of achievement: A study of American, Chinese, and Japanese children. *Monographs of the Society for Research in Child Development, 55* (1–2, Serial No. 221).

Willingham, W. W., & Cole, N. S. (1997). *Gender and fair assessment.* Mahwah, NJ: Erlbaum.

Woolf, B. P., Hart, D., Day, R., Botch, B., & Vining, W. (2000). Improving instruction and reducing costs with a web-based homework system. *Proceedings of the International Conference on Math/Science Education and Technology*, San Diego, CA, March.

Zambo, R., & Follman, J. (1994). Gender-related differences in problem solving at the 6th and 8th grade levels. *Focus on Learning Problems in Mathematics, 16*, 20–38.

Part IV

Family and Consumer Media Models

Chapter 11

The Development of a Child into a Consumer

Patti M. Valkenburg and Joanne Cantor

Over the past two decades, marketers and advertisers of children's products have developed a massive and diverse spectrum of strategies to reach the child consumer (Kline, 1993). They are interested in children for three reasons. First, today's children in western societies have considerable amounts of money to spend on needs and wants of their own, which qualify them as an important *primary* market (McNeal, 1992). Second, children are also a future market (McNeal, 1992). It has been demonstrated that children develop brand loyalty at an early age, and that favorable attitudes toward brands last well into adulthood (e.g., Moschis & Moore, 1981). Finally, children are an important market of *influencers*. Not only do they give direction to daily household purchases, such as snacks, sweets, and breakfast products; as they get older they also have a say in their parents' choice of the restaurant, the holiday destination, and the new car (Gunter & Furnham, 1998; McNeal, 1992).

The increased economic power and influence on family decisions of today's children can be explained by several socioeconomic changes in the 1970s and 1980s. Parents have a larger income and a higher educational level; they often postpone having children and have fewer of them; and there are more single-parent families and dual-working-parent families (Gunter & Furnham, 1998). Together, these factors encourage parents to be more indulgent and to take care that their children do not lack anything (McNeal, 1992).

Another factor that explains the increase in children's influence on family decisions is the liberalization of parent-child relationships in western societies. A few decades ago, child-rearing patterns were characterized by authority, obedience, and respect (Torrance, 1998). In today's families, however, understanding, equality, and compromise are considered to be of paramount importance. The parent-child relationship is no longer regulated by authority and command, but rather by negotiation (Torrance, 1998). In modern western families, children's opinions and participation in decision-making processes are encouraged and taken very seriously. As a result, children have never been as emancipated, articulate, and market-mature as they currently are (Gunter & Furnham, 1998).

Children's consumer behavior has often been studied within the paradigm of consumer socialization, which was developed almost three decades ago (Ward, 1974). Consumer socialization is seen as a rather effortless process by which children learn the skills, knowledge, and attitudes necessary to function as consumers (Ward, 1974). Although there is no single definition of consumer behavior, those that have been employed seem to entail similar characteristics. A consumer is able to (1) feel wants and preferences, (2) search to fulfill them, (3) make a choice and a purchase, and (4) evaluate the product and its alternatives (Mowen & Minor, 1998).

The aim of this chapter is to discuss the phases during which the different characteristics of consumer behavior develop in children, and why they occur at particular ages. To this end, we draw together a number of theories and ideas currently in the literature that may increase our understanding of the development of children's consumer behavior. Our discussion relies on existing cognitive developmental theories (e.g., Flavell, Miller, & Miller, 1993), as well as developmental theories of parent-child interaction (e.g., Kuczynski & Kochanska, 1990), marketing models (e.g., Acuff, 1997; McNeal, 1992), and theories of children's likes and dislikes of toys and entertainment (Valkenburg & Cantor, 2000).

A basic assumption of our discussion is that children of all ages strive to understand their physical and social environment. Moreover, their level of understanding determines to a large extent their tastes and preferences for products, information, and entertainment, and, as a result, their consumer behavior. In addition, we assume that children of different developmental levels vary in their attention and susceptibility to different environmental forces (e.g., commercial media, peer pressure) that influence their consumer behavior and values. We argue that the development of consumer behavior occurs in four phases and that in each phase, one of the above-mentioned characteristics of consumer behavior emerges.

INFANTS AND TODDLERS (BIRTH TO AGE 2): FEELING WANTS AND PREFERENCES

Although little is known about how children's wants and tastes are formed during childhood, it has been shown that even toddlers firmly express their preferences regarding what to eat, wear, watch, or play with

(Bartsch & Wellman, 1995). Some of these wants and tastes seem to be innate; others are formed during childhood.

Researchers agree that babies come into the world with some very definitive preferences for tastes and smells. Newborns seem to come equipped with a preference for sweet substances, whereas sour, salty, or bitter liquids elicit expressions of disgust (Blass & Ciaramitaro, 1994). Infants have also been shown to dislike the same smells that adults consider disagreeable. When they detect an unpleasant smell such as vinegar, they turn their head away or turn up their nose (Rieser, Yonas, & Wilkner, 1976).

Children are also born with an innate tendency to respond to language. The "favorite auditory diet" of a baby is the human voice (Flavell, Miller, & Miller, 1993, p. 276). Babies are especially attentive to a form of speech that is referred to as "motherese," which is characterized by a slower pace, a higher pitch and greatly exaggerated intonations (Flavell et al., 1993; Siegler, 1991). It has been shown that infants as young as four months clearly prefer tape-recorded speech in motherese to speech in standard intonations (Fernald, 1985). This preference lasts for several years. The use of motherese may increase the chance of success of audio and audiovisual stories and programs for this age group (Valkenburg & Cantor, 2000).

Babies also seem to enjoy listening to music, and they prefer rhythmic to non-rhythmic sounds (Siegler, 1991). By the age of 4 to 6 months they start to turn their head in the direction of the source of music, and they have been observed to listen to music with an "unmistakable expression of astonishment and joy" (Moog, 1976, p. 39). Because young children are so responsive to songs, rhymes, and music, these devices are often used to elicit interest in educational and entertainment programs for young children (Wakshlag, Reitz, & Zillmann, 1982) though the song lyrics may not be well understood, even at older ages (Calvert & Billingsley, 1998).

Although babies are quite responsive to music and speech, their visual perception matures more slowly. However, babies do have distinct preferences for certain types of images. They like to watch moving objects with primary colors and sharp contrasts (Acuff, 1997; Jaglom & Gardner, 1981). It is no coincidence, therefore, that toys and entertainment programs for infants and toddlers are often produced in such colors.

When children are 4 to 5 months of age, they start to develop an interest in television programs. Observational studies have shown that they are mostly interested in children's programs such as *Sesame Street* and *The Teletubbies* that have brightly colored fantasy figures, and in commercials (Lemish, 1987; Valkenburg, 1999). Both children's programs and commercials specialize in drawing attention by visual and auditory means, and babies are very sensitive to these kinds of stimuli (Lemish, 1987; Siegler, 1991).

By 8 months of age, most children are able to sit erect without support. At this time, they typically begin to be allowed to sit in the child-seat of the shopping cart, from which they observe and admire the brightly colored products, which are often deliberately positioned at the eye-level of children (McNeal, 1992). After a few months of observing, children start to be able to take products from the supermarket shelves, and between 18 and 24 months of age they start to ask their parents to buy products (McNeal, 1992).

When children are 18 months of age they increasingly recognize familiar objects and faces (Siegler, 1991). By the age of 2, children also start to make connections between television advertising and products in the store when they accompany their parents (Valkenburg, 1999). A recent survey of 360 Dutch parents showed that 40% of the parents of 2-year-olds said their child had recognized an advertised product in the store. This percentage increased rapidly over the succeeding few years. Sixty percent of the 3-year-olds, 84% of the 4-year-olds, and 88% of the 5-year-olds were reported to have recognized an advertised product in the store (Valkenburg, 1999).

Although children up to 18 months of age have been shown to have distinct preferences for smells, colors, sounds, objects, and images, their behavior is still primarily reactive and not very intentional. Although children experience their own wants and preferences, which is an important characteristic of consumer behavior, they cannot yet be considered as true, goal-directed consumers. They are still primarily *children* of consumers. However, this status changes rapidly as they enter the next phase in their development as consumers.

Preschoolers (Age 2 to 5): Nagging and Negotiating

There are several characteristics of the preschooler's mind that determine children's tastes and preferences for products and entertainment and, as a result, their consumer behavior. One of these characteristics is their limited ability to distinguish fantasy from reality. Preschool children often believe that the characters and events that they encounter in the media are real. Two- and 3-year-olds often think that television characters reside inside the TV set (Noble, 1975). Jaglom and Gardner (1981), for instance, observed that some 2- to 3-year-olds ran to get a paper towel to clean up an egg they saw break on television. By the time they are 3 years old, children start to make statements indicating attachment to television personalities (Jaglom & Gardner, 1981). However, because children between the ages of 2 and 5 often do not adequately distinguish between fantasy and reality, they can just as easily focus their attraction on an animal or a fantasy protagonist as on a real-life character.

Preschool-aged children also think the information in commercials is true. They often do not understand the persuasive intent of commercials, and they have trouble distinguishing commercials from television programs (see Buijzen & Valkenburg, in press, for a review). It is not surprising, therefore, that advertising and marketing efforts have been reported to have the highest impact on children below the age of 8 (Acuff, 1997; Buijzen & Valkenburg, 2000).

Because of their immature cognitive capacity, preschool-aged children need more time than adults to interpret and make sense of information and television images. This is the reason why preschoolers often respond best to programs with a slow pace and with lots of repetition (Acuff, 1997)— for example, *Barney and Friends* and *Mr. Rogers' Neighborhood*. For the same reason, preschoolers often prefer familiar contexts and visuals (Lemish, 1987), and objects and animals that they can verbally label, such as a cat, a dog, or a horse. They like to watch programs that show babies and young children (Lemish, 1987), and they especially like nonthreatening real or animated animals, such as kind birds, friendly dinosaurs, and babyish creatures like the Teletubbies (Acuff, 1997; Cupitt, Jenkinson, Ungerer, & Waters, 1998). It must be noted, however, that by the age of 4, children, and particularly boys, often start to prefer more rapid and adventurous entertainment programs and products (Acuff, 1997).

Another characteristic of preschool children that may influence their consumer behavior is *centration*, the tendency to center attention on an individual, striking feature of an object or image, to the exclusion of other, less striking features (Flavell et al., 1993). A qualitative study reported in Acuff (1997) is illustrative of this tendency in young children. In this study, 5-year-old girls were presented with three dolls. Two of the dolls were very expensive, had beautiful and realistic faces, and came with sophisticated mechanical effects. The third doll was cheaply made but had a big, red-sequined heart on her dress. To the surprise of the researchers, the majority of the girls preferred the cheap doll with the sequined heart. This consumer behavior is typical of preschoolers. When judging a product, they focus their attention on one striking characteristic. Preschool children, therefore, have little eye for detail and quality, which is an important characteristic of a mature consumer.

A final characteristic of children in the preschool age group that has implications for their consumer behavior is that they cannot keep their minds off tempting products for long (Metcalfe & Mischel, 1999). Research has shown that although an adult can teach young children how to use certain distractive strategies when presented with a tempting stimulus (Mischel & Patterson, 1976), children under the age of 5 usually do not use such strategies to delay gratification. When they see an attractive toy or snack, they center their attention on the desirable aspects of this stimulus and have great difficulty resisting it (Mischel & Ebbeson, 1970). This tendency in young children can result in embarrassing situations for parents in the supermarket or toy store, as children start to whine, scream, and cry when their parents refuse to buy something they want. The survey by Val-

Figure 11.1
Percentage of Parents Experiencing a Purchase-Related Conflict with Their Child
in a Store

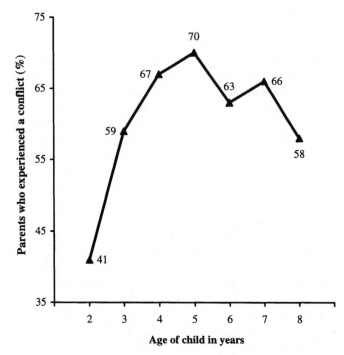

Source: Adapted from Valkenburg, 1999.

kenburg (1999), cited above, asked parents about such conflicts. This survey showed that 41% of the parents of 2-year-olds said they had experienced a conflict with their child during a store visit (see Figure 11.1). This percentage increased rapidly in the age range of 2 to 5 years: 59% of the parents of 3-year-olds, and 70% of the parents of 5-year-olds had experienced such a conflict with their child (see Figure 11.1).

As Figure 11.1 shows, the parent-child conflicts began to decrease again between the ages of 5 and 6. This decline could be due to the fact that at around this age, children become increasingly able to use control strategies (e.g., covering their eyes, inventing a game) to resist temptation (Metcalfe & Mischel, 1999). However, the decrease in parent-child conflicts might also result from children's growing ability to negotiate. By the age of 5, and particularly in homes where negotiation plays an important role in family communication, children possess a sophisticated range of negotiation strategies (Kuczynski & Kochanska, 1990; Kuczynski, Kochanska, Radke-Yarrow, & Girnius-Brown, 1987; McNeal, 1992). Some researchers assume that the development of negotiation strategies in children has its origin in the "terrible twos," when children start to exhibit explicit un-cooperative and noncompliant behavior. This type of overt noncompliance in children is often only temporary, because children soon start to under-stand that these forms of resistance are less effective than the strategy of negotiation. Although direct defiance, whining, and tantrums are still rel-atively common among 3-year-olds (Kuczynki & Kochanska, 1990), chil-dren of this age are already able to provide explanations and excuses, and to offer alternatives or compromises for not carrying out their parents' wishes (Kuczynski & Kochanska, 1990). Soon, they also start to employ such strategies to persuade their parents to respond to their wants and wishes (McNeal, 1992). This might explain why parent-child conflicts in the store decrease when children enter the next phase in their development as consumers.

EARLY ELEMENTARY SCHOOL (AGE 5 TO 8): ADVENTURE AND THE FIRST PURCHASE

Many of the characteristics of preschoolers also hold for early elementary school children. Most children in this age range still exhibit the character-istic of centration, although this tendency is on the decline (Flavell et al., 1993). Children's ability to distinguish fantasy and reality is also in tran-sition. Almost all children by this stage know that Big Bird is a person dressed in a costume (Howard, 1998), and they also judge marked viola-tions of physical reality, such as animation and special effects, as unreal (Dorr, 1983). However, they still consider something that looks real on television as real even if it is not (Wright, Huston, Reitz, & Piemyat, 1994). For example, they think that actors on television have those televised pro-fessions in real life, and they think that the families in television situation comedies are real families (Howard, 1998).

There are a number of changes in early elementary school children, how-ever, that justify segmenting them as a separate age group. First, the atten-tion span of children in this age group becomes considerably larger. Three-year-olds are able to concentrate on a single task for an average of only 18 minutes, and they are easily distracted during this time (Ruff & Lawson, 1990). Five- to 6-year olds, in contrast, are often able to work on a task or game for more than an hour (Ruff & Lawson, 1990).

The development of imaginative play reaches its peak between the ages of 5 and 8 (Fein, 1981). By the age of 3 or 4 years, children's fantasy play becomes more social. Children increasingly play with other children their age. In addition, their fantasy play develops from loose fragments into com-plex plots. Between 5 and 7 years of age, children can enjoy the most elaborated forms of social imaginative play (Valkenburg & Hellendoorn, 1992). They also develop a preference for more adventurous themes in their imaginative play and entertainment programs, such as those with locations in foreign countries or in outer space (Valkenburg & Hellendoorn, 1992).

During the early elementary school years, children also develop a preference for more fast-paced entertainment. They often find slower-paced programs with friendly characters and familiar contexts boring or childish (Acuff, 1997; Sheldon & Loncar, 1996). Because they are able to make sense of far more information, they show persistence with content that is more difficult to understand (Anderson & Burns, 1991). They also become more responsive to verbally oriented information and entertainment, more complicated characters, and more sophisticated forms of humor (Jaglom & Gardner, 1981).

Children around age 5 increasingly make independent purchases. The first independent purchase is usually performed in a supermarket or department store together with the parent (McNeal, 1992). Valkenburg's (1999) survey reported that 54% of 4-year-olds and 74% of 5-year-olds had already made a purchase in the presence of a parent. Children between the ages of 5 and 7 also start to make purchases and independent store visits *without* their parents. The first independent store visit is usually a convenience store or a retail outlet close to home (McNeal, 1992). According to Valkenburg (1999), 21% of 5-year-olds, 35% of 7-year-olds and 48% of 8-year-olds had already made an independent purchase without a parent present.

LATER ELEMENTARY SCHOOL (AGE 8 TO 12): CONFORMITY AND FASTIDIOUSNESS

In the period of ages 8 to 12, the opinions of peers play an increasingly important role. This is also the period in which children's eye for detail and quality develops, and thereby their ability to critically evaluate and compare products and information. In contrast to preschoolers and early elementary school children, 8- to 12-year-old children have fantasies that more often entail realistic and plausible themes. In this period, children develop a sincere interest in real-world phenomena (Mielke, 1983), and they can be highly critical of entertainment and commercials that lack realism (Acuff, 1997; Gunter, McAleer, & Clifford, 1991). They continue to like animals, but they are mainly interested in real-life animals (Mielke, 1983). Because most fantasy characters have been demystified (Fernie, 1981), children in this age group tend to become attached to real-life heroes, such as sports heroes, movie stars, and realistic action heroes (Acuff, 1997).

With the developing ability to decenter, children come to appreciate details. As discussed earlier, children in previous age groups may focus on one striking detail of a toy or a character. For the 8- to 12-year-old child, many characteristics of a toy may be carefully observed, from the face and body to details of the doll's clothing to how it moves (Acuff, 1997). At this age, children become progressively critical of entertainment of low quality, such as those that are poorly produced or repetitious (Gunter, McAleer, & Clifford, 1991). They are no longer content with simple, salient characteristics, such as a colorful cartoon character. Unlike younger children, who are greatly impressed by special effects and characters with special powers, older children seem to agree that special effects by themselves are not enough (Gunter et al., 1991).

Their emergent eye for detail and quality also explains why some children in this age group develop a preference for collecting objects, such as dolls, or cards of their heroes. Whereas younger children may also show a tendency toward collecting, their "collecting" is usually more a matter of "accumulating" (Acuff, 1997, p. 72). Many younger children simply like to gather lots of toys around them. By the age of 7 or 8, however, children start to collect with the aim of making distinctions between the different objects (Acuff, 1997), and also with an eye toward the opportunity for social interaction that collecting may offer.

Another characteristic of children in the later elementary school years is that their ability to recognize and interpret others' emotions improves rapidly. By age 4 or 5, children can provide explanations for why their playmates are happy, angry, or sad, although they tend to rely primarily on visible cues, such as facial expressions (Flavell et al., 1993). As children rely more and more on both internal and external cues to interpret emotions, they improve greatly in their understanding of emotions. For example, they eventually recognize that more than one emotion can be experienced at the same time and that an emotion can be feigned (Flavell et al., 1993). By this age, therefore, children start to recognize, criticize, and dislike poor acting by protagonists in entertainment programs and commercials (Sheldon & Loncar, 1996).

Peer interactions become increasingly sophisticated among older elementary school children (Durkin, 1997). Because children in this age group develop such a strong sense of commitment and loyalty to the norms of their peer group, they are increasingly sensitive to the thoughts, opinions, judgments, and evaluations of other children, and become very sensitive to what's "cool" and what's "in." They, therefore, become alert to how to behave in public and how to avoid being ridiculed with respect to what they wear and even what they prefer to watch on television. For example, older children feel the need to firmly demonstrate their aversion to programs designed for younger children or for shows that feature characters younger than they are (Mielke, 1983).

By the time children are 9 to 10 years old, they start to lose interest in toys and develop a preference for products with a social function, such as music and sports equipment (Buijzen & Valkenburg, in press). At this time, they are also primarily interested in products and entertainment designed for adults (Buijzen & Valkenburg, 2000; Rosengren & Windahl, 1989).

Children's requests for advertised products decrease by 9 or 10 as well (Buijzen & Valkenburg, 2000). Not only do children become more critical about media offerings, their sensitivity to peer influences is at its peak in this period (Costanzo & Shaw, 1966). It is possible that the norms and values that are created in particular peer groups function as a filter for other consumer socializing forces, including advertising.

Because of their increased loyalty to brand names and their increased negotiation strategies, children's influence on household purchases further increases in this period. According to McNeal (1992), by the age of 9 or 10, nearly all children are visiting different types of stores and making purchases on their own several times a week.

Although children's consumer behavior continues to develop during adolescence and adulthood, by age 12 children have become acquainted with all aspects of their consumer behavior, at least in a rudimentary form. Typically, they are able to (1) feel wants and preferences (as early as infancy and toddlerhood); (2) search to fulfill them (as early as the preschool period); (3) make a choice and a purchase (from the early elementary school period on); and (4) evaluate a product and its alternatives (as early as the later elementary school period).

SUGGESTIONS FOR FUTURE RESEARCH

Most research on children's consumer behavior has been conducted by marketing researchers (Kline, 1993). Although these researchers have gathered a wealth of knowledge about children's consumer behavior, their methods and findings are, for economic reasons, often not accessible to the academic world. In academic circles, there has been little systematic research on the different determinants of children's consumer behavior. Many academic studies have been published on the behavioral effects of advertising, but only a few have investigated the development of consumer behavior in a wider context. Moreover, most of the academic studies that have focused on a broader spectrum of determinants of children's consumer behavior were conducted in the 1970s (e.g., Moschis & Churchill, 1978; Moschis & Moore, 1979).

There are several changes in the child's environment, however, that call for a revitalization of research on children's consumer socialization. First, as discussed earlier, the child-rearing and communication styles of today's families have changed significantly from those employed in the early 1970s. Anecdotal observations suggest that children may now be more "sophisticated" in their consumer behavior than were their comparison cohorts from earlier generations (Cram & Ng, 1999), but there is currently no academic evidence to support such claims.

Second, consumer organizations throughout the world have noted increasing commercial pressures on children (e.g., Murray & Westendorp,

1996). Commercial children's programs in the Netherlands, for example, include more than 25 child-targeted television commercials per hour during the Christmas period (Valkenburg, 1999). Many new marketing techniques, such as those using the Internet, kids' clubs, and telemarketing, are increasingly aimed at the child consumer and have the potential to disrupt the privacy of the family (see Chapter 12, this volume).

Because of the wide range of commercial messages meticulously targeted to specific segments of the child audience, children seem to have become less dependent on their parents in learning about consumer values. It is possible that entertainment and advertising aimed at young children shortens the period during which parents are the primary socializing force in the lives of their children. Although today's children and adolescents have the spending power to utilize their consumer skills, they still often lack the maturity to think carefully about buying decisions. Media literacy research is needed to understand how children and adolescents can be taught to make thoughtful consumer decisions as well as how to protect them from commercial pressures to buy quickly and impulsively.

Research on children's consumer behavior has typically been based on one of two types of theoretical models of human learning: cognitive-developmental models and socialization models (Gunter & Furnham, 1998). Studies based on cognitive-developmental models have primarily investigated differences between younger and older children in responses to advertising (e.g., Rubin, 1974; Wartella & Ettema, 1974). Studies conducted within the socialization perspective have attempted to explain children's consumer socialization as a function of environmental influences (e.g., Moschis & Churchill, 1978; Moschis & Moore, 1979).

Socialization studies often seem to have been guided by a simple stimulus-response perspective, where exposure to a socializing agent (e.g., advertising) directly influences children's consumer attitudes. However, a basic assumption in modern theories of media effects is that children are active and motivated explorers of what they encounter in the media (Valkenburg & Cantor, 2000). Another assumption is that any media effect on children is enhanced, channeled, or mitigated by what the child makes of the message (Valkenburg & Janssen, 1999). In order to understand media effects on children, then, it is crucial to gain insight into the different antecedents of children's exposure to different media.

In the consumer socialization literature to date, too few attempts have been undertaken to explore the dynamic elements of child variables in the socialization process. Future research should be derived from more elaborated theoretical models, in which different environmental agents (e.g., media exposure, parent and peer influence, family communication patterns) and child factors (e.g., gender, developmental level, interests and tastes that motivate exposure) operate as interacting determinants of children's developing consumer behavior.

In conclusion, future research on children's consumer socialization should try to integrate the different theoretical perspectives that have been used in previous studies. In addition, there is a need for historical, longitudinal, and cross-national research to investigate and compare the marketing efforts aimed at children in "new" and "old" media, parental attitudes about consumerism, and family communication patterns about consumer values and behavior.

ACKNOWLEDGMENT

Reprinted from *Applied Developmental Psychology*, Vol. 22 (1), P. Valkenburg & J. Cantor, The development of a child into a consumer, pp. 61–72, © 2001, with permission from Elsevier Science.

REFERENCES

Acuff, D. S. (1997). *What kids buy and why: The psychology of marketing to kids.* New York: The Free Press.

Anderson, D. R., & Burns, J. (1991). Paying attention to television. In J. Bryant & D. Zillmann (Eds.), *Responding to the screen: Reception and reaction processes* (pp. 3–25). Hillsdale, NJ: Erlbaum.

Bartsch, K., & Wellman, H. M. (1995). *Children talk about the mind.* New York: Oxford University Press.

Blass, E. M., & Ciaramitaro, V. (1994). A new look at some old mechanisms in human newborns: Taste and tactile determinants of state, affect, and action. *Monographs of the Society for Research in Child Development, 59* (1, serial no. 239).

Buijzen, M., & Valkenburg, P. M. (2000). The impact of television advertising on children's Christmas wishes. *Journal of Broadcasting and Electronic Media, 44,* 456–469.

Calvert, S. L., & Billingsley, R. L. (1998). Young children's recitation and comprehension of information presented by songs. *Journal of Applied Developmental Psychology, 19,* 97–108.

Costanzo, P. R., & Shaw, M. E. (1966). Conformity as a function of age level. *Child Development, 37,* 967–975.

Cram, F., & Ng, S. H. (1999). Consumer socialisation. *Applied Psychology: An International Review, 48,* 297–312.

Cupitt, M., Jenkinson, D., Ungerer, J., & Waters, B. (1998). *Infants and television.* Sydney: Australian Broadcasting Autority.

Dorr, A. (1983). No shortcuts to judging reality. In J. Bryant & D. R. Anderson (Eds.), *Children's understanding of television: Research on attention and comprehension* (pp. 199–220). New York: Academic Press.

Durkin, K. (1997). *Developmental social psychology: From infancy to old age.* Malden, MA: Blackwell.

Fein, G. G. (1981). Pretend play in childhood: An integrative review. *Child Development, 52,* 1095–1118.

Fernald, A. (1985). Four-month-old infants prefer to listen to motherese. *Infant Behavior and Development, 8,* 181–196.

Fernie, D. E. (1981). Ordinary and extraordinary people: Children's understanding of television and real life models. In H. Kelly & H. Gardner (Eds.), *Viewing children through television: New directions in child development, 13* (pp. 47–58). San Francisco, CA: Jossey-Bass.

Flavell, J. H., Miller, P., & Miller, S. A. (1993). *Cognitive development.* Englewood Cliffs, NJ: Prentice-Hall.

Gunter, B., & Furnham, A. (1998). *Children as consumers: A psychological analysis of the young people's market.* London: Routledge.

Gunter, B., McAleer, J., & Clifford, B. R. (1991). *Children's view about television.* Aldershot, UK: Avebury Academic Publishing Group.

Howard, S. (1998). Unbalanced minds? Children thinking about television. In S. Howard (Ed.), *Wired-up: Young people and the electronic media* (pp. 57–76). London: UCL Press.

Jaglom, L. M., & Gardner, H. (1981). The preschool viewer as anthropologist. In H. Kelly & H. Gardner (Eds.), *Viewing children through television: New directions in child development, 13* (pp. 9–29). San Francisco, CA: Jossey-Bass.

Kline, S. (1993). *Out of the garden: Toys, TV, and children's culture in the age of marketing.* New York: Verso.

Kuczynski, L., & Kochanska, G. (1990). Development of children's noncompliance strategies from toddlerhood to age 5. *Developmental Psychology, 26,* 398–408.

Kuczynski, L., Kochanska, G., Radke-Yarrow, M., & Girnius-Brown, O. (1987). A developmental interpretation of young children's noncompliance. *Developmental Psychology, 23,* 799–806.

Lemish, D. (1987). Viewers in diapers: The early development of television viewing. In T. R. Lindlof (Ed.), *Natural audiences: Qualitative research of media uses and effects* (pp. 33–57). Norwood, NJ: Ablex.

McNeal, J. U. (1992). *Kids as customers: A handbook of marketing to children.* New York: Lexington Books.

Metcalfe, J., & Mischel, W. (1999). A hot/cool-system analysis of delay of gratification: Dynamics of willpower. *Psychological Review, 106,* 3–19.

Mielke, K. W. (1983). Formative research on appeal and comprehension in 3-2-1 CONTACT. In J. Bryant & D. Anderson (Eds.), *Children's understanding of television: Research on attention and comprehension* (pp. 241–263). Hillsdale, NJ: Erlbaum.

Mischel, H. N., & Patterson, C. J. (1976). Substantive and structural elements of effective plans for self-control. *Journal of Personality and Social Psychology, 31,* 254–261.

Mischel, W., & Ebbeson, E. B. (1970). Attention in delay of gratification. *Journal of Personality and Social Psychology, 16,* 329–337.

Moog, H. (1976). The development of musical experience in preschool children. *Psychology of Music, 4* (2), 38–45.

Moschis, G. P., & Churchill, G. A. (1978). Consumer socialization: A theoretical and empirical analysis. *Journal of Marketing, 43,* 40–48.

Moschis, G. P., & Moore, R. P. (1979). Decision making among the young: A socialization perspective. *Journal of Consumer Research, 6,* 101–112.

———. (1981). *A model of brand preference formation: AMA Educator's Conference Proceedings*. Chicago: American Marketing Association.

Mowen, J. C., & Minor, M. (1998). *Consumer behavior* (5th ed.). London: Prentice-Hall.

Murray, J., & Westendorp, D. (1996). *Children and advertising*. Den Haag, The Netherlands: Consumentenbond.

Noble, G. (1975). *Children in front of the small screen*. Beverly Hills, CA: Sage.

Piaget, J. (1954). *The construction of reality in the child*. New York: Basic Books.

Rieser, J., Yonas, A., & Wilkner, K. (1976). Radial localization of odors by human newborns. *Child Development, 47,* 856–859.

Rosengren, K. E., & Windahl, S. (1989). *Media matter: TV use in childhood and adolescence*. Norwood, NJ: Ablex.

Rubin, R. S. (1974). The effects of cognitive development on children's responses to television advertising. *Journal of Business Research, 2,* 409–419.

Ruff, H. A., & Lawson, K. R. (1990). Development of sustained focused attention in young children during free play. *Developmental Psychology, 26,* 85–93.

Sheldon, L., & Loncar, M. (1996). *Kids talk TV: "Super wicked" or "dum."* Sydney: Australian Broadcasting Authority.

Siegler, R. S. (1991). *Children's thinking* (2nd ed.). Englewood Cliffs, NJ: Prentice-Hall.

Torrance, K. (1998). *Contemporary childhood: Parent-child relationships and child culture*. Leiden, The Netherlands: DSWO Press.

Valkenburg, P. M. (1999). De ontwikkeling van kind tot consument [The development of a child into a consumer]. *Tijdschrift voor Communicatiewetenschap, 27,* 30–46.

Valkenburg, P. M., & Cantor, J. (2000). Children's likes and dislikes in entertainment programs. In D. Zillmann & P. Vorderer (Eds.), *Entertainment: The psychology of its appeal* (pp. 135–152). Hillsdale, NJ: Erlbaum.

Valkenburg, P. M., & Hellendoorn, J. (1992). Fantasie [Fantasy]. In T.W.J. Schulpen, G. Cluckers, M. Meijer, R. Kohnstamm, R. Willemaers, J. Rispens, & G. A. Bakker (Eds.), *Handboek Kinderen en Adolescenten: Vol. 17* (pp. 1–17). Deventer, The Netherlands: Van Loghum Slaterus.

Valkenburg, P. M., & Janssen, S. C. (1999). What do children value in entertainment programs? A cross-cultural investigation. *Journal of Communication, 26,* 3–21.

Wakshlag, J. J., Reitz, R. J., & Zillmann, D. (1982). Selective exposure to and acquisition of information from educational television programs as a function of appeal and tempo of background music. *Journal of Educational Psychology, 74,* 666–677.

Ward, S. (1974). Consumer socialization. *Journal of Consumer Research, 1,* 1–16.

Ward, S., Wackman, D., & Wartella, E. (1977). *How children learn to buy: The development of consumer information-processing skills*. Beverly Hills, CA: Sage.

Wartella, E., & Ettema, J. S. (1974). A cognitive developmental study of children's attention to television commercials. *Communication Research, 1,* 69–87.

Wright, J. C., Huston, A. C., Leary Reitz, A., & Piemyat, S. (1994). Young children's perceptions of television reality: Determinants and developmental differences. *Developmental Psychology, 30,* 229–239.

Chapter 12

Family Boundaries, Commercialism, and the Internet: A Framework for Research

Joseph Turow

During the past few years, the Internet—especially its World Wide Web graphics interface—has become a fixture in a rapidly growing number of U.S. homes. Although electronic mail and chat rooms are popular, the fastest growing use of the Internet seems to be in its commercial domain. Marketers of all stripes have found the Web a great place to target parents and youngsters with ad messages and products while getting information out of them that can be used for further marketing. These activities have raised controversy and alarm—and even led to new government regulations.

The growing social debate and the rapidly rising presence of the commercialized Web in U.S. households have so far not led to a stream of published studies that attempt to understand its impact on the family. Many writings do exist on the implications of traditional mass media, such as television. That literature, however, barely begins to address a raft of new questions about commercial intrusion and family privacy that the Web raises.

This chapter presents an *information-boundaries* perspective on the family and the Internet with the aim of helping to set the context for child development in the new media environment. Drawing from family studies, sociology, and communication, it lays out a model for viewing the family in relation to the Web. It uses the model to elucidate two views of the Web. One sees the new and enduring commercial dynamics as helping to reinforce divisive tensions that researchers say are features of families throughout society. The other view hails e-mail and related activities as countering this dysfunctional development by strengthening family relationships and reducing stress in households.

To what extent is one tendency triumphing over the other, and how might that change over time? To suggest ways to answer this question, this chapter first lays out the family information-boundaries approach and relates it to the emerging domestic, media, and regulatory environment. It then draws research ideas out of the framework that center on four areas: family communication patterns, filters and monitors, information disclosure practices, and the Internet in the larger media context. Because the Web is a harbinger of an even broader digital interactive media environment, the issues raised about the context of child development through the information-boundaries prism will increase in importance as the new media world takes hold.

THE FAMILY AND THE PRIVATE/PUBLIC REALMS

For the purpose of this chapter, a family will be defined as one or more adults and at least one child or teenager who live together on an ongoing basis. A dominant theme of scholarly discussions of the family centers on the functions of "public" and "private" realms of interaction in society, with the family traditionally dubbed "the private." Thinking of the family as private as opposed to public may seem natural, but the separation is not a very old one (see Zaretsky, 1986). Although writers have traditionally discussed public and private realms as though they were objective, externally observable phenomena, recent scholars have argued that the distinctions are socially constructed and negotiated (Fahey, 1995). The terms *private* and *public* may, therefore, hold different meanings for different family members in different family environments. Some scholars even argue that the boundary between home and work is a false one, for these boundaries are malleable and easily penetrated by the welfare state or even by mass media (see, e.g., Habermas, 1989; Lasch, 1977).

Nevertheless, distinctions between private and public are still extremely important to society's view of the family because people act as if the differences mean something (Fahey, 1995). The epigram that "your home is your castle" continues to survive as a reflection of the adamant social belief that strong boundaries between the two domains should be the norm even if they aren't always the reality. Researchers insist that this belief has crucial consequences. Hess and Handel (1985) argue that strong family relationships evolve through an awareness of boundaries between family members and the rest of the world. In their lives together, parents and children negotiate ideas about how and why they are similar to and different from each other and various other people.

Bronfenbrenner (1975) extends this notion directly to argue that dysfunctional social institutions can, through impact on the family, adversely affect child development. Berger and Kellner (1985) discuss the important role that ongoing conversations among significant adults play in creating a plausible and stable world. As a kind of corollary to these ideas, the Carnegie Council on Adolescent Development (1995) argues that a strong and caring family relationship can be a potent force to help children, adolescents, and parents cope with the fast-changing learning and working conditions in which Americans find themselves at the turn of the twenty-first century. However, dual careers, single-parenting tensions, poverty, and a host of other factors have converged to make strong family units difficult to achieve at a time when they are sorely needed.

The Council also points its finger at the mass media. It asserts that in recent times they have been helping to short-circuit the potential for supportive family relationships to an unprecedented extent. Electronic media have permeated the lives of American youth. Through television, radio, records, films, and videos a "heavily materialistic youth culture has emerged, weakening and challenging parental authority and stable, supportive bonding with a caring adult" (Carnegie Council on Adolescent Development, 1995, p. 36). One obvious solution—more time with parents—is increasingly unrealistic because youngsters' increased media use is accompanied by less family time. "Although there has been less research than the problem deserves, the time that American children spend with their parents has decreased significantly in the past few decades" (1995, p. 36).

Elkind (1994) extends this theme about the way commercial media are implicated in the "splintering" of the U.S. family. He points out that "the entertainment, information, and communication industries have fueled a new and heightened consumerism by targeting and catering to the diverse interests of the buying public" (p. 24). He suggests that the marketing-driven media environment increasingly urges parents and children, men and women, and people of varied ages to consider their differences rather than their similarities. He argues that this target-oriented media world encourages individual interests over family togetherness. It privileges child decision making over parental authority, and it pushes outside marketing influences over parents' influences and, perhaps, values. With the increasing role in children's world-views being shaped by marketers, children's sense of family identity (and through that kids' sense of social stability) may erode.

Elkind (1994) and other writers are important for calling attention to the role that commercial media may play in reinforcing and extending crucial family problems. Ironically, though, the media world that family analysts critique is quickly being eclipsed, and they have not turned their attention to the implications of that change. Taking the place of the traditional electronic environment of radio, videos, audio CDs, and one-way television is a digital interactive world symbolized by the Internet and interactive television. Neglect of these developments is unfortunate because the new technologies that are moving rapidly into U.S. homes raise a raft of new questions about the relationship between family boundaries, commercialism, and information that few family theorists have systematically considered together.

One view of the new technologies leads to the conclusion that their commercially driven dynamics may reinforce the dysfunctional family dynamics that Elkind and the Carnegie Council have bemoaned. It might, for example, cause tension between teens and parents regarding the disclosure of information to web sites that offer free products for valuable information. Other aspects of the Web—e-mail is one—have been hailed as activities that strengthen family relationships and reduce stress in households. To what extent is one tendency already triumphing over the other, and how might that change over time? Virtually no research has spoken to this topic. The first step in addressing it is to pull back and look at the emerging environment.

THE INTERNET AND FAMILY BOUNDARIES

Although the Internet itself dates back to its creation by scientists in the 1950s, its graphical interface, the World Wide Web is much more recent, dating to 1993. The number of U.S. households going online has grown so rapidly that any numbers presented as current are sure to become obsolete quite soon afterwards. In the middle of 1999, Dataquest found that 36% of American households were "online" (Wired, 1999). By the middle of 2000, a variety of sources pegged online households at 44% (Elkin, 2000).

The Web is paradigmatic of the kind of digital interactive technology that will permeate the home during the twenty-first century. It has three features that taken together distinguish it from all past media that bring the outside into the home. First, its digital nature means that parents, children, and outsiders can send, retrieve, transform, and store the material that moves across it. (A 13-year-old can carry on a discussion in a chat room, and the firm that operates it can store the text for future analysis.) Second, the Web's two-way, interactive nature means that family members and outsiders can respond to one another in an ongoing fashion. (The chat room operator can send ads for products that reflect the interests that the teen reveals through the ongoing chat.) Third, its ability to function through sophisticated computer software and hardware means that family members' activities can be tracked, sorted, and predicted through increasingly intelligent agents. (The company hosting the chat room can analyze the discussions and sell the results—and even the opportunity to reach the discussants—to market researchers.)

The Web is becoming a major communication vehicle for much of American society—so much so that trade magazines now refer to an *Internet economy*.[1] Consulting firm estimates in 1998 were that the Internet economy generated $301 billion in revenue and employed 1.2 million Americans. Much of that use is to engage in electronic mail, chat room conversation, and personal web sites. As the Web has matured, however, a larger and larger portion of it—and a larger portion of its use—has related to commercial purposes. The Web's commercial (.com) sector has skyrocketed, outpacing by far the growth rate of nonprofit (.org), educational (.edu), and government (.gov) sites. Electronic commerce is also growing by leaps and bounds. Marketers of all stripes, from soap manufacturers to porn purveyors, have found the Web a great place to deliver their ad messages quickly and efficiently.

Americans are going online in large numbers. A study in early 1999 by Nielsen Media Research and CommerceNet found that 92 million people over the age of 16 in the United States and Canada used the Internet at work or home (Bridis, 1999). Although affluent, highly educated, white males dominated the Web in its first few years, figures near the turn of the century find almost as many women as men online. Moreover, the numbers of African Americans and Hispanic Americans who have online connections have been rising steadily. Although the Web population is still skewed toward the upper-middle class, it is becoming less so as the months pass.

A national survey of parents released in March 2000 found that 28% of all U.S. children access the Internet from home. Parents in 49% of U.S. households reported that their children access the Internet from some location, at home or elsewhere (National School Boards Association, 2000). Around the same time, other studies noted that about 45% of U.S. households had online connections. Marketers saw the Web becoming a hub of activities that is as integral as the telephone with users communicating, learning, and shopping online (Bridis, 1999).

The analogy to the telephone is important beyond its recognition of the Web's centrality. As Marvin (1988) points out, in the telephone's early years many Americans were thrilled with the possibilities of the technology at the same time that they worried about the intrusions it would bring to the home and the private information it might take out. The Internet has also evoked a combination of fear and hope. A national survey of U.S. parents of 8- to 17-year-olds in late 1998 and at the start of 2000 found most American parents deeply conflicted about the Web (Turow, 1999a; Turow & Nir, 2000). Across the nation, parents and the press have heralded the Web as a way to help the family by connecting them to relatives, schools, and informative web sites for homework. Fully 81% of parents with online connections at home said that the Internet is a place for children to discover "fascinating, useful things," and nearly 68% said that children who don't have the Internet are disadvantaged compared to their peers who do. At the same time, over 77% of parents worried that their children might give out personal information and view sexually explicit images on the Internet. Fifty percent agreed that "families who spend a lot of time online talk to each other less than they otherwise would" (Turow & Nir, 2000,

p. 12). In a 1998 survey, 79% said that it bothered them when advertisers invite children to web sites to tell them about products (Turow, 1999a).

Many of these tensions and hopes reflect a desire to properly calibrate the permeable boundaries between the family and the world outside it—particularly when it comes to the protection and socialization of children. Concern about the Web as a conduit for advertisements, "fascinating, useful things," and "sexual images" underscores that familiar program genres make up a key part of the online experience. That, in turn, raises the concerns that Elkind (1994) and the Carnegie Council (1995) have expressed regarding commercialized mass media materials coming into the home. Public worries about children giving out "personal information," by contrast, underscore that digital interactive media challenge family boundaries with respect to another information flow—one *going out* of the home. This challenge to the "private" nature of the family recalls similar fears about the telephone. A close look at marketers' work in the developing digital interactive environment suggests, however, that what is developing is not simply a combination of traditional mass media and the telephone. It is a new commercial domain, with new features and possibly new implications for the family.

The Internet and Information Flows into the Home

Since video, music, and direct mail are easily available online, it is tempting to see Web materials coming into the home as merely an amalgamation of all of these and other mass media. From the standpoint of parental boundary-setting, however, three features of the Web make auditing the flow and enforcing rules about it much more difficult than with previous media. One feature is the Web's virtually unlimited nature; individuals can access literally millions of sites at any time, on subjects from pandas to pornography. A second aspect is the presence of a huge number of commercial sites targeted to virtually any demographic, psychographic, and lifestyle interest one can imagine—including many that aim at children and teens. The third feature of the Web that makes parental auditing more difficult than before is the complexity of the technology. Not only do many adults have trouble with it, many of their own youngsters are more savvy and confident about the digital world than they are. This circumstance may change as the current generation, who is comfortable with the Internet, ages. But then again, youth may be attracted to the ongoing evolution of the digital age, giving the next generation the advantage that our current youth enjoy.

The emphasis on commercial targeting is so great on the Web that concerns about family splintering that Elkind and the Carnegie Council raised regarding traditional media would seem to apply here to a much greater extent. Web technology increasingly allows visitors to sites to "personalize" the material sent to them by specifying what they want. Marketers see today's teenagers as the replacement consumers for their parents, the aging baby-boom generation that so captivated business for 50 years. To the commercial realm, these "echo-boomers" are prime targets for the development of brand loyalties at a particularly sensitive time in their lives. By cordoning off entertainment and advertising areas of the Web with personalized materials that are just for them, and then creating separate consumption arenas for their parents and younger siblings, marketers may well reinforce family splintering in ways that go beyond traditional media.

The potential implications of the Internet as a target marketer's dream have not made it into public discourse about the Web and the family. Instead, the great percentage of concerns centers on the wide availability of sex, violence, and commercialism on the Web (see Turow, 1999a). Web versions of sex, violence, and advertisements, however, are often exactly the same as those on video game cartridges or magazines that an adolescent can surreptitiously bring home through nonelectronic means. What is different is the torrent of objectionable material easily available to the home and the consequent difficulty that parents feel they have in controlling what their children access.

So far, three solutions to concerns about objectionable material have emerged. They involve filters, monitors, and safe-haven sites. Filters are computer programs that parents can use to stop certain words or web sites (or both) from entering the home. Monitors are computer programs that parents can install on computers to track (secretly or openly) where their children go on the Web and what they do when they get there. Safe-haven sites are child-friendly sites on the Web that provide parents with software that ensures children go to them and nowhere else.

Filters have generated considerable controversy. Critics argue that the programs are often severely flawed. Parents who block sites with the word "sex," for example, may find that all educational biology sites are off limits. Moreover, say the critics, many of the firms that create filters don't make clear the ideological biases of their software programs. So that competitors will not steal the data that makes them unique, they are often reluctant to release the names of the sites they block or the filtering terms they use (Hunter, 1999).

A big drawback of monitors and safe-haven sites—and a big drawback of filters as well—is that parents with only basic computer and Web skills may not feel comfortable using them. A drawback of surreptitious monitoring is that it has the potential to violate children's privacy and disrupt their trust in their parents. When used, another drawback is that adolescents can find ways to circumvent or disable many of these attempts to place limits on them. One nontechnological way they do that is simply by accessing the Web from places—friends' homes, libraries—where such barriers don't exist.

The Internet and Information Flows out of the Home

If the Internet creates new control challenges for parents with respect to the commercialized information it brings into the home, these challenges pale next to the ones the Web is creating with respect to commercially useful information about the family that commercial interests *take out* of the home. Until rather recently, the information that marketers could retrieve from children and teenagers at home was limited by the need to go through a parent or school to speak to the youngsters or track their habits. The Internet has changed all that, with implications that family research has hardly begun to consider.

At the center of this activity is consumer profiling for the purpose of direct and relationship marketing. Profiling involves gathering specific demographic, psychographic, and lifestyle intelligence about individuals and families from a variety of public and private databases (Businesses radically rethinking, 1998). Digital technologies enter the home with features that revolutionize the data marketers can get from people. Quite widespread are web sites that offer free information, paraphernalia, phone calls, even cash if the user will enter personal information into a registration window and then visit the web site.

Even when it doesn't appear that web sites are collecting a lot of information about their visitors, it is likely that they are quite busy doing that. A close reading of web "privacy policies" will reveal that virtually all the activities that individuals perform on web sites can be tracked and catalogued. To make web sites particularly attractive to advertisers and visitors, companies are using increasingly sophisticated "cookies" and intelligent agents that determine the interests and habits of the visitors. The sites aim to offer them personalized ad and editorial environments based on an analysis of previous purchases, clickstream interests, and the personal characteristics noted during site registration.

Marketers hope that sophisticated data-gathering and database management will converge in digital media to allow them to actually speak to segments, even individuals, in ways that reflect what they know about them (Turow, 1997). The growing ability to solicit information electronically from people without their full knowledge about its use has, however, drawn enormous concern from parents as well as a gamut of advocacy groups (Turow & Nir, 2000). Advocates see the issue as one of information privacy, in which the individual has control over how personal information is communicated to others (see Westin, 1967). Of particular concern have been attempts by children's web sites to elicit information about parents' incomes and lifestyles. Responding in part, the U.S. Congress in 1998 passed the Children's Online Privacy Protection Act (COPPA), which directed the Federal Trade Commission (FTC) to regulate data collection by commercial web sites that target kids under age 13. The FTC decreed that web sites wanting information from children under 13 years old must get consent from parents. The required nature of the consent varies depending on the site's intended use of the information (Clausing, 1999).

The Family Challenge of Two-Way Commercialism

Although marketers generally support COPPA, they insist that Web users 13 years and older are savvy enough to be able to handle information about themselves. Increasingly, Web executives say, society must move away from the notion that consumers hold that the absolute secrecy of certain types of information about themselves is their fundamental human right. Rather, they argue consumers will give up all sorts of sensitive information to companies if they trust the firms to use it properly and get commensurate benefits in return. They argue further that with the rise of digital interactive media, information is and ought to be an important coin of exchange for the individual in the twenty-first century. As evidence, marketers point to the large numbers of Web users who freely give information about themselves to get information and material goods.

Advocates and academics have weighed in with a variety of opinions about the possible social impact of this "exchange" approach to information privacy. Despite the uproar over children's naïve release of information to web sites, though, few writers have explored the general implications of an individual's barter of information for the family unit. Most see information disclosure on the Web as an issue of individual rather than group information inflow and outflow. Coming at the topic from the standpoint of family information boundaries points to the importance of the latter view. Take the example of a 14-year-old who reveals his parents' favorite web sites to a web site for a "free" gift, not realizing that his parents consider such data sensitive. It turns out his mother has a health problem that is reflected in the list of sites and that might, if revealed publicly, lead to employment discrimination or have implications for health insurance.

Writings on family information privacy suggest that concerns about this and other types of information leakage across their private/public boundaries may have profound impact on the family group as well as on its individual members' psychological well-being. Summarizing a stream of work on the topic, Berardo (1998) posits that society requires some monitoring of individuals and groups in order to enforce social norms. Domestic violence by men against women and children is an example of the dark side of information that families sometimes keep within their boundaries and shouldn't. Yet, argues Berardo, there must be a balance between surveillance and privacy for effective functioning of a social structure. "Full surveillance of activities in a group would become psychologically overwhelming and, as a consequence, dysfunctional for the maintenance and stability of the group as a whole" (p. 8). "Information privacy," he adds, "allows . . . sufficient autonomy from disruptive extra-familial scrutiny to foster a feeling of group cohesiveness, thereby enhancing solidarity" (p. 10).

The possibility that a loss of control over information about the family that goes out of the home—or even the fear of it—can weaken family bonds places a new light on Web privacy. Concern about the integrity of family information boundaries may be heightened when one considers that digital interactive technology provides, for the first time, a media environment where information surveillance and targeting marketing can work together in real-time. Web information and, eventually, television programming, can be personalized to a family member based on volunteered, collected, and purchased data. In turn, creators of that programming collect information about the individual and his or her clickstream while the viewing is taking place. Parents may be concerned both about what information leaves the home as a result of the youngster's clickstream, and about the kinds of materials that he or she is bringing into his computer (or Web TV) as a result of this personalization.

What we have, then, is an unprecedented, continual example of what Shapiro (1997) terms the leakage of personal information from the home accompanied by the intrusion of undesirable parts of the world. If what Berardo, Elkind, the Carnegie Council, and others say is correct, what may be happening over time is a weakening of the family in a spiraling manner. In a general social environment of embattled families, tensions over information leakage may help erode family cohesiveness. That, in turn, may make it easier for target marketing messages to reinforce separatism within the family—which, in turn, may allow for more information leakage and greater family tensions. And so on, in an increasing spiral of family tension and fractionalization created by information leakage.

INTERNET RESEARCH AND FAMILY BOUNDARIES

Evidence to support or refute this scenario about the family in the new media environment is almost totally absent. A recent national random telephone survey of 1,001 parents of children aged 8 to 17 and 304 children aged 10 to 17 attempted to break ground in this area (Turow & Nir, 2000). About half of the youngsters were linked to the parents, and half were not. The authors concluded that in many families the Web is becoming an arena for discord around the release of sensitive information. Their survey found that 45% of U.S. 10- to 17-year-olds are much more likely than parents to say it is OK to give sensitive personal and family information to commercial web sites in exchange for a free gift. Examples of such information include their allowance, the names of their parents' favorite stores, and what their parents do on weekends.

The study also noted that 41% of U.S. parents and 36% of youngsters recall tensions at home over kids' release of information to the Web. Curiously, 69% of the parents say they have had discussions with their children about what kinds of information to give up to web sites, and 66% of the kids say they have had these discussions with their parents. But when interviewers specifically focused on the 150 pairs of parents and kids in the same family, they found that most didn't agree on whether these sorts of discussions had ever taken place. The authors infer that parent-child conversations about Web-privacy issues are fleeting at best, perhaps in the form of "don't give out your name" or "don't talk to strangers" that parents have traditionally urged upon their children. They suggest that it is wrong to think that such simple discussions between parents and kids about what information to give to the Web can easily resolve family tensions over information privacy.

Clearly, there is much more work to do in this area. Existing data that can be brought to bear on the issue is scattered across a variety of studies. The family-boundaries framework presented above can help point research in useful directions. It suggests that questions and hypotheses will usefully center around four general areas: the Internet and family communication; filters, monitors, and the family; information disclosure practices and the family; and the Internet in the general media environment. The following pages will briefly sketch a few key issues in each domain and suggest how they intersect.

The Internet and Family Communication

The proposition that private/public boundaries will likely be constructed differently in different families can serve as a good departure point. A basic hypothesis is that families vary in the extent to which and the way in which they care about what information comes in and what goes out of the house via the Web. This seemingly straightforward statement, however, opens a variety of issues.

A key set of questions centers on what it really means to say that "families vary" in "setting boundaries" regarding the Web information that comes in and goes out of their homes. Who in the family sets the boundaries? Do family members challenge them and force changes? If so, who, when, why, and how?

A major problem is whether it is, in fact, realistic to assume the existence of one private/public information boundary that individuals within a family perceive in the same way. The very idea of social construction makes it likely that what writers call a *boundary* is really a melange of contested statements, actions, and accommodations regarding the Web by family members that not only change over time but that might be described quite differently by various individuals involved. Researchers should describe the dynamic nature of such private/public boundary making within families. Studies may well find that families differ substantially in the nature of their contested, continually changing statements, actions, and accommodations regarding what can come in and go out of the home via the Web.

This basic understanding of these family dynamics will allow for the exploration of the central issue suggested by the family-boundaries perspective: the extent to which the Web's commercialization is reinforcing differentiation between family members, tensions about incoming materials some family members find objectionable, and worries about family information privacy. Also key is whether and how Web benefits such as e-mail, chat rooms, interesting information, and homework help yield a counterbalancing force that supports family unity. Operationalizing words such as *differentiation, tensions, objectionable, worries,* and *counterbalance* will be a challenge and incite debate. Moreover, the work must take place with a textured understanding of the social and historical contexts in which families live.

Filters, Monitors, and the Family

One way in which a growing number of parents have been trying to control family boundaries when it comes to their children bringing objectionable Web materials into the home is by using filters and monitors. Despite vigorous debate about the use of filters in libraries, no research has actually explored the use and implications of Internet filters in homes. Basic questions need to be addressed, with an eye on whether filters really do mitigate the anxieties of the parents involved about the permeability of their families' boundaries. Of special interest is whether parents decide to use filters more out of fears of the Web that they pick up from the press than from bad experiences within their families or the families of people they know. One project found that the opinions of a national sample of parents about the Web mapped quite closely onto the way a national sample of newspapers discussed the family and the Internet (Turow, 1999a). A long tradition of media agenda-setting research as well as a newer stream of framing studies can help to shape work on this important question.

Almost lost in the discussion of filtering is a straightforward alternative that retains adult oversight but does not lock out the Web. It is the use of monitoring software to observe children's behavior, either with or without their knowing it. Someone opposing monitoring might argue that it invades a youngster's privacy. Someone supporting it might reply that use of monitor software is akin to a parent looking over the youngster's shoulder, especially if the child knows that the monitor exists. Careful study of the use of such monitors may stir or calm this controversy.

Information Disclosure Practices and the Family

While research surrounding Web filters and monitors speaks to family boundary negotiations in the face of nervousness about material coming into the home, the topic of information disclosure practices relates to data that marketers and others try to take out of the house. Here lie great opportunities for exploration of the relationship between family information boundaries and changing social environments. It seems logical to assume that families hold norms about information disclosure. Adults may have their own implicit and explicit rules about what to say about family affairs to "outsiders." Parents may tell children not to tell strangers their names, not to talk to telephone marketers, not to talk about certain sensitive family practices. They may elaborate definitions of "outsiders" for their children. Children, in turn, may develop their own rules about disclosing certain kinds of information about themselves, their siblings, or their parents to friends, relatives, teachers, and other outsiders.

Are parents articulating norms about the release of information to the Web—and, if so, how? How sophisticated are different types of families and specific family members when making sure that only the information they want released will go out? The possibility that in some families the greatest knowledge about the Web may lie with the children rather than the parents may make it difficult for some parents to articulate and police certain Web disclosure norms. Wartella (1999) notes that this sort of knowledge asymmetry recalls the predicament of U.S. immigrants, who often find themselves feeling much less savvy than their quickly Americanizing and English-speaking children. The intriguing comparison deserves elaboration with an eye to its implications for younger and older family members' negotiation of, and adherence to, family information boundaries.

The Internet in the General Media Environment

Adults and youngsters constantly monitor their environment. Implicitly or explicitly, they make decisions about what can go in and go out, fight about those decisions, circumvent them, forget them, or ignore them. Researchers' awareness of this process can guide many questions about the Internet and the family.

But researchers also need to recognize that the Internet does not exist on its own. It is part of a much larger web of media and nonmedia activities that relate to the home and the family. This development particularly affects the direction of commercial media. The marketing mandate of the twenty-first century is to follow target audiences wherever they go, on any medium that they use (see Turow, 1999b, ch. 18–19). To truly understand the implications of the Web for the family, researchers must stay on top of media and marketing trends that might affect the family and its members.

How do advertisers understand the family? How and why do advertisers try to target family members in certain ways? How do media firms respond to advertiser interests in their attempts to reach the targets? What do the changing media tactics mean for the commercial blandishments that different family members receive? What do changing marketing tactics mean for information that marketers want to bring in and take out of the home? In what way and to what extent do these tactics affect family boundary-making with respect to the Web and other media?

Addressing these questions will place the Internet, commercialism, and the family into a broad societal context. Doing that will require a close understanding of the media and marketing industries. Studies that explore the historical and cultural roles of media and commercialism in American family life are critical for a proper understanding of the Web's impact. Similarly, assessments of contemporary industry strategies are key to understanding contemporary business strategies toward family information boundaries, the social discourse about it, and the possible large-scale implications of that.

A LOOK AHEAD

There is certainly much to study. Moreover, the Web is changing quickly. Every month, the Web gets bigger, more commercialized, and more quickly accessible to many Americans. The notion of a discrete "Web" in the home is also likely to blur as interactive digital television, radio, and print materials become common via broadband technologies. Along with these new developments will come a wide array of target-marketing activities aimed at youngsters as well as parents and entire families.

To get a good grasp on the nature and implications of these developments, research methods to explore them should vary. Some studies will involve interviewing family members in depth; others may take place through paper-and-pencil surveys; and still others through ethnographic or experimental approaches. Because the United States is only at early stages in adopting the Web, many of the family dynamics may still be too new or too subtle to observe. Longitudinal research on families is therefore warranted, as is research comparing otherwise similar families who have had the Web at home for different lengths of time.

The Web we have now, though, represents the beginning of this new digital realm. It, or versions of it, is here to stay. So is the family, the cradle of child development. How the two relate to one another is a subject that is likely to occupy researchers in the coming century. Looking at these developments through the prism of family information boundaries would seem to be a good way to start.

ACKNOWLEDGMENT

Reprinted from *Applied Developmental Psychology*, Vol. 22 (1), J. Turow, Family boundaries, commercialism, and the Internet: A framework for research, pp. 73–86, © 2001, with permission from Elsevier Science.

NOTE

1. *The Industry Standard*, a popular magazine that focuses on Web business, is subtitled, "The Newsmagazine of the Internet Economy."

REFERENCES

Berardo, F. (1998). Family privacy: Issues and concepts. *Journal of Family Issues, 19*, 4–19.

Berger, P., & Kellner, H. (1985). Marriage and the construction of reality: An exercise in the microsociology of knowledge. In G. Handel (Ed.), *The psychosocial interior of the family* (3rd ed.). New York: Aldine Publishing Company. (Article originally published in 1964.)

Bridis, T. (1999). Net users hit 92 million in U.S., Canada. *Austin American-Statesman*, June 18, p. D7.

Bronfenbrenner, U. (1975). The origins of alienation. In *Influences on human development* (2nd ed.). Hinsdale, IL: The Dryden Press.

Businesses radically rethinking how they view customers, according to Andersen Consulting/Economist Intelligence Unit study. (1998). *Business Wire*, October 13.

Carnegie Council on Adolescent Development. (1995). *Great transitions: Preparing adolescents for a new century*. New York: Carnegie Corporation of New York.

Clausing, J. (1999). New privacy rules for children's web sites. *New York Times*, October 22, p. G11.

Duclaux, D. (1998). Kraft, TCI take the narrow view; Deal would let food giant tailor ads to different segments in the same area. *DM News*, March 16, p 6.

Elkin, T. (2000). How MSN connects to the world of free ISPs. *Advertising Age*, March 27, p. 46.

Elkind, D. (1994). *Ties that stress: The new family imbalance*. Cambridge, MA: Harvard University Press.

Fahey, T. (1995). Privacy and the family: Conceptual and empirical reflections. *Sociology, 29*, 687–703.

Habermas, J. (1989). *The structural transformation of the public sphere*. Cambridge, MA: MIT Press.

Hess, R., & Handel, G. (1985). The family as a psychosocial organization. In G. Handel (Ed.), *The psychosocial interior of the family* (3rd ed.). New York: Aldine Publishing Company. (Article originally published in 1959.)

Hunter, C. (1999). *Filtering the future: Software filters, porn, pics, and the Internet content conundrum*. Master's thesis, Annenberg School for Communication, Philadelphia, PA.

Lasch, C. (1977). *Haven in a heartless world*. New York: Basic Books.

Marvin, C. (1988). *When old technologies were new: Thinking about communications in the late nineteenth century*. New York: Oxford University Press.

Media matrix. (1998). *The Internet Standard*, September 7, p. 46.

National School Boards Association. (2000). *Safe and smart: Research and guidelines for children's use of the Internet*. Alexanderia, VA: National School Boards Association.

Net hookups double in Europe. (1999). *Wired*, June 7. http://www.wired.com/news/business/0,1367,20056,00.html.

Shapiro, S. (1997). Places and spaces: The historical interaction of technology, home and privacy. *The Information Society, 14*, 275–284.

Turow, J. (1997). *Breaking up America: Advertisers and the new media world.* Chicago: University of Chicago Press.

———. (1999a). *The Internet and the family: The view from parents/The view from the press.* Report No. 27. Philadelphia, PA: The Annenberg Public Policy Center of the University of Pennsylvania.

———. (1999b). *Media today: An introduction to mass communication.* Boston: Houghton Mifflin.

Turow, J., & Nir, L. (2000). *The Internet and the family 2000: The view from parents/The view from kids.* Report No. 33. Philadelphia, PA: The Annenberg Public Policy Center of the University of Pennsylvania.

Wartella, E. (1999). Personal communication, December.

Westin, A. (1967). *Privacy and freedom.* New York: Atheneum.

Zaretsky, E. (1986). *Capitalism, the family, and personal life* (2nd ed.). New York: Perennial Library.

Chapter 13

A Family Systems Approach to Examining the Role of the Internet in the Home

Amy B. Jordan

Children today live in environments that are highly saturated with media. Virtually every American home has at least one television set and over half of all children have a TV in their bedroom (Stanger & Gridina, 1999). In the last two decades, television has been joined by several new media technologies that extend the capabilities of the medium. Nearly every family (97.8%) has a videocassette recorder and more than three-quarters (77.4%) have cable or satellite television. In addition to the ubiquity of television, there are more household media available to children in their homes than ever before, including video-game equipment (67%) and home computers (68.2%). Into this media mix comes the Internet—an extension of the television screen or home computer that brings a new dimension of the outside world into the inner sanctum of the home.

Families make available certain kinds of media within the home but also provide notions about *how* and *when* to use the media (e.g., the Internet is for socializing and television is for entertainment) and how to interpret media content (e.g., newspaper stories are real, TV situation comedies are pretend). Much of this socialization does not occur through the explicit directives of parents. Instead, the interactions of family members subtly create patterned ways of thinking about and using the media. These patterns become habits, and these habits become the stuff of everyday experience. As Berger and Luckman have argued: "The reality of everyday life maintains itself by being embodied in routines" (1967, p. 137). In today's family, the media have become part and parcel of the routine of family life.

One might take any one of a number of approaches to integrate ideas about the family into media research. Some family researchers emphasize the *roles* the individual members assume in their families (Morley, 1986).

Others examine the way families construct a common social reality by building meaning through repeated, patterned interactions (Berger & Luckman, 1966; Pollner & McDonald-Wilker, 1985). Still others think about the family through its individual and collective life cycles, tracing the changes in structure and function over time (Aldous, 1978).

Each of these approaches is helpful for understanding how families assimilate, adapt, and accommodate to new media. Yet as a research framework, the family systems theory approach incorporates elements from each of these perspectives and provides researchers with terms and tools for exploring Internet usage within the totality of the family's experience.

FAMILY SYSTEMS THEORY: A BRIEF HISTORY

Family systems theory grew out of the broader general systems theory, which adheres to the basic premise that one must study "wholes" rather than "parts" in order to understand how the system functions (Bavelas & Segal, 1982; Vetere & Gale, 1987). Early research in the area of systems theory was conducted by Von Bertalanffy, a biologist interested in how organisms maintained and adapted to their changing environments. A decade later, general systems theory was applied to military technology and organizational behavior (Vetere & Gale, 1987). It wasn't until the 1950s, however, that clinicians in psychology began to apply systems theory concepts. Most notable were Bateson and his colleagues, who extended the theory to schizophrenic symptoms (Bateson, Jackson, Haley, & Weakland, 1956). With the systems approach, a schizophrenic's behavior came to be viewed as an adaptive response to a dysfunctional family environment (Bavelas & Segal, 1982).

During the next 20 years, general systems theory became a strong component when thinking about "normal" families (Bochner & Eisenberg, 1987). Individuals were conceptualized as members of an ecological system. Family members are seen as sharing physical and emotional closeness and as mutually influential. Moreover, the emerging cadre of family systems theorists recognized the importance of identifying how the distinct members and dimensions of the family work to establish and regulate the functioning of the whole, despite internal and external pressures to change. As Bochner and Eisenberg state:

[This] represented an epistemological turn away from thinking of "forces" or "causes" and toward thinking of "relationships" and "contexts"; away from emphasizing what "goes on under the skin" or "inside the head" and toward a focus on the communicative behavior that takes place between people; away from linear models and toward recursive or circular descriptions. (1987, p. 4)

Systems theory has come to span the physical, biological, cognitive, and social worlds (Rosenblatt, 1994). Its application to family life encourages the study of whole families and focuses on the process by which family life emerges as patterned and meaningful to its members. Family systems theory provides the researcher interested in family and media with a new way to think about relationships within the home. It attempts to account for all family members and their reciprocal influences on one another, as well as the monitoring and negotiation of how the external world should be rejected, assimilated, or accommodated. Finally, it emphasizes the importance of family communication and family relationships in defining media use rather than focusing on the technology itself as driving patterns of behavior.

The family systems framework examines how the family creates patterns of media use that "fit" with the norms, values, and beliefs that define the family system. It draws out components of the family system that provide important contexts for behavior—for example, family boundaries and members' roles. From this perspective, researchers consider mass media within a larger structure of patterned behaviors and relationships. It posits that in order to truly understand media in children's lives—and for the purposes of this chapter, children's use of the Internet—one must understand the medium's role in family life and the variety of contexts that will determine its meaning.

Strictly speaking, family systems theory is more a conceptual framework than a theory. As Rosenblatt (1994) has pointed out, the systems approach—particularly as it is applied to the family—does not offer integrated or comprehensive propositions, nor does it offer much in the way of predictive value. One might argue that it does, however, offer explanations for retrospectively observed patterns of phenomena. Like Rosenblatt, I will use the terms "conceptual framework" and "theory" interchangeably.

STRUCTURAL AND SOCIAL DIMENSIONS OF THE FAMILY SYSTEM

The numerous components of family life can be considered for the ways in which they shape and reflect the "whole" of the family system. As a heuristic device, this section divides the home into two domains of family life: the "structural dimension" (how space and time are organized), and the "social dimension" (the family member's acquisition of identity, roles, rules, and interactions).

Time and Space within the Home

The structural domain of family life contains those aspects of the home which provide the family with notions about where and when day-to-day living should be carried out. The importance of space to human interaction and functioning has been recognized by social scientists, most notably Edward Hall who argued that there are both norms for the distances people keep between one another and the implications of the spatial construction of any given social environment for human behavior (Hall, 1966).

The idea that space within the home is meaningful and consciously constructed has implications for the role media will play in family life (Ashcraft & Scheflin, 1976; Lull, 1980). In their ethnographic study of television and VCR use in the home, Lindlof and his colleagues revealed that rooms are arranged around television sets while allowing for other, simultaneous activities, such as eating or ironing (Lindlof, Shatzer, & Wilkinson, 1988). Television, for example, occupies a central position in many family gathering areas, leading one scholar to dub it the "electronic hearth" (Tichi, 1991). Furniture is arranged not for ease in conversation or interaction but for ease in viewing (Leichter, Ahmed, Barrios, Bryce, Larsen, & Moe, 1985).

Others have argued that the visibility of a medium in a room is related to the importance of the role it plays in a family. Studies from the early 1980s, for example, found that the accessibility of the TV set was related to the amount of viewing done by families. Bryce and Leichter (1983) write that "television sets that were visually and aurally accessible from the centers of social interaction were on more often . . . were viewed more often and were more available for family mediation than were sets in socially isolated locations" (p. 132).

Later researchers have found that the rise of multitelevision households has altered the ability of families to centrally locate themselves around the TV (Lawrence & Wozniak, 1989; Wartella & Mazzarella, 1990) and the means by which parents oversee their children's TV consumption (Huston, Donnerstein, Fairchild, Feshbach, Katz, Murray, Rubenstein, Walcos, & Zuckerman, 1992). Research also indicates that children with bedroom sets are less likely to have rules about the medium and are more likely to watch programs their parents would not approve of (Holz, 1998). This relationship may be the result of tacit approval of the medium (i.e., parents who think television to be a harmless or positive force are more likely to approve bedroom TVs) or the consequence of spatial arrangements (since bedroom TV viewing is outside of the purview of the parents). These trends with television may provide insight into the role of the Internet in the family system's spatial structure.

Studies also show that computers are often located in children's bedrooms. According to a recent study by the Kaiser Family Foundation (Roberts, Foehr, Rideout, & Brodie, 1999), approximately 16% of American children have computers in their bedroom and 7% have online access in there. Though bedroom computers are not as common as bedroom TVs, many "experts" recommend that Internet-linked computers be kept in a central location in order to aid parental oversight of the medium (Carlson, 1999; Stroh, 1999). They argue that without such monitoring, children may accidentally or purposefully access sexually explicit sites that are disturbing to children or participate in chat rooms that are inappropriate or potentially compromising to their safety.

In addition to the potential relationship between the spatial location of the online computer and parents' monitoring capability, the systems approach calls for a consideration of the arrangements of the room that encourage or discourage children's use of space and time in particular ways. At a recent Annenberg Public Policy Center Conference, industry insiders discussed the increasing tendency of children to use multiple media simultaneously. One television executive argued that since many online computers are located in rooms equipped with television sets, children should be encouraged to provide instantaneous online feedback to the producers of television programs they are watching (Woolf & Allen, 2001).

Family members' notions about time—its importance and its ideal use—can vary within and between homes. Time can be seen as a scarce resource that must not be wasted or as an abundant commodity that needs to be filled. Time can even be both scarce and abundant, depending on the situation (e.g., work verses vacation) or the family members' responsibilities (parent vs. child). Notions of time may lead to varying temporal structures within and across family systems. In his cross-cultural studies, Hall (1959) uncovered a dichotomy of temporal orientation: "monochronic" cultures—which emphasized segmentation of activities, focus, and promptness; and "polychronic" cultures—which reflected multiple, and simultaneous tasking and emphasized the importance of completing transactions. One can see a variety of temporal orientations within the culture of the family as well.

In an ethnographic study of the role of media in family life, I have found that the temporal ideologies of families varied according to their socioeconomic status (Jordan, 1991). Parents' orientations toward time (polychronic versus monochronic) were reflected in the ways they socialized their children to use media, particularly television viewing. Children from more affluent and well-educated homes tended to be socialized to view time as a precious resource, one that should not be "wasted" with excessive amounts of viewing. Though children from less-affluent homes also had some restrictions on time spent viewing television, their parents' rules were more likely to be centered around content (what they could watch). This difference could be traced to parents' own valuation of time and experiences with managing time within the workforce (Jordan, 1991). Parents with occupations that offer autonomy but demand self-motivation (e.g., professors, lawyers, writers) were more likely to try to instill in their children notions of managing and scheduling time than parents whose jobs were externally controlled (e.g., factory workers, secretaries, and firefighters). Others have demonstrated the relationships between education and workplace experiences and child-rearing practices as well, most notably in the domain of discipline (Kohn & Schooler, 1983).

Parents' conceptions of time (how it should be valued, how it should be used) are likely to be reflected in their views of their children's use of the Internet. For those who see the World Wide Web as a potentially enriching resource for information and/or a valuable educational tool, Internet use may be encouraged as a productive leisure-time activity. Parents' views of the Internet's educational promise, however, may be driven by their own experiences with it. Turow (1999), for example, found that parents who use the Web for work are much more "gung ho" about it (and more likely to bring it into the home) than parents whose jobs do not involve the Internet. In addition, it is possible that, in general, parents are more likely to use the Internet for work while children use it for entertainment. This may impact conceptions of online time use. Unlike television, which is more likely to be seen as a monolithic medium (with little variation in use and content), the Internet provides a variety of experiences for children—from chat rooms to encyclopedias to pornography. Thus, it is critical to examine how the form and content of the medium intersect with parents' judgments of its value. In addition, it is important to explore how parents' judgments of the Internet's value shape the ways children perceive it and ultimately use it.

Research thus far seems to indicate that the majority of children do not spend much time online. A 1999 Kaiser Family Foundation survey of children's media use indicates that only 3% of children ages 2 to 16 spend more than one hour a day online while 64% spend more than one hour per day with television. In fact, on average, children spend only about eight minutes per day on the Internet. However, adolescents spend far more time online than younger children do. As more and more families get online, and more and more children become comfortable surfing the Web, the amount of time children spend on the Web may increase dramatically. In addition, it is difficult to get an accurate measure of online time through self-report. It is also difficult to get up-to-date statistics on children's time with the Internet, given the exponential growth of availability both in and out of the home. With these caveats, it should be noted that the majority of parents with children online say that they restrict when their children can access the Internet and how much time they can spend online (Turow, 1999).

The technological capacity of the Internet itself may begin to shape how children use the medium. It is possible to engage in multiple activities simultaneously online. For example, children researching a term paper for social studies can minimize several sites and bring them up on demand, while, at the same time, engage in instant messaging (IM) with their friends without ever closing out of a window.

The Social Dimensions of the Home

The uses of media within the social domain of the home have historically been of interest to media researchers, in part because of concerns over the impact of media on family relationships (Liebert, Sprafkin, & Davidson, 1982; Maccoby, 1954). In the following section, family patterns of interaction, the development of gendered roles and individual identities, and the mediation practices of parents are separated for discussion here in order to consider the Internet in the social dimension of the family system. It is recognized, however, that the structural and the social dimensions of family life are tightly intertwined.

Interaction

One of the most frequently expressed concerns about children's use of the Internet in both the press and in national surveys is the fear that children's connections to a "machine" and the development of relationships that are disconnected in physical space will create a generation of children who have no social skills (Turow, 1999). Indeed, much of the early commentary on television's ill effects centered around fears of creating children who were isolated and "drugged" into a zombie-like stupor (Winn, 1977). There were also fears that television created a home environment in which children no longer talked with one another or their parents (Schramm, Lyle, & Parker, 1961). Over the years, researchers have found that while family interaction decreases to some degree as a result of TV viewing, physical closeness (Medrich, Roizen, Ruben, & Buckley, 1982) and common conversational agendas (Lull, 1980) are often retained when TV viewing is a shared activity.

Interestingly, many of the same fears about the isolating effect of television have reemerged with the Internet. In 1998, Kraut and his colleagues released research that indicated that the use of the Internet was associated with a decline in communication with family members in the household. Another study found that nearly half of online parents agree with the statement that "Families who spend a lot of time online talk to each other less than they otherwise would" (Turow, 1999). Yet as with television, the relationship between Internet use and social avoidance has become less clear. Kraut has recently reported that the same online users, three years later, show no signs of the negative effects of Internet use that were initially present when Internet use was novel to them (Guernsey, 2001).

Lull's research (1980) on the social uses of television by the family illustrates that, in fact, families may be assimilating the Internet into the family system in ways that are not easily measured through survey and interview questions. His observations of families illustrated that television content often found its way into conversations between family members at times outside of the viewing context. Similarly, Messaris (1983) argues that "mediation" in the form of "interaction" may be difficult to pick up since so much of it is unconscious behavior. Nevertheless, the Internet is less likely than television to be a shared medium. Unlike television, Internet content tends to cater to the specialized interests of family members—for example, web sites for trading baseball cards or for researching a term paper on Henry Hudson. And unlike television, the Internet allows its users to "chat" in telephone-like situations (dyads) or party-like situations (groups of like-minded chatters). For these reasons, one is unlikely to see parallel use by members of the same family the way one might observe the patterns around TV. Rather, the Internet may provide a literal and figurative space in which family members are isolated and private. As Livingstone (1992) writes: "If television once brought the family together around the hearth, now domestic technologies permit the dispersal of family members to different rooms or different activities within the same space" (p. 128).

One interesting facet of Internet use is that it takes on unique social forms depending on the person within the family system who uses it. As others have written (see Chapter 1, this volume), the Internet has become a socially useful tool for adolescents who have appropriated it as a postmodern telephone. Adolescents have found ways to connect with one another in real time though the Internet (e.g., instant messaging), although perhaps at the expense of time that might be spent in face-to-face communication with one another and with other family members. This has yet to be examined carefully and is an important direction for future research.

Different family members may feel differing senses of efficacy with the Internet. The prevailing belief is that, in these early days of Internet use, children may often feel more comfortable with the technology than parents (Connolly & Schwartz, 1999; Schmitt, 2000; Stroh, 1999). Children may therefore be using computers (and by extension, the Internet) in isolation and may be living in homes where parents, who are less familiar with the medium, do not know how to use or even talk about the medium with them (Murdoch, 1992).

Gender Roles

In family systems theory, each member of the family contributes in unique ways to the family system and, as such, maintains "roles" that may be patterned by age, gender, or other characteristics of the individuals (Rosenblatt, 1994). One must recognize the reciprocal nature of the roles, and the functionality of them for the developing child and the organization of the family.

Researchers in media studies have long recognized that there are gender-related patterns surrounding the technologies, particularly in the domestic setting. Seiter (1999), for example, has written of men's tendency to dominate decision-making around the television set by dominating the remote control. Similarly, Gray (1992) found that the acquisition and use of the videocassette recorder by families in England was gendered; specifically, males typically decided upon the necessity of the machine, researched the options available, and set up the device within the home. The time-shifting function of the VCR is rarely used, in part because mothers never mastered the ability to program the device (Gray, 1992; Lin, 2001).

Computers have also been associated with gender-related behaviors. Turkle (1995) writes of the "computerphobia" and the interest and expertise men show relative to women vis-à-vis the technology. Gershuny's (1992) index reveals that the more "high tech" the device is, the more likely it is to be male-dominated in its use. Although the adoption and early use of new innovations may be gendered, there is also a tendency for discomfort to be transitional, particularly in the case of entertainment media which are eventually used by all family members (Gershuny, 1992; Gray, 1992; Turkle, 1995).

When a new technology such as the Internet is brought into the domestic sphere, it is important to consider not only which family members adopt or use the new technologies, but which family members set up the guidelines about how, when, and where it is used. In the case of television, research indicates that mothers typically set up the rules and restrictions with respect to children's TV viewing (Jordan, 1990; Schmitt, 2000), perhaps because she plays a greater role in the everyday supervision of children's activities (Hochschild, 1989). Fathers, in turn, frequently "un-do" these guidelines (Jordan, 1990; Schmitt, 2000). Similarly, fathers typically make decisions about computer purchases and online access and, presumably, fathers feel they know the technology best. Yet, it is mothers who historically socialize children's media use. Will mothers feel less comfortable supervising online than television activities? Will they have a sense of how to construct guidelines and the capacity to enforce them, particularly if mothers don't know how to use the Internet well?

Adolescent Identity Development

According to many developmental psychologists, most American children go through a period during which they "separate" from adults. We call it adolescence. Media remain important to children in adolescence, though television use declines substantially and lower emotional involvement takes place when they watch TV (Comstock, 1991). Studies suggest that during adolescence, television viewing becomes associated with the family. In his research on adolescent media use, Larson (1995) writes that "TV viewing reflects, or may be deliberately used, to maintain close emotional bonds to the family" (p. 542).

Generations of adolescents have used their bedrooms as sites of refuge and spaces in which they can express and explore their identities. These sites of identity formation are filled with cultural products and pathways to the world outside the home. Not surprisingly, children's bedrooms are increasingly becoming media centers (Roberts et al., 1999; Livingstone, 1999; Stanger & Gridina, 1999). The increasing diversity of media targeted specifically to adolescents allows young audiences greater specificity in choosing media that suit their moods and their passing interests, often in isolation from other family members (Arnett 1995). For adolescents seeking to "find themselves," television viewing becomes a more solitary activity (Larson, 1995); music listening becomes associated with the process of disengagement from the family (Larson, 1995; Roe, 1987); magazines provide teenage girls with exemplars of beauty (Steel & Brown, 1995); and telephones (or online chat rooms) offer social connection to peers (Steel & Brown, 1995). Introducing the Internet into the plethora of choices for adolescents allows for an even greater ability to specifically address teens' issues, concerns, and interests. But it also provides an opportunity to connect with virtual social worlds outside of the family system. (See Chapter 3, this volume, for a more in-depth discussion of the Internet and identity formation.)

Parental Mediation Strategies

Andreasen (2001) has observed that television use is predicted by family rules rather than television rules—an observation that underscores the importance of recognizing the family as a system in which patterns are interwoven with media practices. Television scholars now have strong evidence that parents' mediation strategies vis-à-vis their children's television viewing are linked to larger norms; values and beliefs both reflect and shape what happens with the medium in the home.

Many researchers have considered "co-viewing" (parents and children watching together) to be a mediation strategy that would allow parents to monitor their children's choices and provide opportunity for discussion about TV-related content (Dorr, Kovaric, & Doubleday, 1989; Messaris, 1983). But what leads parents to sit down and watch television with their children? Research has uncovered some interesting trends. First, it turns out that when parents and children watch television together, they are much more likely to watch adult than children's programming (Huston et al., 1992; Lin & Atkin, 1989). Second, parents who co-view with their children tend to have a greater affinity toward the medium, that is, they like watching television (Austin, Bolls, Fujioka, & Engelbertson, 1999). Thus, it appears that co-viewing as a mediation strategy may say more about parents' habits with television than any conscious strategy they have devised to "protect" or "inform" their children.

Experts have argued that it is important for parents and children to "co-view" the Internet (Connolly & Schwartz, 1999; Stroh, 1999)—that is, spend time together exploring and discussing Internet content and activities. While this may be a natural and comfortable process with television, the Internet may present more of a challenge. One obstacle is that parents who are not comfortable online may be less likely to use the medium as a way to share leisure time with children. Moreover, research on television co-viewing illustrates that parents watch TV with their children because they enjoy the content. Since Internet web sites are created with highly specific audiences in mind (e.g., fourth graders who love Harry Potter, soccer moms who don't have time to shop), it is less likely that there would be content that is of mutual interest to both parents and children. In many ways, the Internet is designed to provide an individualistic rather than a shared experience (Montgomery, 2001).

This pattern may be age-dependent. By necessity, very young children have to come online with their parents. Nick Jr., for instance, has a site with content directed at preschool children and their parents. Mothers and fathers do many of the activities on the child site with their own child (e.g., reading online stories). In addition, there is a parent section of the site where Nickelodeon provides information for parents, such as activities to do with their child. By adolescence, children's and parents' interest in going online together will predictably wane, as adolescents increasingly assert their independence from parental control.

Another mediation strategy that has been explored by researchers is parents' practice of prohibiting and recommending programs for their children. Many of the restrictions parents have for children's television viewing involve children's exposure to violent (Cantor, 1999) or scary (Valkenburg, Krcmar, Peeters, & Marseille, 1999) content. However, research also indicates that there can sometimes be a discrepancy between what parents say they "protect" their children from and what children sometimes watch. Holz's (1998) focus group discussions with children reveal that though restrictions are in place, they are not consistently enforced—a finding which may partially explain the consistently high viewer ratings of violent programs such as *WWE Wrestling, Cops,* and *Walker, Texas Ranger* among children ages 2 to 12 (A. C. Nielsen, 1999).

Issues with the Internet arise when parents worry that their children may visit age-inappropriate sites or unwittingly have their names added to e-mail lists. "Spam" (which is similar to "junk mail" in the nonvirtual world) is a phenomenon that has been perceived as dangerous and annoying as robots harvest names from chat rooms and then spam all e-mail addresses. In this way, unwanted sexually explicit material and links can come to children anonymously through their own e-mail accounts (Calvert, 2000).

In addition to forbidding or discouraging content that they don't want their children to see, parents may also positively direct children's media use; for example, they make specific recommendations for television programs their children should watch. In one study, nearly 42% of 10- to 17-year-old children said there are specific programs their parents encourage them to watch. Interestingly, the programs they listed were not targeted to children but were programs for a general audience—for example, the news, *Touched by an Angel*—or specific channels—for example, PBS or The Discovery Channel (Stanger, 1997). It is possible for parents to provide the same sort of direction with the Internet as well, for example, parents can use the bookmark function on Internet service providers to direct children to desirable sites.

Research on parental mediation of television, however, indicates that in order for parents to be effective in shaping the media habits of their children, they must be familiar with the way the technology works and the kind of content that is available. Many parents of school-age children, however, do not even seem to know enough about what is on television to be able to recommend specific program recommendations. In several recent studies, parents were virtually unaware of any of the educational programs being offered by the major networks to satisfy their public interest obligations to children (Holz, 1998; Stanger & Gridina, 1999).

Obstacles to active mediation of the Internet are even higher when one considers the range of content available through this medium. Though parents may be able to use filtering devices to screen children from potentially harmful content, recent studies indicate that the majority of parents do not employ them (Turow, 1999). Moreover, there appears to be little consistently available information about the quality and content of web sites appropriate for children (such as the information one might get from *TV Guide*). Turow suggests that parents track children's online visits in order to monitor and discuss the appropriate use of the Internet (and provide reminders to children that their parents care about where they go and what they do on the Web). This, he argues, may offer a mechanism for inculcating the norms and values of the family system into children's online habits (see Chapter 12, this volume).

Such recommendations, however, may not fit with existing systems of family norms that value, for example, privacy. In addition, children entering adolescence need to develop a measure of autonomy, which may be expressed through choices of media that are counter to what parents would choose for their children or choose for themselves (Larson, 1995).

CONCLUSION

Family systems theory holds that family norms, values, and patterns of the system will both reflect and shape the general approach children take to media and the particular role the Internet will have in the individual and collective lives of family members. The home environment provides structural dimensions of space and time—domains of family life that reflect larger social values and orientations to media. Space within the home is a constructed element of the system that—consciously or not—provides family members with a sense of that which is shared (e.g., living room sofas arranged around the electronic hearth [Tichi, 1991]) and that which is personal (computers with only one chair in front of them). Within this domain, children learn to think about the nature of time and the value of time. Such learning is subtly woven into the patterns of the family's day but also explicitly expressed through statements about the best ways to spend time and manage time. Children are socialized to beliefs about how much time to devote to online activities and whether "going online" is a productive way to spend time within this larger system.

Children's online choices and habits may also reflect and shape the social dimension of the family system. Mass media use in general may alter patterns of interactions between family members; and Internet use may give rise to unique issues—including the extent to which family members can share space, time and content in ways that promote family functioning and individual expression. New media such as the Internet are also assimilated into family members' ongoing need to define their role within the system (often in gender-patterned ways) and develop a personal identity (a process that is particularly salient for adolescent family members). Finally, the mediation strategies parents use in the new multimedia environment of the home may not only reflect the kinds of mediation strategies they employ with television and other media, but also reflect their ongoing interest in socializing children to the larger norms and values of the family system.

Missing from this discussion of children's use of the Internet is the fact that children's knowledge of and expectations about the medium may be *external* to the family. Many children are now being exposed to computers for the first time in schools and, because of the E-rate which provides Internet service to schools at a discount, children may be introduced to the Web through peers and teachers—systems that are outside of the context of the home. One recent study conducted in Belgium found that quite often it is the children who initiate the demand for Internet access in the home and serve as the family experts on navigating the Web (Struys, Roe, & van Rompaey, 2001). Such dynamics in the family system—the openness of the family to external agents of change, the fluidity of roles vis-à-vis the Internet—likely have important implications for how the Internet shapes and is shaped by the home context. Ultimately, the family system is nested within larger social and cultural systems that impact the Internet's role in the familial setting.

REFERENCES

A. C. Nielsen. (1999). Nielsen television index ranking report: Top 100 demographics for the period 11/02/98–11/08/98. Custom report to the Annenberg Public Policy Center.

Aldous, J. (1978). *Family careers: Developmental change in families*. New York: John Wiley and Sons.

Andreasen, M. (2001). Evolution in the family's use of television: An overview. In J. Bryant & A. Bryant (Eds.), *Television and the American family*. Mahwah, NJ: Erlbaum.

Arnett, J. (1995). Adolescents' uses of media for self-socialization. *Journal of Youth and Adolescence, 24*, 519–533.

Ashcraft, N., & Scheflin, A. (1976). *People space: The making and breaking of human boundaries*. New York: Doubleday.

Austin, E., Bolls, P., Fujioka, Y., & Engelbertson, J. (1999). How and why parents take on the tube. *Journal of Broadcasting and Electronic Media, 43*, 175–193.

Bateson, G., Jackson, D., Haley, J., & Weakland, J. (1956). Toward a theory of schizophrenia. *Behavioral Science, 1*, 251–264.

Bavelas, J., & Segal, L. (1982). Family systems theory: Background and implications. *Journal of Communication, 32*, 99–107.

Berger, P., & Luckman, T. (1967). *The social construction of reality*. New York: Doubleday.

Bochner, A. (1976). Conceptual frontiers in the study of communication in families: An introduction to the literature. *Human Communication Research, 2*, 381–397.

Bochner, A., & Eisenberg, E. (1987). Family process: System perspectives on family communication. In C. Berger (Ed.), *Handbook of communication science*. Beverly Hills, CA: Sage.

Brody, G., & Stoneman, Z. (1983). The influence of television viewing on family interactions. *Journal of Family Issues, 4*, 329–348.

Brown, J., Dykers, C., Steele, J., White, A. (1994). Teen room culture: Where media and identities intersect. *Communication Research, 21*, 813–827.

Bryce, J. (1988). Family time and television use. In T. Lindlof (Ed.), *Natural audiences: Qualitative research of media uses and effects*. Norwood, NJ: Ablex.

Bryce, J., & Leichter, H. (1983). The family and television: Forms of mediation. *Journal of Family Issues, 4*, 309–328.

Calvert, S. L. (2000). Is cyberspace for all girls? Paper presented at the annual meeting of the American Psychological Association, Washington, DC, August.

Cantor, J. (1999). Ratings for program content: The role of research findings. *Annals of the American Academy of Political and Social Sciences, 557*, 54–69.

Carlson, M. (1999). Do not enter: Filters, monitoring software help control kids' Internet use. *Hartford Courant*, May 27, pp. F1, F4.

Comstock, G. (1991). *Television and the American child*. San Diego, CA: Academic Press.

Connolly, C., & Schwartz, J. (1999). Gore lets parents in on children's Internet safeguards. *Washington Post*, May 5, pp. A6–A7.

Dorr, A., Kovaric, P., & Doubleday, C. (1989). Parent-child co-viewing of television. *Journal of Broadcasting and Electronic Media, 33*, 35–51.

Gershuny, J. (1992). Revolutionary technologies and technological revolutions. In R. Silverstone & E. Hirsch (Eds.), *Consuming technologies: Media information in domestic spaces*. London: Routledge.

Gray, A. (1992). *Video playtime: The gendering of a leisure technology*. New York: Routledge.

Guernsey, L. (2001). Professor who once found isolation online has a change of heart. *New York Times*, July 27.

Hall, E. (1959). *The silent language*. Greenwich, CT: Fawcett Press.

———. (1966). *The hidden dimension*. New York: Doubleday.

Hochschild, A. (1989). *The second shift: Working parents and the revolution at home*. New York: Viking Books.

Holz, J. (1998). *Measuring the child audience: Issues and implications for educational programming*. Report No. 3. Philadelphia, PA: The Annenberg Public Policy Center of the University of Pennsylvania.

Huston, A., Donnerstein, E., Fairchild, H., Feshbach, N., Katz, P., Murray, J., Rubenstein, E., Wilcos, B., & Zuckerman, D. (1992). *Big world, small screen: The role of television in American Society*. Lincoln: University of Nebraska Press.

Jordan, A. (1990). The role of the mass media in the family system: An ethnographic approach. Unpublished doctoral dissertation, The Annenberg School for Communication, University of Pennsylvania.

———. (1991). Social class, temporal orientation, and mass media use within the family system. *Critical Studies in Mass Communication, 9*, 374–386.

Kohn, M., & Schooler, C. (1983). *Work and personality: An inquiry into the impact of social stratification*. Norwood, NJ: Ablex.

Kraut, R., Patterson, M., Lundmark, V., Kiesler, S., Mukopadhyay, T., & Scherlis, W. (1998) Internet paradox: A social technology that reduces social involvement and psychological well-being? *American Psychologist, 53*, 1017–1031.

Larson, R. (1995). Secrets in the bedroom: Adolescents' private use of media. *Journal of Youth and Adolescence, 24*, 535–550.

Lawrence, F., & Wozniak, P. (1989). Children's television viewing with family members. *Psychological Reports, 65*, 395–400.

Leichter, H., Ahmed, D., Barrios, L., Bryce, J., Larsen, E., & Moe, L. (1985). Family contexts of television. *Educational Communication Technology Journal, 33*, 26–40.

Liebert, R., Sprafkin, J., & Davidson, E. (1982). *The early window: Effects of television on children and youth*. New York: Pergamon Press.

Lin, C. (2001). The VCR, home video culture, and new video technologies. In J. Bryant and A. Bryant (Eds.), *Television and the American family*. Mahwah, NJ: Lawrence Erlbaum Associates.

Lin, C., & Atkin, C. (1989). Parental mediation and rulemaking for adolescent use of television and VCRs. *Journal of Broadcasting and Electronic Media, 33*, 53–67.

Lindlof, T., Shatzer, M., & Wilkinson, D. (1988). Accommodation of video and television in the American family. In J. Lull (Ed.), *World families watch TV*. Newbury Park, CA: Sage.

Livingstone, S. (1992). The meaning of domestic technologies: A personal construct analysis of familial gender relations. In R. Silverstone & E. Hirsch (Eds.), *Consuming technologies: Media information in domestic spaces*. London: Routledge.

————. (1999). Personal computers in the home: What do they mean for Europe's children? *Intermedia, 27,* 406.

Lull, J. (1980). The social uses of television. *Human Communication Research, 6,* 197–209.

Maccoby, E. (1954). Why do children watch television? *Public Opinion Quarterly,* Fall, 239–244.

Medrich, E., Roizen, J., Rubin, V., & Buckley, S. (1982). *The serious business of growing up: A study of children's lives outside of school.* Berkeley: University of California Press.

Messaris, P. (1983). Family conversations about television. *Journal of Family Issues, 4,* 293–308.

Montgomery, K. (2001). Digital kids: The new on-line children's consumer culture. In D. Singer & J. Singer (Eds.), *Handbook of children and the media.* Newbury Park, CA: Sage.

Murdoch, G., Hartmann, P., & Gray, P. (1992). Contextualizing home computing: Resources and practices. In R. Siverstone and E. Hirsch (Eds.), *Consuming technologies: Media information in domestic spaces.* London: Routledge.

Pollner, M., & McDonald-Wilker, L. (1985). The social construction of unreality. *Family Process, 24,* 241–254.

Roberts, D. F., Foehr, U. G., Rideout, V. J., & Brodie, M. (1999). *Kids and media at the new millenium: A comprehensive national analysis of children's media use.* Menlo Park, CA: Kaiser Family Foundation, November.

Roe, K. (1987). The school and music in adolescent socialization. In J. Lull (Ed.), *Popular music and communication.* Newbury Park, CA: Sage.

Rosenblatt, P. (1994). *Metaphors of family systems theory: Toward a new construction.* New York: The Guilford Press.

Schmitt, K. (2000). *Public policy, family rules and children's media use in the home.* Report No. 35. Philadelphia, PA: The Annenberg Public Policy Center of the University of Pennsylvania.

Schramm, W., Lyle, J., & Parker, E. (1961). *Television in the lives of our children.* Stanford, CA: Stanford University Press.

Seiter, E. (1999). *Television and new media audiences.* New York: Oxford University Press.

Stanger, J. (1997). *Television in the home: The 1997 survey of parents and children.* Survey No. 2. Philadelphia, PA: The Annenberg Public Policy Center of the University of Pennsylvania.

Stanger, J., & Gridina, N. (1999). *Media in the home 1999: The fourth annual survey of parents and children.* Survey No. 5. Philadelphia, PA: The Annenberg Public Policy Center of the University of Pennsylvania.

Steele, J., & Brown, J. (1995). Adolescent room culture: Studying media in the context of everyday life. *Journal of Youth and Adolescence, 24,* 551–576.

Stroh, M. (1999). Safeguarding kids on the net. *Sarasota Herald-Tribune,* May 27, pp. 1E, 4E.

Struys, K., Roe, K., & van Rompaey, V. (2001). Children's influence on the family purchase of media. Paper presented at the 51st annual conference of the International Communication Association, Washington, DC, May.

Tichi, C. (1991). *Electronic hearth: Creating an American television culture.* New York: Oxford University Press.

Turkle, S. (1995). *Life on the screen: Identity in the age of the Internet*. New York: Simon and Schuster.

Turow, J. (1999). *The Internet and the family: The view from parents/The view from the press*. Report No. 27. Philadelphia, PA: The Annenberg Public Policy Center of the University of Pennsylvania.

Valkenburg, P. M., Krcmar, M., Peeters, A., & Marseille, N. (1999). Developing a scale to assess three styles of television mediation: "Instructive mediation," "restrictive mediation," and "social coviewing." *Journal of Broadcasting and Electronic Media, 43* (1), 52–66.

Vetere, A., & Gale, A. (1987). *Ecological studies of family life*. New York: John Wiley and Sons.

Wartella, E., & Mazzarella, S. (1990). An historical comparison of children's use of leisure time. In R. Busch (Ed.), *For fun and profit*. Philadelphia, PA: Temple University Press.

Winn, M. (1977). *The plug-in drug*. New York: Viking Books.

Woolf, K., & Allen, J. (2001). *The fifth annual conference on children and media: A summary*. www.appcpenn.org, May.

Index

"Adaptive instruction" and computer-based teaching, 183–84; examples from AnimalWatch project, 186–90

Aidman, Amy, 143

Alphaworld, 65

American Medical Association, health web sites recommendations, 81

America Online, 19, 20

Annenberg Public Policy Center, University of Pennsylvania, 1, 10, 87, 170

AnimalWatch project, 184–85; development, 186–90; formative research, 190–92; support for teachers, 192–94; theoretical framework, 185–86

Barbie Fashion Designer, 9–10

Barney and Friends, 205

Bill Nye, the Science Guy, 170, 179

Blue's Clues, 145

Breakout, 24

Buddy System Project, 15

Carnegie Council on Adolescent Development, 217, 220

CDS (Child Development Supplement), 38. *See also* Research study in children's television/interactive game use by age and gender

Chat rooms, 18–19, 20

Child development and dysfunctional social institutions, 216–17

Children as consumers, 201–10; and centration, 205; collections, 209; early elementary school, 207–8; infants to toddlers/preferences, 202–4; later elementary school, 208–10; and media saturation, 231; and negotiation strategies, 206–7; preschoolers, 204–7; profiling for direct and relationship marketing, 222; research directions, 210–12; theoretical underpinning, 202

Children's Online Privacy Protection Act (COPPA), 222–23

Children's Television Act of 1990 (CTA), 145, 165; impact, 146, 178. *See also* E/I programming; Three-Hour Rule

Civics education: as a goal of public education, 84–85; and private/tailored programs, 85–86

Classroom of Tomorrow, 15

Cognitive skills development and computer games, 11, 26; and Animal-

Watch research, 190–92; iconic
skills, 12; spatial representation, 11–
12; visual attention, 12–13

Columbine High School violence, 24;
and violent video games, 103

CommerceNet, 219

Computer-based teaching, 194; and
adaptive instruction, 183–84. *See
also* AnimalWatch project

Computer games, 4; core audience, 8;
and girl market, 9–10; impact on violent behavior, 24–26, 27; and military training, 25, 26; and nonverbal
(performance) IQ, 13; as precursor
to computer literacy, 9; short-term
transfer effects, 25. *See also* Cognitive skills development and computer
games

Computer literacy: and computer game
playing, 9; and gender differences,
168

Concentration, 12

Conjecture, 12

Cro, 147

Cybergate, 65

Cybersex, 24

"Digerati," 126

"Digital divide," 72; and computer
utilization in schools, 183; concerns
about in adolescent Internet health
information study, 76

Doom, 24

Doug, 180

Duke Nukem, 24, 25

Dungeons and Dragons, 61

"Echo-boomers," 221

E/I programming, 145–46, 165–66; hypotheses about, 168; study methods,
169–71; study results, 171–73, 176–
78

"Electronic friendships," 15

Electronic media and children: active
versus passive processes, 36; age differences, 36–37; choices, 35; gender
differences, 37; genre and content
importance, 35; research study re-

sults, 50–51; weakening family
bonds, 217. *See also* Children's Television Act of 1990; Research study
in children's television/interactive
game use by age and gender; Television viewing; Violent video games

E-mail, as primary Internet application,
17

The Empire Strikes Back, 24

E-rate programs, 72

Erikson, E.: application to social interactions on the Internet, 65–66; concept of unitary identity, 58–59;
identity confusion/diffusion concept,
67; search for mature sexual identity, 63

Evers, Frank, 9

Experience Sampling Method, 5

Families and the Internet: communicating boundaries, 225–27; information-
boundaries perspective, 215–16, 218–
20; information flow into the home,
220–21; information flow out of the
home, 222–23; "public" and "private" realms of interaction, 216; research, 224–25, 231–32;
"splintering," 217, 220; two-way
commercialism, 223–24; use of, 218

Family systems theory, 232–33, 242–
43; as a conceptual framework, 233;
social dimension, 237; social dimen-
sion/adolescent identity development,
239–40; social dimension/gender
roles, 238–39; social dimension/in-
teraction, 237–38; social dimension/
parental mediation strategies, 240–
42; structural dimension/time and
space organization, 233–36

"The Fifth Dimension" project, 14–15

Filters, 221; and families, 226

"Furby," 22. *See also* Virtual pets

General Aggression Model (GAM),
104–7

General systems theory, 232

Georgetown Hoya TV Reporters, 62,
64, 169

Ghostwriter, 147
GI Joe, 166

Hall, Edward, 233–34
Hammond project, 4
Health-related content on the Internet, 72–73; and adolescent use of (study), 75–81; CyberIsle, 74–75; Not-2-Late, 75; qualities of sites, 78–81; Zaphealth, 73–74
Hey Arnold!, 179–79, 180
Home computers: and academic performance, 13–15; parents' position, 14; usage statistics, 3. *See also* Perceptions of reality; Social development/relationships and computer use; Time-use data
HomeNet study, 4, 5, 8, 13, 16–20

Identity, 57–58, 60; and adolescence, 58, 239–40; and biological sex, 62–63; confusion/diffusion, 67; Erikson's perspective, 58–59; exploration on the Internet, 59; issues for young online players, 66–68; Jung's perspective, 59; role playing and social interaction, 65–66; social interactionists' perspective, 59–60
"Information-age" preparation, 3
Information privacy: exchange approach, 223; leakage of personal information, 224
Instant messaging, 16–17, 20
Internet access (adult and teen): bi-directionality, 124; commercial domain, 215; and e-mail, 17; MUDs and chat rooms, 18–19; public, 71–72, 78; purposes, 6–7. *See also* Families and the Internet
Internet access (children): children's preference for, 3; computer location, 234–35; displacement of other activities, 10–11; expectations external to the family, 243; by gender, 9; and multiple identities, 23; and new marketing techniques, 211; parents' positions, 3, 123; time online, 236
Internet access (teens): and declining

social involvement, 17–18; and e-mail/instant messaging, 16–17; by gender, 8–9; and health information study, 75–81; and identity exploration, 58, 59, 68; as a postmodern telephone, 238; site qualities to attract users, 79–80; social usage, 5
Internet use: democratic global learning community (*see* Junior Summit); by ethnic groups, 72; by gender, 125, 219; in general media environment, 227–28; and Internet economy, 218; as a research tool, 180; telephone analogy, 219–20; and voice, 124–26

Jung, C., archetypal images and construction of a unitary self, 59, 61
Junior Summit program, 124, 142–43; action, 137–39; evaluation issues, 139–41; format/differences from other programs, 130–33; language, 135; outcomes/contributions, 141; participants/differences from other programs, 127–30; representation, 135–37; role of adults/differences from other programs, 133–34; technologies, 133; underdetermined design, 126–27; voice issues, 126

Kidsnet Media Guide, 170
"Kids Voting USA," 85–86

LambdaMOO, 23, 62; "Mr. Bungle," antisocial role-playing persona on, 67
Lucas Learning, focus on boy users, 9

Mace, 24
Magic School Bus, 179
Marble Madness, 12
Monitors, 221; and families, 226
Mortal Kombat, 24, 25, 102
Mr. Rogers' Neighborhood, 145; appeal to preschoolers, 205; study, 167
MUDs (Multi-User Domains), 18–19, 20, 57, 60–61, 68; and antisocial behavior, 67–68; and "Bots," 67; and gender identity, 63–64; personae

construction, 61–65; role playing, 22, 59, 65; social, 61

Nickelodeon, 241
Nick Jr., 241
Nielsen Media Research, 219

Office of Population Research, 75

Pac-Man, 110
PAID (Panel Study of Income Dynamics), 38–39. *See also* Research study in children's television/interactive game use by age and gender
Parents' positions: fear of sexual exploitation of children via the Internet, 66; on home computers as an academic resource, 14; ignorance about violent computer games, 24–25; on Internet access by children, 3; on time and use of the Internet, 236
Perceptions of reality (impact of electronic games/Internet), 21; simulation, 21–24
"Plugged In" program, 72
Political socialization, 83, 84; as a goal of public education, 84–85; and the Internet, 83–84; and mass media, 86–87; using technology to address apathy, 96. *See also* "Student Voices" program
Pong, 24
PsycINFO computer database, 107

Research study in children's television/interactive game use by age and gender, 38, 238–39; data/results, 41–49; discussion, 50–51; method, 38–41
"Rock the Vote," 86

Saved by the Bell, 179
Safe-haven sites, 221
School District of Philadelphia, 87
Sesame Street, 145, 147, 161, 165, 166, 203
SimAnt, 21
SimCity, 21
SimFamily, 51

SimLife, 21
Social development/relationships and computer use, 15, 27; communications, 16–18; effects over time, 19–21; impact on family dynamics, 16; impact on friendships, 15–16; role playing and social interactions, 65–66; "strong tie" versus "weak tie" relationships, 18–19
Soldier of Fortune, 102
Sonic the Hedgehog, 111
Street Fighter, 102
"Student Voices" program, 84, 87; citizenship education, 84–86; effectiveness, 95–97; evaluation method, 90–93; evaluation results, 93–95; key features, 88–89
Super Mario Brothers, 101

TeenNet, 74
Teletubbies, 203, 205
Television viewing, 162, 165; advertising and toddlers, 204; and computers, 10–11; "co-viewing" (parents and children), 240–41; "electronic hearth," 234; and Internet usage fears, 237–38; parents' mediation, 242; and research on learning, 147–48, 161–62, 167; violence/stereotyping research study/methods, 148–52; violence/stereotyping research study/results, 152–53, 160. *See also* E/I programming
Tetris, 13
Three-Hour Rule, 146; and prosocial programming, 160–61, 178–79; science emphasis in academic programming, 161, 180
Time-use data, 4; collection methods, 5, 26; usage by age/gender/ethnicity/social class, 5, 8–9
TinySex, 66–67

Violent video games, 101–2, 115–16; knowledge structures changed by violent media, 105–7; long-term effects of media violence, 105; magnitude of effects, 115; meta-analysis study (basic), 107–8; meta-analysis study (new), 109–12; potential negative effects, 103–4; research directions, 116; research designs, 112–14; and youth access, 102–3. *See also* General Aggression Model (GAM)

Virtual pets, 21–22
"Voice," 126
Von Bertalanffy, L., 232

Wishbone, 179
Wolfenstein 3D, 102
World Wide Web, 215, 218, 228

About the Editors and Contributors

SANDRA L. CALVERT, Ph.D., is a Professor of Psychology, the Director of the Children and Media Project at Georgetown University and the Director and co-founder of the Children's Digital Media Center which is located at Georgetown University, the University of Texas at Austin, Northwestern University, and UCLA. She is a fellow of the American Psychological Association and author of *Children's Journeys Through the Information Age* (1999). Dr. Calvert examines the impact of media on children's cognitive and social development as well as policy issues in the children's media area.

AMY B. JORDAN, Ph.D., is Senior Research Investigator at the Annenberg Public Policy Center of the University of Pennsylvania. She directs the research on the impact of public policy on children's television, and has been the primary author of the annual "State of Children's Television" reports for the past several years. Dr. Jordan has written extensively about the economic and regulatory forces that shape children's television and is the 2001 recipient of the International Communication Association's Award for Best Applied/Policy Research.

RODNEY R. COCKING, Ph.D., was Program Director of Developmental and Learning Sciences in the Division of Behavioral and Cognitive Sciences at the National Science Foundation. Dr. Cocking was co-editor of *Interacting with Video* (Ablex, 1996), *Cross-Cultural Roots of Minority Child Development* (1994), and *The Development and Meaning of Psychological Distance* (1993). He was co-editor and co-founder of the *Journal of Applied Developmental Psychology* He passed away in February 2002.

CRAIG A. ANDERSON, Ph.D., is Professor and Chair of the Department of Psychology at Iowa State University. He is a fellow of the American Psychological Society, the American Psychological Association, the International Society for Research on Aggression, and the American Association of Applied and Preventive Psychology. Dr. Anderson's current research focuses on the potentially harmful effects of exposure to violent video games.

IVON ARROYO has a master's degree from the School of Education at the University of Massachusetts at Amherst, and is currently a doctoral candidate in the Department of Computer Science. Her research focuses on how educational software can be tailored to student characteristics such as gender and cognitive style.

CAROLE R. BEAL, Ph.D., is Professor of Psychology at the University of Massachusetts at Amherst. Her research interests are in the area of cognitive development and education, with a particular focus on educational technology. She is also interested in gender development and is the author of *Boys and Girls: The Development of Gender Roles* (1994).

DAVID S. BICKHAM, M.A., is a graduate student in Human Development and Family Sciences in the Department of Human Ecology at the University of Texas at Austin and a member of the Center for Research on the Influence of Television on Children. His research interests include online identity development and television rating system effects on children's viewing patterns.

DINA L. G. BORZEKOWSKI, Ed.D., is an Assistant Professor in the Department of Population and Family Health Services at the Johns Hopkins Bloomberg School of Public Health. Her area of expertise is children, media, and health. Dr. Borzekowski is currently conducting national and international research on how different media can be used to improve the health of children and adolescents.

JOANNE CANTOR, Ph.D., Emeritus Professor of Communication Arts at the University of Wisconsin–Madison, is the author of *Mommy, I'm Scared: How TV and Movies Frighten Children and What We Can Do to Protect Them* (1998). Her research focuses on developmental differences in how children respond to television and on strategies for reducing media-induced harm.

ALLISON GILMAN CAPLOVITZ is a graduate student in Human Development and Family Sciences in the Department of Human Ecology at the University of Texas at Austin. She is also a member of the Center for Research on the Influence of Television on Children.

JUSTINE CASSELL, Ph.D., is an Associate Professor at the MIT Media Lab, where she directs the Gesture and Narrative Language Research Group. Dr. Cassell designs computational systems that have some of the same kinds of social and communicative competencies that we do, and that can therefore support sociocognitive development in children, and communication among adults. She is co-editor of *Embodied Conversational Agents* (2000) and *From Barbie to Mortal Kombat: Gender and Computer Games* (1998).

JONATHAN FINKELSTEIN worked as a Research Associate on the Panel Study of Income Dynamics Child Development Supplement (PSID-CDS) at the Institute for Social Research at the University of Michigan during the 1997 wave of data collection.

MELISSA FRIEDMAN graduated with a B.A. in Psychology from Georgetown University, where she was a member of the Children and Media Project. She currently works for a non-profit national service organization in Seattle, Washington.

EDWARD GONZALES, M.A., graduated with a degree in Communications, Culture, and Technology from Georgetown University and is a member of the Children and Media Project and the Children's Digital Media Center. He currently is a web developer at Q-Industries.

PATRICIA M. GREENFIELD, Ph.D., is Professor of Psychology at the University of California, Los Angeles. She is a past recipient of the American Association for the Advancement of Science Award for Behavioral Science Research, a fellow of the American Psychological Association, and a co-founder of the Children's Digital Media Center. She is co-editor of *Interacting with Video* (Ablex, 1996) and *Cross-Cultural Roots of Minority Child Development* (1994), and author of *Mind and Media* (1984).

ELISHEVA GROSS is a graduate student in the Department of Psychology at the University of California, Los Angeles. She has worked extensively with several non-profit organizations to develop Internet-based programs for minority children. Ms. Gross is currently interested in the social relations developed in various Internet forums.

PHILLIP HAMMACK graduated with a B.A. in Psychology from Georgetown University, where he was a member of the Children and Media Project. He currently attends graduate school at Loyola University in Chicago.

MATTHEW HAMMAR graduated with a B.A. in Psychology from Georgetown University, where he was a member of the Children and Media Project.

SANDRA HOFFERTH, Ph.D., was the project director for the 1997 wave of data collection for the Panel Study of Income Dynamics Child Development Supplement (PSID-CDS) at the Institute for Social research at the University of Michigan. She is currently a Professor of Family Studies at the University of Maryland.

ALETHA C. HUSTON, Ph.D., is the Priscilla Pond Flawn Regents Professor of Child Development at the University of Texas at Austin. At the University of Kansas, she was Co-Director of the Center for Research on the Influence of Television on Children (CRITC). She is lead author of *Big World, Small Screen* (1992) and numerous articles on the influences of educational and prosocial media on children.

JENNIFER A. KOTLER, Ph.D., graduated from the University of Texas at Austin and recently completed a postdoctoral fellowship at the Children and Media Project in the Department of Psychology at Georgetown University. Her research interests include the effects of educational television on social and academic development as well as the effects of parental mediation of children's television use. She is currently a Senior Staff Associate at the School of Public Health at Columbia University.

ROBERT KRAUT, Ph.D., is Professor of Social Psychology and Human Computer Interaction at Carnegie-Mellon University. He has broad interests in the design and impact of computing on people.

JUNE H. LEE is a graduate student in Human Development and Family Sciences in the Department of Human Ecology at the University of Texas at Austin and is a member of the Center for Research on the Influence of Television on Children.

WILLIAM F. MURRAY completed a B.A. degree from the Department of Psychology at Georgetown University, where he was a member of the Children and Media Project. He designed and created the original web site for the Georgetown Hoya Reporters. He currently works as a computer programmer at FactSet Research Systems.

CHRISTINE PACES graduated with a B.A. in Psychology from Georgetown University, where she was a member of the Children and Media Project. She currently attends law school at Georgetown University.

VAUGHN I. RICKERT, Psy.D., is an Associate Professor of Pediatrics at The Mount Sinai School of Medicine and Director of Research and Training for the Mount Sinai Adolescent Health Center. Dr. Rickert has authored or co-authored over 75 articles, reviews, or book chapters in the area of adolescent health. He has done research on substance use, contraception, clinically based interventions in primary care medical settings, and factors affecting health service utilization among adolescents.

KRISTIN SAVOYE graduated with a B.A. in Psychology from Georgetown University, where she was a member of the Children and Media Project. She currently attends the postbaccalaureate premedical program at Columbia University.

RONDA M. SCANTLIN, Ph.D., graduated from the University of Texas at Austin in 1999 with a doctoral degree in Child Development and Family Relationships. She is currently a postdoctoral fellow at the Annenberg Public Policy Center at the University of Pennsylvania, where she studies children's media policy.

KELLY L. SCHMITT, Ph.D., works in Education & Research at Sesame Workshop. She completed her Ph.D. at the University of Massachusetts and was a research fellow at the Annenberg Public Policy Center of the University of Pennsylvania.

ERIN SHOCKEY graduated with a B.A. in Psychology from Georgetown University, where she was a member of the Children and Media Project.

KAVERI SUBRAHMANYAM, Ph.D., is an Assistant Professor in the Department of Child and Family Studies at California State University, Los Angeles, and a member of the children's Digital Media Center. She is particularly interested in gender issues in children's use of the computer and the Internet.

JOSEPH TUROW, Ph.D., is Robert Lewis Shayon Professor of Communication at the University of Pennsylvania's Annenberg School for Communication. His books include *Breaking Up America: Advertisers and the New Media World* (1997) and *Media Systems in Society: Understanding Industries, Strategies, and Power* (1997).

PATTI M. VALKENBURG, Ph.D., is a Professor and a Dutch Royal Academy Fellow in the Amsterdam School of Communications Research, the Netherlands. Her research interests include children's likes and dislikes in entertainment, children's development as consumers, and the effects of media on children's emotional and social development. Her work has appeared in numerous communication and psychology journals, including *Journal of Communication, Communication Research, Psychological Bulletin,* and *Developmental Review.*

ELIZABETH A. VANDEWATER, Ph.D. is an Assistant Professor of Human Ecology in the division of Human Development and Family Sciences at the University of Texas at Austin, Co-Director of the Center for Research on the Influence of Television on Children (CRITC), a member of the Advisory Board for the Panel Study of Income Dynamics Child Development Supplement, and co-founder of the Children's Digital Media Center. Her research focuses on children's electronic media in the context of family interactions.

ELLEN A. WARTELLA, Ph.D., is Dean of the College of Communication, the Walter Cronkite Regents Chair in Communication at The University of Texas at Austin, and co-founder of the Children's Digital Media Center. Dean Wartella serves on editorial boards for numerous journals and has co-authored or edited numerous books in the children and media field. Dean Wartella recently completed a comprehensive review of research on children and interactive media funded by a Markle Foundation grant.

SUSAN WEIGERT, Ph.D., completed her doctoral work in the Department of Psychology at Georgetown University. She currently works as an adjunct professor in the Department of Psychology at Georgetown University.

EMORY H. WOODARD IV, Ph.D., is an Assistant Professor of Communications at Villanova University. He is a graduate and former research fellow from the University of Pennsylvania, where he worked at the Annenberg Public Policy Center. Dr. Woodard is interested in the uses and effects of television and new media technologies.

JOHN C. WRIGHT, Ph.D., was Professor and Director of the Center for Research on the Influence of Television on Children (CRITC) at the University of Kansas, and Senior Lecturer and Senior Research Scientist at the University of Texas at Austin. He authored numerous articles and monographs investigating the educational potential of television and electronic media for young children's learning and development.